EMIGRATION AND DISENCHANTMENT

Portraits of Englishmen Repatriated from the United States

EMIGRATION

&

DISENCHANTMENT

Portraits of Englishmen Repatriated from the United States

Wilbur S. Shepperson

UNIVERSITY OF OKLAHOMA PRESS : NORMAN

BY WILBUR S. SHEPPERSON

British Emigration to North America
(Oxford and Minneapolis, 1957)
Samuel Roberts: A Welsh Colonizer in Civil War Tennessee
(Knoxville, 1961)
*Emigration and Disenchantment: Portraits of Englishmen
Repatriated from the United States* (Norman, 1965)

LIBRARY OF CONGRESS CATALOG CARD NUMBER: 65–11248

Copyright 1965 by the University of Oklahoma Press, Publishing Division of the University. Composed and printed at Norman, Oklahoma, U.S.A., by the University of Oklahoma Press. First edition.

TO STANLEY CARLYLE

 PREFACE

Immigration has always commanded the
attention of Americans, and in the twentieth century, the
sociological, economic, literary, and historical aspects of the
movement have received considerable study. But the subject of
the returning immigrant has generally been overlooked. Recent
publications have contributed to an understanding of the Nor-
wegian and the Greek pattern of repatriation; however, for most
of Europe, both detailed analysis and broad synthesis is needed.
The present work proposes to investigate the magnitude and
significance of the British return movement to 1865, to offer
abbreviated sketches on some seventy-five returnees, and to explore the personal circumstances which led fifty of the would-be
immigrants to leave America. Although the reactions of fifty or
seventy-five persons do not necessarily typify the motivation of
the large and anonymous mass of the undistinguished, one is led
to suspect that thousands of Britons were similarly distraught and
only less articulate.

Americans think of the growth and settlement of their continent as a spectacular series of successes. They cling to the tales
of heroes and pioneers and, even when disillusioned, refuse to
paint sardonic pictures of the past. Nevertheless, some of the
most imaginative immigration and colonization projects were
stillborn. From Sir Walter Raleigh's Roanoke colony to the
official attempts to populate Alaska, scores of migration schemes
collapsed. But success was often a by-product of failure. Frances

Trollope failed as an immigrant, but gained recognition as an author. Henry M. Stanley was renaturalized a British subject, yet his gifts to the world were American inspired. It is apparent that the American tendency to admire only immigrants who managed to express confidence and optimism, and to honor only those who prophesied an Augustan age, has blinded the people to a complete understanding of the immigration movement and denied them the chastening values of disapproval.

Americans have assumed that immigration, from the point of view of the immigrant, was a great human triumph. The United States provided "a shelter for the hunted head" and opportunity for "the homeless, the tempest-tost." Yet public concern with the problems of ethnic groups has often resulted from prejudice, tension, or other negative reactions within society. National and racial minorities have commonly been noticed only at times of conflict or at the point of social breakdown. There have been surprisingly few inquiries into the success and failures of American immigrants. Did their dreams mature into reality? Did they achieve their goal? Or was their goal obliterated by a new way of life which in its own peculiar way rendered the New World as unyielding as the Old?

Many British arrivals demanded more of society than it was able to give. Others were unwilling to make necessary adjustments and refused to accept what was offered. Some immigrants were vagabonds, destined to spend their lives moving from hope to hope. And, of course, many had viewed the movement as a solution to all their problems and not as a decision entailing very real risks. The inability of a few newcomers to compound their dream with the American experience often resulted from trifles and personal foibles, not from fundamental disagreement. But as a matter of course, the vast majority of British immigrants accepted the new society, some because it provided them with hitherto unrealized opportunities, some because economic necessity, at least for a while, forestalled the possibility of return, and some because pride would not allow them to admit defeat. Obviously, the new life as it unfolded in America was not a linear series of achievements; rather, it was a complicated experience influenced by diverse and involved circumstances. The feedback to Europe, when placed in historical perspective, became a normal sequel to the more extensive migration to America.

I am grateful to Augustana Library Publications for permission to use material previously published in Chapter XIII of *In the Trek of the Immigrants* (1964) and to the *Bulletin of the Historical and Philosophical Society of Ohio* for permission to re-use parts of my April, 1961, article on William Bullock. Professors Harold Kirkpatrick and George Herman of the University of Nevada have been particularly helpful on matters of both content and style. Of the many persons who have contributed ideas and material to the study, special thanks are due Fred Reichman and John G. Folkes, who as graduate students rendered valuable research assistance.

WILBUR S. SHEPPERSON

Reno, Nevada
July 5, 1965

CONTENTS

	Preface	*Page vii*
I.	*Immigration, A Two-Way Movement*	3
II.	*Land Without Plenty*	31
III.	*Uncertain Reward*	62
IV.	*The Search That Failed*	98
V.	*Unsevered Ties*	141
VI.	*A Diversity of Causes*	178
	Bibliography	197
	Index	205

EMIGRATION AND DISENCHANTMENT

Portraits of Englishmen Repatriated from the United States

IMMIGRATION, A TWO-WAY MOVEMENT

From the first landing of colonists in the seventeenth century to the present, the transatlantic migration of peoples has been a two-way movement. Obviously, the main current flowed toward North America, but a steady though lesser drift constantly bore Europeans back to their native shores. Englishmen were uniquely conscious of the opportunities afforded by the wealth of the New World, and many came to envision America as a land which could supply material and spiritual wants unattainable at home. But the migrants differed in what they sought, and many grew impatient with American inadequacies. Furthermore, England's historical depth, the strength of her national sentiment, and her pride in race evoked intangible barriers which were not logically explained or easily defined. The homesick or disappointed usually exalted instinct more than reason and feeling more than logic. Over the centuries, thousands of Britons undertook American settlement only to "starve in the land of abundance."

Even during the first crucial decades of settlement, the return of immigrants provoked concern in seaboard communities. Governor Thomas Hutchinson once declared that throughout much of the seventeenth century, more people were drawn back to the mother country from Massachusetts than migrated to the colony. While Hutchinson obviously exaggerated the backward flow, modern research suggests that a major exodus did create considerable anxiety in New England after 1640.[1] During the following century, letters and reports indicate that the more cautious immigrants sailed with enough money to finance the second crossing should they choose to return. Colonial governors explained that both affluent settlers and common laborers recrossed the Atlantic in surprisingly large numbers. In 1751, Benjamin Franklin declared that an extensive exodus from America was counterbalancing the influx from Britain. By the early 1770's, influential Englishmen proposed that troopships carrying soldiers from Britain be used on the return voyage to provide free passage home for the many disappointed migrants.[2]

As long as the American colonies were attached to Britain, few political or psychological issues faced the immigrant who wished to return, but with the formation of the United States, international antagonisms and economic competition forced dissatisfied Britons to justify and explain their actions. Despite political hostility and a conflict of loyalties, economic pressure led to a startling increase in migration after the Napoleonic Wars. Naturally, as more persons arrived in America and as the cost, danger, and hardships of the voyage decreased, the number likely to return increased. Unfortunately, the records maintained by British and American officials open up few avenues for profitable investigation. Not only did the statistical methods vary, but the figures provide only rough approximations. Immigrants, tourists, businessmen, and others aboard a vessel were commonly lumped together as migrants. Nevertheless, scattered documents, newspapers, and immigrant literature suggest that the British movement led to a high incident of return.

By the late nineteenth century, the influx and exodus of migrants from southern and eastern Europe resulted in a great national debate, with increased notice being given to the return movement. Contemporary records show that the British were

1 William L. Sachse, "The Migration of New Englanders to England, 1640–1660," *American Historical Review*, Vol. LIII (January, 1948), 251.

2 Mildred Campbell, "English Emigration on the Eve of the American Revolution," *American Historical Review*, Vol. LXI (October, 1955), 6, 18–19.

also contributing to the backward flow. In 1891, Joseph Powderly, an investigator for the American Commissioners for Immigration, estimated that four-fifths of the Scottish migrants who sailed for the United States returned the same year. Clearly, Powderly exaggerated the return movement; however, figures furnished by the British Board of Trade indicate that a substantial percentage of the British migrants to the United States during the last three decades of the century sailed for home.[3] Between 1881 and 1889, for example, 370,697 British and Irish aliens left the United States, and in the year 1889, while 240,395 British and Irish entered the country, 71,392 returned to the United Kingdom.[4] In the year ending June 30, 1908, the first period for which complete and exact statistics were kept, a total of 49,056 English immigrants entered the United States and 5,320 left; 17,014 Scots arrived and 1,596 returned; 2,504 Welsh disembarked and 163 embarked for Britain.[5]

Although mass immigration was prohibited in the early 1920's, the depression year 1931—for the first time since the exodus of the United Empire Loyalists—saw more persons leaving America than entering. In that year, 43,000 aliens arrived in the United States and 89,000 departed. During early 1932, the mass of disappointed humanity crowding the ports led authorities to estimate that four persons left the country for every one who entered.[6] Of those leaving, the British represented one of the highest incidences of return. For the year ending June 30, 1932,

[3] *Parliamentary Papers, House of Commons*, XCIII, 1896, Emigration and Immigration, "Report to the Board of Trade," Tables X, XI, XIX, and XX. See also *ibid.*, XCIV, 1894, Emigration and Immigration, "Report to the Board of Trade," Table XI.

[4] "A Report of the Commissioners of Immigration upon the Causes which Incite Immigration to the United States," 52 Cong., 1 sess. (1891–92), *House Executive Document 235*, Part I, 260, 282.

[5] *Annual Report of the Chief of the United States Bureau of Statistics on Foreign Commerce and Navigation*, 889. Warner A. Parker (comp.), *Annual Report of the Commissioner-General of Immigration for the Fiscal Year Ending June 30, 1908*, 63–65.

[6] Louis I. Dublin, "A New Phase Opens in America's Evolution," *The New York Times*, April 17, 1932, Sec. 9.

records show that 2,155 British aliens entered the United States and 12,311 departed.[7] By 1937, the percentage of foreign-born in the United States had fallen to a lower point than at any time since the early days of the Republic; even the greatly reduced immigration quotas were not being filled.[8] Approximately 500,-000 aliens reimmigrated during the depression decade. The picture changed substantially after World War II; however, during the late 1940's and throughout the 1950's, between 10,000 and 15,000 aliens returned home each year. In the mid-1950's, Oscar Handlin estimated that there were scattered throughout Europe perhaps 3,000,000 persons who had experienced life in the United States.[9]

A large number of the migrants from southern Europe sailed for America with very real hopes for quick financial success and vague plans for eventual return. Most Continental nationalities tended to follow, and indeed were forced into, a rather rigid and limited settlement pattern. As newly arrived migrants congregated together for mutual assistance, they also tended to preserve Old World habits, languages, and customs. Such practices hindered their Americanization and substantially increased the chances for their reimmigration. The probability of return was further heightened by the fact that the overwhelming majority of the immigrants from southern and eastern Europe arrived in America within the brief span of fifty years.

Conversely, British immigration represented a fairly constant movement in which approximately fourteen million persons deserted the United Kingdom for the United States between 1815 and 1914. The British were also the most heterogeneous of all immigrant groups. Persons from every profession, trade, and occupation, as well as from all economic and social classes, participated in the adventure. The rarity of co-operative or group-settlement patterns and the similarity of ideologies rendered

[7] *Annual Report of the Commissioner-General of Immigration, 1932*, 58–59.

[8] "Alien Population Is Smallest in Years," *The New York Times*, June 13, 1937, p. 10e.

[9] Oscar Handlin, "Immigrants Who Go Back," *The Atlantic*, July, 1956, p. 70.

the British the most difficult nationality in America to isolate
historically or culturally. A few English and Welsh parties
co-operated in founding loosely organized agricultural communities, but these were seldom successful and never became "Little
Englands" standing aloof in a foreign land. With a rare diversifi-
cation of talents and interests, the British accepted employment
in eastern cities and pushed into the interior, became day
laborers, and built great businesses. They founded the American
theater, made biological discoveries in American forests, and
filled American pulpits. They helped to construct and operate
the textile mills of New England. They settled on small farms
and entered the mines of Pennsylvania. They sought the trade
and participated in the mellow life of the Old South. They helped
to break the sod and build the towns of the Middle West. They
purchased cattle baronies on the Great Plains, dug ore in the
western mountains, and invested in the fruit groves of the Pacific
Coast. Not all were to find an Elysium.

The issues impelling the return of Britons were quite removed
from the sociological forces which led Italians, Greeks, or Yugo-
slavs to recross the Atlantic. Since many Britons were trained in
a profession or were highly skilled in a craft, it was necessary for
fewer of them—fewer Britons, in fact, than members of any other
national group—to enter American life at the lowest level. The
British seldom left the United States because of congestion,
trouble with the law, labor-organization difficulties, nativist dis-
crimination, or resentment of their religion, speech, color, or
culture. They were not one of the submerged minorities. But
since the British found immigration a less disruptive ordeal than
other Europeans, by the same token, they were better equipped
to understand and judge America, make sharp comparisons,
and indulge in enlightened criticism. They also recorded their
opinions more readily and found publishers on both sides of the
Atlantic eager to set their works in print.

Of the seventy-five returning immigrants studied in the following chapters, all but nineteen published works on their New
World experiences. For twenty-six, the American odyssey was

7

their only book; two prepared two reports each, and three wrote a series of letters which friends or scholars later published. The remaining twenty-five back-trailers published nearly four hundred books and pamphlets on a wide assortment of subjects, but all wrote of their return from America. Twenty published at least one complete book on the subject, and five recorded their impressions in articles or in books devoted to other subjects. In short, the compulsion to express an opinion, to reveal a trend, or to expose a fallacy about America was overpowering for the returnees; yet not more than three or four of the seventy-five became authors by profession, while at the time of their sojourn in the United States, only William Cobbett and Charles Hooton admitted to being writers. The books of the immigrants, therefore, were not preconceived literary undertakings, and although occasionally adopting the form of travel accounts, the writers were motivated by quite different circumstances.

Much attention has been given to the unfavorable portrait drawn of America by British travelers and of the biased reviewing by leading British journals. Despite the implication of failure, however, the reports by returning immigrants were not a series of temperamental retrospections or negative prognostications. Of the fifty-six who personally recorded their evaluations of American society, some twenty-four remained friendly to the New World after return and at least five others, while temporarily indiscriminate in their criticism, quickly mellowed into balanced reporters. William Cobbett cursed the Republic and its base institutions when he left New York in 1800, but within ten years he had again become a great admirer of most things American. Annoyed by the general lack of taste and distraught by her marital scandal, Frances Kemble found little attractive about the United States, yet after a few months of European reflection, she wrote in *Year of Consolation*: "Oh, my poor dear American fellow citizen! How humbly on my knees do I beg pardon."[10] Both Miss Kemble and Cobbett returned again to attempt life in

10 James Playsted Wood, *One Hundred Years Ago* (New York, Funk and Wagnalls, 1947), 35.

the New World. Community-makers like William Bullock and Samuel Roberts eventually withdrew from their American experiments, not so much because they were disappointed in what they found as because their countrymen failed to follow them to their terrestrial retreat. David Mitchell was not displeased by his decade of business experience in Virginia. Even in a remote Welsh valley, the Reverend John Griffiths found he had no wish to divorce himself from his American-acquired habits. And the versatile William Hancock believed that a few years in America provided the necessary stimulation for a richer and fuller life. Taken as a whole, the works of the fifty-six reporters on things American add up to a balanced story, but as individuals they portrayed widely divergent sentiments.

Despite the lack of literary experience, the American story tended to be the best or at least the most popular work published by the returnees. Frances Trollope followed her *Domestic Manners of the Americans* with thirty-four novels and eight travel books, but none excited the English-speaking world like her description of life in Cincinnati, Ohio. Conversely, William Bullock had written scientific papers and museum guides and his European and Mexican travel books had been translated into many languages, yet it was his last work, *Sketch of a Journey Through the Western States of North America*, that became a labor of love and a guide to a new utopia. As a retired naval officer, John Oldmixon had enjoyed *A Lounge in the Tuileries* and during the Crimean War hastened from *Piccadilly to Pera*; however, it is neither French art nor the Turkish army but, rather, his American experiences for which he is best remembered. Between the 1820's and the 1870's, Richard Beste wrote fifteen books, yet only *The Wabash* received literary acclaim. The critical *Athenaeum* gave Beste one favorable review: it declared that *The Wabash* "can never be out of date anymore than Sterne's *Sentimental Journey* or *Robinson Crusoe*."[11]

What factors elevated mediocre scribblers into popular artists? How were technical and professional men enabled to excite

11 *The Athenaeum*, 1870, p. 258.

9

public fancy when they portrayed their personal reactions to America? What prompted the insatiable demands for such litera- ture? How were total novices stimulated to add to the already lengthy shelf of American description? The *North American Review* explained the phenomena as mainly personal economics. In reporting on William Faux's *Memorable Days in America*, the reviewer pointed to a half-dozen British immigrants who had sought an easy path to riches and when disappointed had at- tempted to compensate for their folly by the sale of a diatribe against America:

> We treated it [*Memorable Days*] as we have generally done the Fearons, the Jansons, the Howitts, and the various other paltry adventurers, who came over to this country to make their fortunes by speculation, and being disappointed in the attempt to jump into riches without industry, without principle, without delay, return to England and pander to the taste for American calumny, in order to pay the expenses of the expedition, by the sale of their falsehoods.[12]

According to the *North American Review*, Faux fell into the same class as "the swindler Ashe, the gardener Parkinson, and the stocking weaver Fearon, and a half dozen others, whose names and trades we forget."

In reviewing *Memorable Days, Blackwood's Magazine* thought it less financial failure than an original misunderstanding of the political and social organization of America that prompted the return. Faux was merely "a capital specimen of a village John Bull, for the first time roaming far away from his native valley." As a radical at the beginning of the journey, a republican about the middle, and a Whig at the end, *Blackwood's* believed he typified the returning Englishman.[13] The political theme was commonly emphasized as the reason for repatriation. *Fraser's Magazine* noted that Frances Trollope left England in the com- pany of Fanny Wright, the "Red lover," and "she made the usual transit in the course of her travels, having gone out Whig and

12 *North American Review*, Vol. XIX (1824), 92–93.
13 *Blackwood's Magazine*, Vol. XIV (1823), 564–65.

come back Tory, ready with anti-Jacobin, in the Robespierrian days in Paris, to cry out D—— liberty! I hate its very name."[14]

The British journals somewhat oversimplified the transformation from Whig to Tory. No doubt many British immigrants had subconsciously embraced theories popularized by Jeremy Bentham and James Mill and had assumed that freedom represented the lack of economic, social, and governmental restraints. To submit to individualistic goals and to yield to personal ambition was to provide greater happiness, therefore greater good. A short experience in a foreign environment revealed, however, that immigrants were not atoms who could separate themselves from their native society to pursue strictly independent or materialistic ends. They found neither freedom in individualism nor happiness in diversity. Their isolation in America tended to destroy them as human beings. They slowly came to understand that self-realization, hence real freedom and happiness, was possible only through identifying themselves and their interests with a sympathy born of tradition and inheritance and respect for the social whole.

Perhaps it was the essential difference between the somewhat similar societies of the parent and the child which invited much of the controversy and stimulated the unprecedented interest. At any rate, travel accounts were generally second only to divinity among the listings in the *London Catalogue*. Marveling at the sustained demand for travel literature, *Fraser's* noted in 1860 that "within the last quarter of a century they [travel books] have been launched forth from the press till their name is legion, and each year adds to the number."[15]

Although writers and critics have been called "the pathfinders for society," the fifty-six generally inexperienced immigration chroniclers who wrote on their American experiences produced few complex literary themes. Many of their observations were frivolous and unimportant, and their tendency to offer facts and technical data often reduced their works to mere geographical

14 *Fraser's Magazine*, Vol. V (1832), 336.
15 *Ibid.*, Vol. LXI (1860), 276.

guides. All too often their vertical shafts into the American environment failed to penetrate beneath the obvious or to be interlaced with an enriching sensitivity. The single-mindedness and parochialism of some of the returnees portrayed a peculiar unawareness of the temper of the New World and its historic relationship to Britain. Despite the length of many of the accounts, so little is said, so much left unexplained. Yet, as anxious and uncertain foreigners in a strange land, the immigrants reveal in their reports much of the habits of mind, the fierce devotion to homeland, and the blind loyalties which prompted their return.

The immigrant books that became significant did so because of the sheer force of the author's personality. Such works were designed, not as professional documents, but as emotional and subjective revelation. Not a few writers unconsciously adopted the Sterne or Dickens approach and portrayed themselves as sentimental Englishmen who could delight in the sublime, the picturesque, and the pathetic but who had found America rent with shattered illusions and futile dreams. By placing man's emotional response to American life on a level with his intellectual understanding, the romantic notions, which played their part in the migratory movement, became more effective. Travel and the accounts of distant perils had been the "mainstay of the romance in all ages"; consequently, the immigrant experience in America, even if declared a tragic failure, spurred the imagination and provided the New World with greater magnetism. For three centuries, the Americas had been a land of quests, and nineteenth-century romanticism found its new institutions, new freedoms, and new society irresistible.

Many of the returning immigrants quickly published their evaluations of the United States, but few attempted to express their views in the more provocative form of the novel. It was an age of serious reading; religious books commonly led all other categories on the printers' lists. Of the works carried in *The Athenaeum* about mid-century, fiction trailed behind religion, travel, history, and geography. Approximately four hundred books were written by fifty-six returnees, yet only seven might be classified as novels dealing with the American scene. In fiction, the author could have dug nearer the deeper truth than in the largely documentary immigrant report. He could have devised a more complicated, subtle, and penetrating technique to describe what he saw and felt. The sophisticated treatment of a novel could have illustrated American life without violating fact and by placing emphasis on selected points. Only Horace Vachell, Frances Kemble, Frances Trollope, Charles Janson, and Charles Hooton fictionalized their impressions of the New World.

Vachell wrote some 105 books after his late nineteenth-century ranching career in the American West, and at least a score of the volumes cite personal experiences. Nevertheless, his reflective and descriptive novel-like sketches were little more than light nostalgic essays designed to deal with his romanticized reactions to California. *Distant Fields, Fellow Travellers, Twilight Grey,* and *Now Came Still Evening On* reveal beauty and sensitivity, but they, like *Methuselah's Diary* and *More from Methuselah,* were more an autobiographical recalling of events than fiction. For more than fifty years after his return to England, Vachell reminisced on the harsh delight of his experiences, but the studies do little more than offer entertainment and provide an understanding of the author's refined and vital response to a youthful land.

Frances Kemble's only novel, *Far Away and Long Ago,* was written when the famous actress was eighty years of age and forty years after she had first lived in the Berkshire Hills. The setting and the plot reveal the strange, wild, emotional force which America exerted on the spirit of a vaguely disillusioned octogenarian. Her evocations of nature revealed that she remembered New England well, but as a guest, not as a Yankee. Although she lived in the Berkshires for more than a decade, they remained a vacationland and London remained home.

Months before *Domestic Manners of the Americans* was published, Frances Trollope had turned to the American theme for her first novel, *The American Exile,* later renamed *The Refugee in America* (1832); but the failure of the work was almost as complete as was the success of *Domestic Manners*. Although she had recently returned from a residence of almost four years in the United States, the American setting for the book was obviously unfamiliar and the handling of American ideas disorderly and overdrawn. But her English gentlemen and aristocrats were more glaringly out of character than were American smugglers and gossipy old ladies. British journals that had praised *Domestic Manners* found the novel a worthless hodgepodge, while *The American Monthly Review*, which had heaped scorn upon the earlier immigrant account, thought *The Refugee* faintly amusing and rather coquettishly suggested that its "gentle satire" upon the American character was not only harmless but might have a beneficial "moral effect."[16] Mrs. Trollope returned to the American theme in 1836 with *The Life and Adventures of Jonathan Jefferson Whitlaw*. Although propagandistic in aim and lacking in taste, the work rather perceptively depicted American slavery a decade and a half before *Uncle Tom's Cabin*.

The Widow Barnaby (1839) was well received and quickly ran through several editions; therefore, Mrs. Trollope married the widow to a swindler and produced *The Barnabys in America* (1843). Major Barnaby represented a cheap fourflusher who outbluffed the Americans at their own game. He used snobbery, swagger, and the pulpit to succeed in a society that drew the unprincipled adventurer, the fake promoter, the chameleon, and the bully. *The Old World and the New* (1849) presented the unattractive story of an English family's search for fortune in the New World. They eventually settled in a utopian-like community, but instead of being drawn by an ideal of perfection and rebirth, they were driven by failure and despair. The two later novels were artistically superior, but lacked the blunt meaning of *Jonathan Jefferson Whitlaw*. The works rather effectively characterized America as the land of the crude and the coarse. They offered a predigested message, and, much like the unsophisticated immigrant reports, they told the reader what he ought to think

16 *The American Monthly Review*, Vol. III (1833), 301.

and constantly intruded upon his imagination. Nevertheless, they succeeded in their over-all design of portraying the United States as a nation offering little hope for the prospective British immigrant.

Charles Janson's one attempt at fiction, *Edward Fitz-Yorke*, immediately followed his travel account of America. As a ponderous four-volume partial autobiography set in the United States it possessed no literary merit. Young Fitz-Yorke, after studies at Cambridge and trouble with an adopted father, sailed from Liverpool to seek his fortune. But American females provoked him, the American climate weakened him, and American manners appalled him. American traders had the finesse of a peddling Jew, American sentiment had become Gallic, and liberty was a clever plot hatched by slaveowners. *Edward Fitz-Yorke* revealed the character of Charles Janson, but the book contributed little to an understanding of the forces which drew most Britons to America or motivated their return.

Charles Hooton, like Mrs. Trollope and Janson, was baffled and embarrassed by immigration. All three had toyed with republicanism, all threw themselves into a frantic American search for gain, yet each remained an outsider. Hooton, like his compatriots, met with defeat and humiliating failure. Upon returning to England in 1842, he was in desperate need of money; therefore, like Mrs. Trollope, he wrote from necessity, and after publishing "Rides, Rambles, and Sketches in Texas" in serial form, he turned to the preparation of a novel. *Woodhouselee; Or the Astrologer*, later published as *Launcelot Wedge*, supplied autobiographical incidents from the author's youth and touched on his experience with immigration. The book was a failure. *The Athenaeum* explained that, since he was a "realist," his style possessed "a certain aridity of manner" and was of a "depressing nature."[17] Hooton's poems, ballads, and short stories published in *Ainsworth's* and *The New Monthly Magazine* were more successful and at times represented rather penetrating reflections on American life as he had observed it in Texas and Louisiana. "The

17 *The Athenaeum*, 1847, p. 201.

Exploits of Moreno the Texan" told of violence, murder, sadism, and witches. After a father and two sons killed several guests at an inn and threw the bodies to the alligators, justice was restored through lynch law. "Soul Le Blanc; or the Slave's Lesson" depicted the brutality of a plantation family when it was discovered that the son was part Negro. "A Fight in the Dark" was equally intense, with a duel being attempted in a darkened room. "The Two Frontiersmen; or Lynch Law" continued the slavery theme and at the same time attacked the English, who, with their "telescope eyes," could pick out every detail of wretchedness across the Atlantic without seeing the same monster when at arm's length. Hooton's preoccupation with the evils of slavery ran much deeper than that of such immigrant returnees as factory owner Peter Neilson and clergyman Samuel Roberts, both of whom published moralistic essays on the subject.

The main drift of criticism by returnees is easy to identify; it adds up to a not unusual British caricature of America. The Republic was peopled by men of action who cared little for the deeper meaning of life, who were blind to the beauties of their natural environment, and who were hostile to refinement and sensitivity. The blot of slavery and its deleterious effects on society, the false message of community-makers, the massive imprint of the wilderness, and the buffoonery, brutality, and uncertainty provided the theme for the novels as well as for much of the literature of return. Of course, not all was captious criticism; Mrs. Trollope made American girls into heroines, Hooton found that justice arose from the violence of the mob, and Janson discovered hospitality in the crudest log cabins. The writers were excited, amused, and disgusted in turn, but concluded that the New World was not a pleasant place to live. Much civilizing would be needed before America became more than "the poor man's country." Britons who made their way to the fringe settlements returned because the region was not yet ready for them. Mrs. Trollope wrote about Ohio, Hooton about Texas, and Janson, in part, about the Carolinas. They sensed, but were unable to understand, the myth of rebirth, of moral effort, and of material reward that spurred so many to withstand the hardships, hardships which for the frontiersman merely confirmed the worthiness of his mission and gave proof of the morality to be derived from nature and the peculiar fitness of free men to advance it. Most British returnees saw, but were not challenged by, the primitive aspects of America; they sought the good life now, not in some uncertain and distant future.

There was, however, often a subtle meaning or a counter-trend in the comments of the more perceptive returnees. Rather than vigorous, they found America boring; rather than questioning and vital, republican communities were suspicious and moribund. Although they were often unemployed, Americans boasted of their economic advantages; although they condemned politicians, they defended the political system; although they advocated freedom, they enforced conformity. A dedicated socialist explained: "If I had known the actual state of things, with the horrible restraint that is imposed on one, I should not have come. I believe there is more real liberty in the most aristocratic part of England, than in the most democratic part of America."[18] Nor had the frontier ennobled man. Americans found it amusing to cheat "green horns" and "smart" to misrepresent when engaged in trade. The knife and pistol were often carried, "but the strongest weapon wielded . . . was an ignorant public opinion." The self-restraint necessary if the immigrant was to be accepted "became most galling," but refraining from speaking on public issues and social customs was not enough, for "one must be like them, or be disrespected."[19]

The absence of European papers, the need for intellectual interplay, and the lack of artistic controversy left America without challenge, without variety, without eccentrics, and without freedom to choose. Sensitive Britons like the writer Charles Hooton, the physician Elizabeth Blackwell, the actress Fanny Kemble, and the communist John Alexander discovered that the values, the mores, and the subconscious trammels of the American community tended to dwarf rather than exalt the imagina-

18 *The Reformer*, No. 5 (May 26, 1849), 35.   19 *Ibid.*

tion. The strength of British tradition often supplied stature and meaning in the Old World, whereas the myth of utopia gave hope but little direction in the New. The myth was like a palimpsest upon which every man had inscribed his sentiments. But for many British immigrants, the image was blurred by the puzzling inconsistencies of American society.

Why did the British return? Was it simple economic determinism? Or were they unwilling or unable to perform the labor which would have given them the necessities, perhaps the conveniences, possibly the luxuries, of life? Did they lack the venturesome and industrious spirit necessary to flourish in the New World? Some Americans asserted that those who left were limited by the artificial manners and restricted by the decadent mores of their youth. Or were they sensitive persons who could not assess self-advancement on the basis of material wealth? Perhaps they sensed the need for the more subtle touchstones of grace, dignity, and forbearance. Wherein did the American dream of personal independence and the high hope for true republicanism prove illusory?

A satisfactory assessment cannot be made of the return movement until more is known about the many forces which induced the British to leave home in the first place. For example, the rate of return seems to have been particularly high among those who accepted public funds to finance their migration. Such assistance stemmed from one of three sources: landlords who wished to clear their estates of pauperized tenants; parish relief committees and church wardens who hoped to reduce poor rates by sending out habitual indigents; and the more official aid given under authority of the Poor Law Act of 1834. The 1834 law legalized the use of parish rates for emigration, and an 1851 act allowed Scottish landlords to borrow government funds to defray the expenses of transporting tenants. Officially, all persons sent out at public expense were to go to the colonies, but until the midforties, a sizable number went to the United States.

Objection to the parish program first developed during the 1830's. The opposition contended that in southern England, where officially financed migration had been most extensive, a "majority" of the single men returned home within a few years. British procedures created consternation in American port cities, and the United States Senate eventually demanded an investigation. By the time reports were secured from American consuls in Britain, the depression of the late thirties had prompted a major return movement and the issue was dropped. Years later, a writer for the *Colonial Magazine and East India Review* estimated that in 1836, "as many as 10,000 returned to this country." The article went on to condemn assisted emigration on the grounds that it did not accomplish its objective.[20]

In 1844, the well-known aristocrat-humanitarian Lord Ashley helped to found the London Ragged School Union. The express purpose of the school was to train and transport orphan and pauper children. A government grant to help finance the project was secured in 1848, and in 1849, many of the aristocracy, including the Queen and the Prince Consort, contributed to the emigration charity. Criticism quickly developed in the United States, and with the return of many of the migrants, opposition became widespread in England. When it was learned that two boys who had returned from America were being transported for the second time, sponsors of the program forced its cessation.[21] Ragged School returnees were not all undesirables, as is indicated by the case of a young lady who called upon Lord Ashley and explained that the Union had financed her migration. She had prospered, married a wealthy merchant, and with her husband had returned to England.[22]

Another factor which dislodged many Britons was the misrepresentation of American opportunities given by ship's brokers

[20] "Present System of British Emigration," *The Colonial Magazine and East India Review*, Vol. XXI (1851), 235.

[21] *Tenth Annual Report of the Ragged School Union* (London, 1854), 9.

[22] "Emigration of Girls as Well as Boys to Canada," *The Ragged School Union Magazine*, Vol. IX (1857), 156–58.

in an attempt to secure passengers. Transport companies were quick to see that immediate and direct profits could be gained from extensive migration. Human freight traveling west added a welcome complement to the larger and bulkier eastbound cargoes. As early as 1827, outbound vessels for British North America had an unused capacity of 400,000 tons.[23] Many journals issued warnings against notices which offered lucrative employment in America. *The Times* (London) of September 9, 1837, cited 350 returnees who had just arrived in Liverpool as typical victims of the false advertising. The writer emphasized that

> all of them arrived in Liverpool bitterly denouncing the base arts of swindling captains and shipowners, who had induced them to leave their happy homes, by advertising in Europe that "labourers in America were gaining from three to four dollars per day" and other lying and delusive statements, to tempt and betray poor emigrants into greater miseries than they would be likely, in the worst of times, to encounter in their native land.[24]

Although land was the one commodity America had in abundance, agricultural migrants often joined with fellow Britons in declaring the life unrewarding. As early as 1817, Scotsmen complained that "labourers in husbandry" had the choice of returning or accepting American charity. Between March 10 and May 10, 1817, the British consul in New York gave passports to eighty-seven British farmers and thirty-one agricultural laborers to enable them to proceed to Canada. A large number of farm laborers were assisted in sailing for home.[25]

Land salesmen and promoters of American settlement were indirectly responsible for the return of many agriculturists. Owners of the sparsely inhabited mountainous area extending from Pennsylvania to Georgia and agents representing Texas land interests were among the most active in their sales campaigns. Such projects often lured Englishmen to America but seldom provided them with a permanent home. Three salesmen

23 *Remarks on Emigration* (London, R. Clay, Cheapside, 1831), 10–11.
24 *The Times* (London), September 9, 1837, p. 6.
25 *Ibid.*, July 19, 1817, p. 2. col. 5.

who converged on England in 1848 typify the pattern. Samuel Saunders, as the agent for the United States Land and Emigration Society, was able to attract a substantial number of Englishmen to the company's barren Virginia hills. Not only did most of the party return, but one of the duped immigrants succeeded in having Saunders imprisoned.[26] Thomas Rawlings, former editor of the *Cheltenham Chronicle* and later of *The Old Countryman and Emigrants' Friend* of New York, also sold western Virginia properties throughout Britain. Because of his acquaintance with newspaper publishers, Rawlings' articles and brochures received wide circulation. His promotion was cut short, however, when most of the Welsh and English settlers he had sent to Virginia deserted their farms and sailed for home.[27] Also in 1848, Richard Keily became London representative for the Georgia Emigration Company. His persuasive salesmanship was reported in such widely separated papers as *The Times* of London, *The New York Journal of Commerce*, and local Georgia publications. But the Englishmen who purchased Georgia lands quickly accepted financial loss and personal embarrassment to return to Britain.[28]

Arthur Wavell, Robert Owen, and other leading Englishmen fostered Texas immigration during the twenties. Arthur Ikin, a Threadneedle Street financier, persuaded a party of Yorkshiremen to migrate to Texas in 1839. In Galveston they found that the land script they had purchased from Ikin was worthless, whereupon many returned.[29] The Robins agency of Covent Garden, the Tietkens agency of Great St. Helens, Bishopsgate,

[26] *The Emigrant and Colonial Gazette* (London), February 17, 1849, p. 422; *Manchester Examiner and Times*, November 24, 1849, p. 6, and December 1, 1849, Supplement, p. 1; *Liverpool Mercury*, June 10, 1851, p. 453.

[27] Thomas Rawlings, *Emigration: An Address to the Clergy of England, Ireland, Scotland, and Wales, on the Condition of the Working Classes* (Liverpool, Charles Wilmer, 1846); *Liverpool Mercury*, July 6, 9, 13, 1847.

[28] Richard Keily, *A Brief Descriptive and Statistical Sketch of Georgia, United States of America* (London, James Carroll, 1849); *The Emigrant and Colonial Gazette* (London), November 18, 1848, p. 213; February 24, 1849, p. 434; October 6, 1849, p. 827.

[29] Arthur Ikin, *Texas, Its History, Topography, Agriculture, Commerce* (London, Sherwood, Gilbert and Piper, 1841).

and the Rowed-Makery agency of London and Dorsetshire were all responsible for the migration and subsequent return of many Britons. The city of Kent, founded in late 1850 in Bosque County, Texas, lasted less than a year. Many of the original party returned to England within a few days after their arrival at Galveston, and others drifted back over the following months.[30]

A short time before William Kennedy traveled to Galveston to fill the post of British consul, he published a controversial history of Texas. On the first page of the work, Kennedy borrowed from Goethe's *Wilhelm Meisters Lehrjahre* to compare Britain's northern latitudes with sunny Texas:

Know'st thou the land where the lemon-tree bloom—
Where the gold orange glows mid' the deep thicket's gloom,
Where a wind, ever soft, from the blue heaven blows,
And the groves are of laurel, and myrtle, and rose?[31]

The book, along with other promotional literature on the Southwest, sparked a lively response from Britons who had migrated to the region only to find it utterly desolate. One article advantageously displayed on the first page of *The Emigration Gazette and Colonial Advocate* was entitled "Emigration Texas: Caution":

> The writer of this CAUTION TO THE PUBLIC is one of three survivors out of ninety-seven Englishmen who were induced to emigrate to the inhospitable swamps called Texas, in 1841. To detail the misery and hardships that the present writer and his deluded associates were exposed to on their arrival in the country, and the CERTAIN SICKNESS IF NOT DEATH that awaits those who may be tempted to emigrate to the land of fevers and disease of all kinds, would be quite impossible within the limits of this caution; which is meant simply to warn the working classes against the manifold schemes now put forth by a base set of YANKEE TEXAS LAND SHARKS, to delude them.[32]

30 Wilbur S. Shepperson, *British Emigration to North America* (Oxford, Eng., Basil Blackwell, 1957), 55ff., 86ff.
31 William Kennedy, *Texas: The Rise, Progress, and Prospects of the Republic of Texas* (2 vols., London, R. Hastings, 1841), I, 1.

Artisans, mechanics, and itinerant laborers provided the largest contingent of British returnees. Before the Civil War, the manufacturing and industrial branches of the American economy were too rudimentary to absorb large influxes of skilled workmen. Yet during the same period, the Industrial Revolution was transforming the British Isles from an essentially agricultural and commercial society into a predominantly industrial and financial society. The philosophy of *laissez faire* was being popularized, and the staggering human adjustment proceeded with little thought for the jobless. The old paternalism of earlier centuries was dying, while the new socialism of a later generation had not yet matured. Periodic recessions further complicated the employment picture and led thousands of skilled and semiskilled workers, even against their better judgment, to seek technical employment in agricultural America. The results were often disastrous.

Within a year after the end of the Napoleonic Wars, a significant reverse migration set in. On August 24, 1816, Captain Beveridge of the *Cheerful* reported that workingmen whom he had carried from Leath to New York were soliciting return passage on the same vessel.[33] By the autumn of 1816, James Buchanan, His Majesty's consul at New York, had received more than 4,000 applications requesting assistance.[34] *The Times* stressed the gravity of the situation: "Ten of the miserable emigrants referred to in Mr. Buchanan's letter published in *The Times,* October 1, 1816 have arrived at Liverpool in the *Venus.* They have been rescued from starvation by the humanity of Mr. B. and sent to their native land."[35] In a dramatic gesture, Thomas Reid appeared before a notary public and "made oath on the Holy Evangelists" that as a linen weaver he could find no employment in the New York area, therefore was forced to leave America. Thomas Boyd swore that as he left the United States,

[32] *The Emigration Gazette and Colonial Advocate* (London), June 18, 1842, p. 1.
[33] *The Times* (London), October 9, 1816, p. 3, col. 4.
[34] *Ibid.*, October 25, 1816, p. 2, col. 4.
[35] *Ibid.*, October 3, 1816, p. 2, col. 5.

"there were immense numbers of them [immigrants] most anxious to return."[36] By May 30, 1817, Buchanan had forwarded 1,658 persons from New York to Canada and had financed the return of many others.[37] Throughout 1819, shiploads of returning workingmen offered "a melancholy account" of the entire movement, and thousands were "prevented from returning merely for want of means to pay their passage home."[38]

Informed British publications like *Sidney's Emigrant Journal* forewarned mechanics and skilled tradespeople that nine out of ten migrants to the United States would be obliged to enter agricultural or pastoral pursuits.[39] The careful observer of American life Charles MacKay emphasized the point when he explained that the New World was swarming with unwanted and unneeded industrial and clerical workers.[40]

Technicians and craftsmen were repeatedly cautioned that American employers lured workers into immigration so that their technical skill could be exploited and job competition induced. In 1845, when the ironmakers and machinists at Pittsburgh resisted a reduction in wages, the importation of workers was attempted. Many of the English mechanics returned when they found that they were to be used as strikebreakers.[41] Whether the British were recruited for the construction of the Chesapeake and Ohio Canal, engaged to mine anthracite coal in Pennsylvania, induced to work for New York clothing manufacturers, secured to cut the stone for the Texas capitol, or employed to lay steel rails in Iowa, many sailed for home upon the completion of the project.

Perhaps the largest British exodus before the Civil War grew out of the series of economic panics of the 1840's and 1850's. After the sharp recession of the late 1830's, the return movement

36 *Ibid.*, October 5, 1816, p. 3, col. 1.
37 *Ibid.*, July 19, 1817, p. 2, col. 5.
38 *Ibid.*, October 8, 1819, p. 2, col. 4.
39 *Sidney's Emigrant Journal*, No. 1 (October 5, 1848), 1.
40 Charles MacKay, *Life and Liberty in America* (London, Smith, Elder, 1859), II, 315ff.
41 *Emigration, Emigrants, and Know-Nothings*, 32.

became a normal phenomenon. Tension before the Webster-Ashburton Treaty of 1842 and changes in American naval regulations led Britons who had served with the United States Navy to augment the backward flow. The *Doncaster Chronicle* stressed the misery of "a considerable number" of mechanics and weavers who "escaped from republicanism" to return to the near-by village of Barnby. Many were ill from starvation. One man attempted to walk from the Liverpool docks but collapsed on the road a few miles from Barnby.[42] Other newspapers emphasized the trend by capitalizing on the case of the *Hottinguer* and the *New York*. In September, 1842, the two vessels arrived at Liverpool only a few hours apart, one with 250 and the other with over 300 returning Britons on board. On the following voyage, three months later, the *Hottinguer* carried 200 persons back to Britain, while the *Liberty* docked the same week with 120 returnees.[43]

British industrial expansion in the era of the Crimean War and American political uncertainty in the fifties intensified the return movement. A Liverpool workhouse committee reported in August, 1858, that destitute immigrants whose return passage had been paid by friends in the United States were creating problems for the city's relief agencies.[44] The outward rush from America led the Colonial Land and Emigration Commissioners to prepare a special account of the movement for the House of Commons. Official figures indicate that 18,814 immigrants returned from North America to the United Kingdom in 1858. The momentum continued through 1860, when 17,798 persons from the United States and 1,098 from British North America recrossed the Atlantic.[45]

British trade-unions often organized emigration societies in an effort to create a scarcity of trained employees or to rid themselves of idle workers. Quite commonly those migrants who were

---

42 *The Times* (London), December 6, 1842, p. 4, col. 5.

43 *Ibid.*, September 20, 1842, p. 4, col. 3; December 13, 1842, p. 4, col. 5.

44 *Ibid.*, August 20, 1858, p. 9, col. 1.

45 *Parliamentary Papers, House of Commons*, Nineteenth General Report of the Emigration Commissioners, 1859, Sess. 2, XIV (2555), 5, and *ibid.*, Twenty-first General Report of the Emigration Commissioners, 1861, XXII (2842), 16.

assisted to leave found America unable to absorb their specialized skills, and many refused to adjust to new occupations.
Workmen sent out by the National Typographical Emigration
Society and the London Compositors Emigration Fund often
returned. Many of the potters forwarded by the Potter's Joint
Stock Emigration Society remained in Wisconsin but a few
months. Approximately half of the seven hundred immigrant
members of the British Temperance Emigration Society and
Savings Fund made their way back to England.[46]

Emotional dissatisfaction and psychological discontent rivaled
unemployment as a contributor to reimmigration. To many of
both the knowledgeable and the unsophisticated returnees, the
true wonders of England emerged, not from a glorious empire,
not from the Island's triadic associations, not from its commercial and industrial wealth, not even from its famed show
places, but to countless thousands, England was some private
place that could never engage a general admiration, a bare sheep-
walk, a cottage folded in a gully which had been the home of
their father and their father's father. They longed for the comfortable assurance of status, for the constricting yet unifying
habits of dress, of speech, of religion, and of social life. They
missed the music, the singing, the mellow, full, and poetic drama
of village life. They missed respect for the land, loyalty to class,
dedication to craft, permanency of employment. For many, the
very thought of home became a flight of the imagination rather
than the recollection of a reality. They stood rooted in the past,
no longer with a desire to free themselves, even from its debris.
They felt an urgency to escape from the cataclysm of America.

In short, many persons were temperamentally incapable of
giving their adopted land a fair trial. Even a personal success was
rationalized as a failure. Such migrants were literally observers of
republican life. They could not undergo the shock of living in a
strange land and postponed their return only for financial reasons or to prove to themselves that they had thoroughly investigated the New World and found it wanting. A few returned

46 *The Reformer* (London), May 26, 1849, p. 37.

almost as if by instinct. They wished to escape from the world in which they were nurtured, yet they were unwilling to break with it. They were like homing pigeons, ignoring adversity, material loss, and danger for the sake of reaching familiar surroundings. Most Englishmen who left America had one thing in common: they failed to become a part of the new society. Basic human instinct and innate tradition did not permit them to belong, to participate, to adjust. They lived, worked, and contributed to the community but could not grow new roots with which to anchor themselves. They easily mastered the details of American life but found it difficult to fill the emotional void which immigration had created.

Others migrants did not exercise conscious intelligence. They threw themselves blindly against the unknown and trusted to luck that the result would be satisfactory. An English gentleman farmer who planned to retire on the Iowa frontier echoed the disappointment of hundreds. "Soon we awakened to a painful realization that our imagination had run away with our judgment."[47] Too often, immigrants were psychologically ill equipped for life in a strange land. The incident at Tattershall Bridge was indicative of the hyperemotional individual who should never have left his native village. In mid-October, 1834, three men appeared at a tavern near Tattershall Bridge. They had disembarked at Boston, Lincolnshire, and traveled some ten miles up the Witham River by boat. After eating and drinking at a tavern, one failed to pay his bill. He explained that three years in America had left him penniless and in rags. As he spoke, he became nervous and excited. Finally, he dashed out the door and attempted suicide by throwing himself into the river. Near-by boatmen dragged him from the water while other tavern patrons paid the bill. The three proceeded on toward their long-deserted families.[48]

The Hull newspaper editor George Sheppard insisted that it was temperament, not conditions, intangible legacies, not genu-

[47] Harcourt H. Horn, *An English Colony in Iowa*, 24.
[48] *The Times* (London), October 25, 1834, p. 2, col. 6.

ine disappointments, which led immigrants to return.[49] As Sheppard conducted a party of Englishmen to Clinton County, Iowa, in 1850, he sensed, even before reaching New York, the inability of many to become Americans:

> Of more than 600 souls who now approach the great republic with the view of finding residences there, how many will realize the objects of their change? I fancy that it would not be difficult to pick out now a few who are altogether unadapted to the mode of life they are about to adopt, who will fail or be otherwise disappointed, and who will return to the "old country" at no distant day, with false estimates of almost everything belonging to America. Of all assailants of the United States, the most virulent and vindictive are those who figure as "returning emigrants." Yet it is certain that in nearly every case, the members of this class ought never to have entertained any notion of emigration. Without aspiring to the character of a prophet, I venture to predict that one-tenth of my fellow-emigrants will leave the United States, and return to their native land, before the expiration of eighteen months from this date. I imagine that I could now name several of these parties, and sure I am that the causes of their disappointment or failure are to be found in themselves, and not in the country which they will hereafter endeavour to depreciate and decry.[50]

In a letter of June 4, 1819, John Quincy Adams outlined the mental and emotional transition necessary before becoming an American. The Secretary of State admitted that, in the first instance, immigrants sailed for the New World hoping to benefit themselves and not to promote the welfare of their adopted country. Nevertheless, Adams contended, if they were to be happy in their new environment, they would have to adopt "that spirit of superiority" which characteried the American people.

[49] James J. Talman, "George Sheppard, Journalist, 1819–1912" *Transactions of the Royal Society of Canada*, Vol. XLIV (June, 1950), 119–34.

[50] Grant Foreman, "English Emigrants in Iowa," *The Iowa Journal of History and Politics*, Vol. XLIV (October, 1946), 397–98. Sheppard's letter of June 15, 1850, was published in *The Eastern Counties Herald*, Hull, England, on July 25, 1850.

"A life of independence" and the "means of obtaining easy and comfortable substance" were not enough.

> To one thing they [immigrants] must make up their minds, or, they will be disappointed in every expectation of happiness as Americans. They must cast off the European skin, never to resume it. They must look forward to their posterity rather than backwards to their ancestors; they must be sure that whatever their own feelings may be, those of their children will cling to the prejudice of this country, and will partake of that proud spirit, not unmingled with disdain, which, you have observed is remarkable in the general character of this people. . . .
>
> If they cannot accommodate themselves to the character, moral, political and physical, of this country, with all its compensating balances of good and evil, the Atlantic is always open to them to return to the land of their nativity and their fathers.[51]

Of the relatively few British political refugees who sought republican shores, several were ideologically inflexible and did not possess the ability to adjust to the political patterns of a new society. After a few months or years in America, political reformers often were quite willing to go home a good deal less hostile to crown and bishop and decidely more critical of republicanism. Some Britons failed to recognize that the United States had developed a distinct identity. Conservatives believed it to be only a youthful and greatly enlarged model of Old England. They were disappointed. Paradoxically, radical utopians assumed that the Western world had discovered the secret of perfectionism and was transforming the wilderness into a democratic paradise. They, too, were disappointed. Many Britons were irritated by the nationalism of Americans, by the confidence, which verged on arrogance, and particularly by the constant demand that all Englishmen offer unqualified praise of the new order.

Naturally, a few returnees possessed no national or group loyalty and could not identify themselves with any group anywhere. The traveler Arthur Young once observed that certain men were either of an unsettled disposition or so active and

[51] *Niles' Weekly Register* (Baltimore), April 29, 1820, pp. 157–58.

enterprising that they could not remain attached to any system. Frontier communities were notorious for instability and recklessness. Certainly, the difficulties and rigors of the return voyage did not deter the dissatisfied pioneers, the misfits, or the malcontents. In 1851, Professor James Johnston of Durham University declared that once this type was dislodged from stable Britain, they rarely stopped drifting and seldom settled permanently in capricious America. With their return to Britain, they took their emptiness with them and often later recrossed to America.[52]

No single explanation can account for the return of British immigrants. There were the utopian iconoclasts, who envisioned a world inhabited by generous, alert, forward-looking people who, although proud, were capable of self-chastisement, introspection, and self-negation. There were the libertarian reformers, who hoped to enhance man's appreciation of life by breaking the trammels, conventions, and compulsions so basic to British society. There were the ambitious, to whom the lure of the unknown was the expectation of financial gain; they sought immediate economic success and rapid ascent of the social ladder. There were the marginal workers, who, always on the periphery of society and buffeted by the economic pressures, were driven solely by the search for employment. Finally, there were the infrequent types who built a material and spiritual home in America but through a sense of personal duty, loyalty, or necessity returned to Britain.

Clearly, the sociological implications to be drawn from a study of immigration are endless. Nor can history ignore the leading participants in a movement so distinctly personal and intimate. In the following chapters, returnees will be grouped and studied on the basis of their major occupation, but emphasis will be placed on the human characteristics of individual migrants. At the same time, an attempt will be made to point up statistically some of the factors which led to return.

52 James F. W. Johnston, *Notes on North America, Agricultural, Economical, and Social* (Edinburgh, William Blackwood and Sons, 1851).

2

LAND WITHOUT PLENTY

Only weather, war, and infrequent epidemics interrupted the prosperous and stable life of eighteenth-century Britain. The wood lot with the common pasture and the three-field system with the narrow strips of tillable land were still the basis for the semicommunal system. By the end of the century, however, Lord Townshend, Jethro Tull, Robert Bakewell, and others had introduced scientific methods in agriculture, and the small industrial towns were beginning to create a new demand for farm products. Between 1761 and 1801, two thousand English estates were enclosed so that the owners might take advantage of the new agrarian techniques. Hundreds of inefficient rural tenants lost the use of the village commons. Evicted from their primitive cottages, they drifted to the new factory communities, or, if able to secure financial assistance, sometimes accepted the alternative of emigration.

Once in America, relatively few British agricultural laborers returned to their homeland. With the exception of unencumbered males, most workers found it impossible to accumulate sufficient capital to undertake the return journey. By the time they were financially able to return, it no longer seemed the wise thing to do. The displaced British agricultural worker had nothing to which he could return. If he settled in the interior of America or remained an agricultural laborer, the possibility of his return was even more remote. Furthermore, America's greatest appeal was to those who had enjoyed little opportunity or possessed few goods in the Old World. Cultivated Europeans with top hats or a plentiful supply of banknotes were often sensitive to the new societies' crudities, while immigrants with bent backs and calloused hands sought work and food and dignity.

The exodus of agricultural laborers should not be confused with the migration of independent British farmers. The latter were a notch higher on the social scale. As middle-class yeomen, they had become the basis of the new agrarian organization. They leased the estates of the landlords, employed agricultural labor as needed, and became the managing specialists who directed the techniques and methods of farming. The American and Napoleonic wars increased the demand for agricultural products, but after 1815 many of the manager-farmers found the long-term cash rents demanded by the landlords ruinous. The enclosures were also on the increase—as many as 853 between 1810 and 1819—thus creating a unique demand for leasable farms in the midst of an agricultural recession. Although the number of enclosures steadily declined after 1819, the recurring depressions of the twenties, thirties, and forties led an ever increasing stream of farmers to seek a more profitable outlet for their skills. The yeoman-farmer migrated with the hope of purchasing a small holding and becoming an independent proprietor. Others sought an opportunity to engage in agricultural experimentation and at the same time increase their income through an enlarged managerial operation. Owners of coastal estates and southern plantations early recognized the progressiveness and scientific abilities of the leading British farmers and, soon after the American Revolution, began to publicize attractive offers for farm administrators.

In 1797, Richard Parkinson, a farmer-manager from near Doncaster, called on an old friend, Sir John Sinclair, president of the Board of Agriculture. While discussing farming, Sinclair showed the Yorkshireman a letter of February, 1796, from George Washington in which the General proposed letting out his Mount Vernon lands to British overseers. Parkinson was immediately intrigued with the idea of supervising a fertile estate for the great American. He wrote Washington and tentatively agreed to take over the management of a 1,200-acre section of Mount Vernon known as the River Farm.

Born in 1748, the son of a Lincolnshire grazier, Parkinson became fascinated by contemporary developments in agriculture. In the tradition of Coke of Holkham, William Marshall, and as a close friend of Arthur Young, he began to experiment with agricultural machinery, the selected breeding of livestock, and the use of fertilizers. After his marriage, he moved to a farm near Doncaster where he continued his practical research and in 1797 completed an expansive but quite readable two-volume work entitled *The Experienced Farmer*. The study was encyclopedic in scope, dealing with such diverse topics as the breeding of horses, the raising of rabbits, the hatching of poultry, and the growing of hedges. Well acquainted with the agricultural reports which Jefferson, Washington, and others had sent to Arthur Young, the fifty-year-old Parkinson appeared to be an ideal manager for the Mount Vernon estates.

After chartering a ship for £850, the Englishman purchased choice livestock, including the famous race horses "Phenomenon" and "Cardinal Puff," and with his wife and five children sailed for Virginia on September 3, 1798. The servants and attendants who were to accompany the Parkinsons either refused to put to sea because of illness or were impressed by the British navy a few hours out of port. The voyage, therefore, became a tiresome and hazardous experience. The captain proved incompetent, many of the horses died because of inadequate care, and when at last Norfolk harbor was sighted in mid-November, the country appeared bleak and desolate. After a few days in Norfolk, the family moved up the Potomac to Alexandria. Although the populace seemed pleasant and friendly, Parkinson found the Mount Vernon lands far below his expectations and, after visiting the estates several times, finally decided not to contract for the River Farm. He experienced a minor disagreement with Mrs. Washington over the best type of livestock for the Virginia lands and climate, but thought the General exceptionally considerate, despite his formality and personal correctness. Indeed, after Parkinson decided not to accept the River Farm, Washington gave him a sum of money to compensate him in part for the trouble and expense of traveling to America.

The number of large landholders who were poor convinced Parkinson of the aridity of American soil. The heavy frosts, the almost complete lack of clover or other cover crops, the lightness and poor quality of grains, the scrawniness of livestock, and, particularly, the many and feverish attempts by landowners to rent their farms further indicated that American farming must be an unprofitable occupation. After examining the real estate business in the new capital city of Washington, estimating the profits to be derived from a brewery, and even considering the prospects for success on the frontier, Parkinson eventually leased a small dairy farm in Maryland. On May 1, 1799, the family took up their residence at Orange Hill, three miles from Baltimore.

It quickly became apparent that no truly large-scale or intensive agricultural enterprise could be conducted because of the impossibility of securing reliable labor. Parkinson refused to use slaves and found free Negroes and Irishmen to be dishonest and shiftless. The social equality demanded by native workers rendered them unbearable. They entered the house with their hats on, slept after the employer arose in the morning, smoked, and even remained seated while ladies were standing. Liberty and equality had "destroyed the rights of the master."

Since the Parkinson children could operate the farm in slack seasons, Richard devoted much time to a study of the country. After inspecting Maryland's Eastern Shore and other near-by districts, he visited Philadelphia, where he arranged for the printing of an American edition of *The Experienced Farmer.* Later, while delivering copies of the work to subscribers, he had an opportunity to observe many phases of the national economy. Particularly attracted to the brewing business, Parkinson accepted a partnership in and became technical director for a brewery in Baltimore. He had helped to devise an instrument which measured the saccharin content of barley, and compiled

34

detailed statistics on costs and prices in American beer production. Parkinson's tables and calculations demonstrated the economic opportunities to be realized from a carefully operated brewery. After returning to England, he specified beer as one of the most lucrative fields for American enterprise, "and the only one I know likely to come to anything worth notice."[1]

In September, 1799, Mrs. Parkinson and four of the five children became ill with yellow fever. In semidelirium, members of the family spoke of their homesickness and indicated their unhappiness in America. Parkinson resolved that "should God spare them, I would return as soon as I possibly could."[2] The large number of dissatisfied migrants increased the Parkinsons' anxiety. Most were unable to finance their passage home; others who were able to do so hesitated because of the scorn and gossip which would brand them a failure. "To put us in spirits, now and then an Englishman would come and tell us a most lamentable story of what suffering he had undergone, that he had been cheated out of his money, and how poor the land was." Upon leaving the house, the visitors would sigh and remark, "The devil's own country to be sure."[3] Parkinson became convinced that his countrymen were universally displeased. "I never met an Englishman in that country, of whatever rank in life he might be, that liked it, but wished himself at home again."[4]

Parkinson decided that he was like Robert Bakewell in having pursued agricultural investigation to the brink of personal bankruptcy.[5] Well read and unusually skilled in the new scientific farming, he sensed that he was failing to use his capital and knowledge to the best advantage. Slowly he came to the realization that land in America presented different opportunities and demanded different handling than land in England. After two years of growing inferior grain, shearing light wool fleeces, and

---

1 Richard Parkinson, *A Tour in America, in 1798, 1799, and 1800,* I, 238.
2 *Ibid.,* 178.   3 *Ibid.,* 167.   4 *Ibid.,* 28.

5 Parkinson generally disapproved of Bakewell's ideas and actions. See Richard Parkinson, *Treatise on the Breeding and Management of Livestock* (London, Cadell and Davies, 1810), I, Introduction.

cultivating gullied fields, he expressed bewilderment that so many Americans were willing to eke out what was at best a miserable existence on the land. He insisted that Michel Guillaume Jean de Crèvecoeur's *Letters from an American Farmer* demonstrated that the author knew nothing about farming, while the writings of Joseph Priestley, Thomas Cooper, and Thomas Paine showed that they knew nothing about America. Equally astonishing to the Englishman was the limited knowledge leading Americans possessed about agriculture in other parts of their own country, in England, or on the Continent. Even intelligent and well-trained observers like Jefferson were unscientific in agricultural studies and totally ignorant of great discoveries that were being made in Europe.

Lower-class Americans, of course, proved particularly annoying. With little show of diplomacy, the strenuous Englishman argued with his less versatile neighbors, debated in the taverns, and assured all that the United States was not and never could become either a great agricultural or a leading manufacturing nation. As a result of the intemperate remarks, petty mischief-makers and community pranksters deliberately harassed the Parkinsons. Unable to understand American society and lacking in frontier humor, the Englishman was at a complete loss to explain such annoyances to his family.

Parkinson returned to Liverpool in 1801 with five hundred unsold copies of *The Experienced Farmer*, but was shocked to find that British authorities would not allow him to take ashore a work printed in America. Thereupon he sailed for Dublin and after several weeks of negotiations settled on the farm of the Earl of Conyngham in November, 1801.[6] Holding the Irish in low regard, Parkinson found the managing of Irish laborers intolerable. After two years with the Earl, he accepted the stewardship of a farm belonging to Sir Joseph Banks and returned to Lincolnshire. In 1805, Parkinson completed and published at least three

6 Richard Parkinson, *The English Practice of Agriculture, Exemplified in the Management of a Farm in Ireland, Belonging to the Earl of Conyngham* (London, Longman, Hurst, Rees and Orme, 1806), 1.

different edition of *A Tour in America in 1798, 1799, and 1800*. The following year, *The English Practice of Agriculture* was published; *Practical Observations on Gypsum* appeared in 1808 and a treatise on the *Breeding and Management of Livestock* in 1810. In the meantime, he had been engaged by Arthur Young, secretary of the Board of Agriculture, to prepare a government survey of farming by counties. Parkinson published his study of the county of Rutland in 1809, Buckinghamshire in 1810, and Huntingdon in 1811. Shorter works dealing with grain farming and a clear description of the "Parkinson cultivator" and "corn cutter," invented while he was in Maryland, have not been preserved.[7] Parkinson died at Osgodby, Lincolnshire, on February 23, 1815.

Although none of Parkinson's later writings equaled *The Experienced Farmer* in analytical quality or wealth of experimental knowledge, it was *A Tour in America* which established him as an agricultural authority and provided for his entry into scientific and governmental circles. Much of the second volume of *A Tour*, compiled after the return to England, was hackneyed and contradictory; nevertheless, the work represented one of the first lengthy reports on the undesirability of American settlement and led Parkinson to be "reckoned one of the best practical writers on agriculture."[8] The author recounted dozens of stories of Englishmen being lured to America only to be fleeced of their capital and left stranded, destitute, and miserable. With neither physical comfort nor mental happiness, why should anyone, inquired Parkinson, wish to undertake the venture of emigration? "Laws, they have none; religion, none; produce on an acre, about one in five compared with ours."[9] But perhaps the greatest misfortune of all was American independence: those who "argue the most strenuously for liberty for themselves are the most absolute to

[7] J. C. Loudon, *An Encyclopaedia of Agriculture* (London, Longman, Hurst, Rees, Orme, Brown and Green, 1825), 1168.

[8] John Donaldson, *Agricultural Biography: Containing a Notice of the Life and Writings of the British Authors on Agriculture* (London, privately published, 1854), 83–84.

[9] Parkinson, *A Tour in America*, II, 623.

others."[10] Parkinson also observed that "liberty and equality may truly be said to destroy all civil magistracy, and to take away all the graces so well spoken of by Lord Chesterfield."[11] Although thousands of British agricultural laborers and farmers prospered in the young republic and admired its institutions, Richard Parkinson appears as a forerunner of the dissatisfied hundreds who throughout the nineteenth century warned their country-men of the indifferent husbandry, degenerate habits, and cultural barrenness of the Western world.

America's greatest economic asset was an abundance of land. The necessity of taming the frontier and clearing the wilderness made all agriculturists an object of considerable national worth. Furthermore, American backwoodsmen were uniquely mobile, constantly deserting partially cleared estates on the fringes of civilization to push farther west. Immigrant farmers, represent-ing the second and third waves of settlement, tended to fill the vacuum created by the migratory habits of the earlier settlers. In the decade following the War of 1812, the American frontier expanded rapidly; thus hundreds of semi-improved farms from western New York and Ohio to Kentucky and Tennessee were open for purchase.

America's agrarian expansion coincided with British contrac-tion following the Napoleonic Wars. Indeed, embittered Eng-lishmen sometimes suggested that only in America could the truly independent English farmer be preserved. As a whole, the migration of agriculturists was a success. Nevertheless, social, political, and, particularly, economic disappointment took its toll even among agriculturists. The American recession of 1819 and the financial uncertainty that followed were particularly illustrative of a period of immigrant disappointment. Persons leaving the United Kingdom for the United States increased from 1,209 in 1815 to 10,674 by 1819, but the depression brought a two-thirds reduction in British departures for 1820, and, even more significant, it served to stimulate a return movement of major proportions.

10 *Ibid.*, 612.   11 *Ibid.*, 734.

Charles H. Wilson was one of the many farmers who arrived in New York at the depths of the 1819 depression and after a year's adventure and misadventure determined to retrace his course to Yorkshire. A limited income, a growing family, and trouble with relatives first led Wilson to consider life in the New World. After reading several emigrant tracts and newspaper reports, he accepted the advice of friends and in May, 1819, sailed from Liverpool. Embittered, self-conscious, and arrogant, Wilson found every phase of his journey irritating. The ship's captain was rude, quarantine regulations were galling, New Yorkers were braggarts, the streets were dirty and infested with hogs, and every tavern wall was covered with deceptive land advertisements.

Wilson eventually decided to purchase a farm in Pike County, Pennsylvania, but before he had completed the negotiations, he was deterred by a fellow Yorkshireman who argued that they should first travel the eighty miles to inspect the property. Before arriving at their destination, persons whom they chanced to meet along the route dissuaded the north-countrymen from continuing on to Pike County and redirected them to other estates. The result was a series of ill-advised inspection tours which convinced Wilson that the entire region was "barren, savage and wild." "So rude and ruinous is the appearance of the land, with its uncouth and rough fences, a melancholy waste of fine timber, that it gives the contradiction to the American apology—which is, that it is a young country, dawning into existence; for it more resembles an old country, yawning out of existence, as exhibiting the wreck of time, or the expiring remains of a deluge, or some other revolutionary devastation of nature."[12]

To Wilson, as to many British farmers, the American type of agriculture was a sacrilege against nature. He understood the fundamental choices of purchasing partially improved and semi-impoverished lands or pushing on in the vanguard of the pioneers, and he readily admitted that he was not fitted for the latter. "I am apprehensive the wilderness is little understood in England. Let me observe, it is a bold undertaking to seek in the

[12] Charles H. Wilson, *The Wanderer in America,* 26.

mazes an English home. The Americans are excellent forest pioneers; with axe on shoulder, and no men can use that instrument like them [sic], they face the labyrinth—not so John Bull—he wants neighbours shaped something like himself; not the gaunt wolf, or rugged bear."[13]

During the autumn and winter of 1819–20, Wilson moved his family to Albany, later to Buffalo, and finally to Canada, but the British colonies were no more hospitable and were even less advanced than the United States. In the spring of 1820, he traveled with a glass manufacturer to Philadelphia, Baltimore, Washington, and Charleston and found himself rather admiring Yankee enterprise and southern courtesy. Yet there was a barrenness of intellect, an excess of democracy, nothing to gratify the philosopher or man of taste, bigotry among Catholics and nonconformists alike, a frightful prejudice against Indians and Africans, and a harrying climate of materialism which led to financial deception. But it was "the many disappointed and ruined returned emigrants . . . from the Western States of Ohio, Illinois, Tennessee, Indiana and Missouri" who convinced Wilson of the uselessness of further search.[14] Although well educated and observant, Wilson was an opinionated and boorish north-countryman who would have found it difficult to adjust to any society outside his native Yorkshire.

Although he was from the same social and occupational strata as Wilson, Joseph Pickering's reasons for emigration were somewhat more rudimentary and compelling. A farmer of Fenny Stratford, Buckinghamshire, Pickering had once moved "in a respectable sphere." In 1813, he took a farm on the usual seven-year lease, but with the cessation of the war found himself unable to pay the high rent. The expiration of the seven-year contract left Pickering ruined financially. A further failure as a storekeeper seemed to leave emigration the only alternative to "privation, and its consequent distress." Leaving London in October, 1824, Pickering traveled steerage to Baltimore, where he immediately set about studying opportunities in the surround-

13 *Ibid.*, 48.   14 *Ibid.*, 70.

ing countryside. At first he hoped to purchase a small farm, but finding himself short of cash, he later determined to secure a position as steward of an estate or plantation. No offers were forthcoming, however, and he moved, in turn, to Philadelphia, New York, Albany, and Buffalo. Although pleased with the picturesqueness of the countryside, Pickering grew fearful of his ability to compete with the natives. Basically, he could not understand the social character of Yankees. Annoyed by their claims of superiority, shocked by their indifference to natural beauty and the simple pleasures of life, and confused by their incessant activity, Pickering at length decided that he could never swear allegiance to American institutions. After an extended residency in Canada, he returned to Britain in October, 1829.[15]

The challenges presented by the new society were many and varied. Inevitably, America failed to fulfill the expectations of many immigrants. It was largely an egalitarian and only partially educated democracy striving to survive, expand, and mature simultaneously. Many of the citizenery were not intent on furthering or even preserving European standards of culture. Much public thought was devoted to the simple matter of felling trees and building cabins. Opinions, attitudes, and responses were shaped and distorted by the crude demands of necessity or expediency. The national mind and imagination, while impregnated with faith and emotion, were, nevertheless, nurtured on reality and tinted with pragmatism. It is not surprising, therefore, that to Parkinson, Wilson, Pickering, and hundreds of other sensitive British farmers, America seemed a broad wilderness peopled by suspicious woodsmen and crafty land salesmen. To predict that a wealthy, stable, and constructive society would evolve over the following generations seemed to be boastfulness bred of uncertainty, not robust vision.

Although British immigrant farmers generally followed the

[15] Joseph Pickering, *Emigration or no Emigration; Being the Narrative of the Author, an English Farmer, from the Year 1824 to 1830.*

established pattern of filling in behind the pioneer Americans, the lure of virgin lands occasionally led them to throw caution aside and proceed into the undeveloped interior. The famous Birkbeck-Flower Colony of Albion and Wanborough, Illinois, was a classic example of such an undertaking. In April, 1816, George Flower, son of a moderately affluent landowner and brewer of Marden Hall, near Hertford, sailed for the United States. After visiting Dr. Priestley's Susquehanna settlement at Sunbury, he traveled throughout the West during the summer and autumn, but returned to the East in early winter. Quite by chance while at the home of former President Madison, Flower met Edward Coles, a future governor of Illinois. Coles had recently returned from a mission to Russia and, while stopping over in England, had become acquainted with Morris Birkbeck, a well-to-do tenant farmer from near Guilford, Surrey. As an enterprising Quaker who supervised a 1,500-acre farm, Birkbeck had grown resentful of a government which taxed him but denied him the vote, which levied tithes for a church he would not attend. Although Birkbeck was twenty-four years older than Flower, the two were close personal friends. In 1814, they had traveled together for three months while making a study of French agriculture.

In the spring of 1817, as Flower was making plans to return to England, he received word that his old friend Morris Birkbeck, with a few relatives and assistants, had landed at Norfolk. Flower immediately joined the group, and during the summer of 1817 the little party of ten made their way to Edward Coles's much publicized Territory of Illinois. By September, 1817, Flower had married one of the young migrants and with his bride was ready to start back to England to advertise the settlement. The young Englishman's migration activities were reinforced by Birkbeck's *Notes on a Journey in America* (Philadelphia, 1817) and *Letters from Illinois* (London, 1818). In the winter of 1817–18, Flower and Charles Trimmer of Yeatley, Surrey, recruited a party of some forty-five farm workers and along with James Lawrence, a merchant-tailor of Hatton Garden, London, Flower organized a party of some forty-eight tradespeople. The two groups sailed from the port of Bristol in early March, 1818. In April, a second contingent, including George Flower's parents and younger brother and a wealthy Englishman by the name of Fidler, also started for Edwards County, Illinois.

Although the colony grew rapidly and by August, 1819, contained about four hundred persons, some of the migrants began to return to Britain as early as the summer of 1818. For example, as Fidler traveled west from Pittsburgh on horseback, he "experienced many annoyances—bad roads, swollen streams, bad cooking, buggy beds—altogether enough to put an elderly gentleman a little out of sorts."[16] At last reaching Vincennes, Indiana, only about forty miles from his destination, Fidler stopped to recuperate. Stories of sickness, swamps, and still greater hardships to be faced on the English Prairie were commonplace. Many such stories were deliberately circulated in an effort to attract migrants to the near-by English community of Saundersville, Indiana. Nevertheless, Fidler decided that his £40,000 would purchase more comfort in England than in America, whereupon he rode directly back to Pittsburgh, hurried on to the coast, and recrossed the Atlantic without even inspecting the Illinois lands.

James Lawrence, leader of the party of London tradespeople, soon followed Fidler to England. Even Charles Trimmer, the young bachelor farmer from Surrey, became discouraged and returned after two years of enduring coarse food, coarse clothing, and log huts.[17] Neither Birkbeck's eldest son nor George Flower's younger brother, Edward, remained in America.[18] Elias Pym

16 George Flower, *History of the English Settlement in Edwards County, Illinois, Founded in 1817 and 1818, by Morris Birkbeck and George Flower*, 151.

17 *Ibid.*, 78, 79, 123.

18 Gladys Scott Thompson, *A Pioneer Family: The Birkbecks in Illinois, 1818–1827* (London, Jonathan Cape, 1953), 17. As a youth of nineteen, Edward Flower decided to become a brewer in England rather than a farmer in Illinois. His father, Richard, traveled back to Britain with him, but later recrossed the Atlantic to America. Edward became a brewer in Hertford, but later founded a very successful brewing business in Stratford-on-Avon. As four-time mayor of Stratford, he was particularly hospitable to Americans when they attended the Shakespeare tercentenary in 1864. Indeed, for some years Mayor Flower divided his time be-

Fordham, a twenty-nine-year-old cousin of George Flower, was one of the original party of ten who traveled to Illinois during the summer of 1817.[19] Although he was a promising engineer, he had become discouraged with both economic and political trends in England and was happy to join Birkbeck's family and friends when they sailed from Gravesend in April, 1817. By a fortunate coincidence, Fordham's letters home from May 8, 1817, to October 30, 1818, have been preserved. Not only do they chronicle conditions on the English Prairie, but, more important, they show how the faith and optimism of a reasonable man were worn down.

During the first months in America, Fordham cheerfully accepted deprivation and inconvenience and argued that time and effort would transform the frontier into a prosperous and enlightened region. In addition to operating a farm and keeping a store, he surveyed and laid out the new town of Albion. He planned its streets, jail, courthouse, chapel, and public square. Fordham explored and marked the section lines on the prairie, dug wells, and built windmills. He even informed a visiting Englishman that only as a rich man would he return home, and should he fail in Illinois, he would "turn hunter and live by his rifle on the frontier."[20] Fordham's last ten letters, dated between February 3 and October 30, 1818, show a diminishing enthusiasm. On May 6, he wrote, "I often think of you in this land of dirt, bad cooking, and discomfort of every kind."[21] Two months later, he offered a brief evaluation of American politics. "Liberty is the watchword of the popular or democratic party, and in their vocabulary it means anything and everything. It has no limits but

---

tween encouraging Shakespeare festivals and fostering English emigration to Illinois.

[19] Fordham's ancestors, who could be traced back to the time of King Stephen, had for eight centuries held extensive estates in Cambridgeshire and Hertfordshire. Elias' father had turned from Trinitarian minister to brewer, to farmer, to Unitarian preacher. His mother died in 1808, and the two sons and five daughters were forced to become self-sufficient at an early age.

[20] William Faux, *Memorable Days in America*, 268.

[21] Elias Pym Fordham, *Personal Narrative*, 204.

the weakness of man, no boundary but that of his desires. To right oneself by violence, to oppose force by force, is reckoned a virtue here; and woe to the man who is suspected of cowardice."[22] English governments squandered the people's money, yet "there are in England, comforts, nay, sources of happiness, which will for ages be denied to those half-savage countries, good houses, good roads, a mild and healthy climate, healthy, because the country is old, society, the arts of life carried almost to perfection, and laws well administered."[23]

Fordham squarely opposed the philosophy of the eighteenth-century nature worshipers, who believed that man remained pure when undefiled by law and society. After revealing that frontiersmen were often guilty of robbery, murder, and brutality, he wrote:

> Instead of being more virtuous, as he is less refined, I am inclined to think that man's virtues are like the fruits of the earth, only excellent when subjected to culture. The force of this simile you will never feel, till you ride in these woods over wild strawberries, which dye your horse's fetlocks like blood yet are insipid in flavour; till you have seen waggon loads of grapes, choked by the bramble and the poisonous vine; till you find peaches, tasteless as a turnip and roses throwing their leaves of every shade upon the winds, with scarcely a scent upon them. Tis the hand of man that makes the wilderness shine. His footsteps must be found in the scene that is supremely and lastingly beautiful.[24]

The exact date of Fordham's return to England is unknown, but over the succeeding years, he was appointed engineer to the Cinque Ports and eventually enjoyed a high reputation as civil engineer and technical assistant to the famous locomotive builder George Stephenson.

The Birkbeck-Flower disagreement which split the colony in 1818, the extended drought of 1818–19, and the rigors of frontier life caused many settlers to return. Under normal conditions, they would have destroyed the magnetism of the English Prairie. The economic and political dissatisfaction in Britain was un-

[22] *Ibid.*, 221.   [23] *Ibid.*, 227.   [24] *Ibid.*, 225.

usually intense, however, and the letters and pamphlets issued by the colony's founders tended to make western settlement an expression of hope for thousands of Britain's yeomen farmers. Dozens of Englishmen from all ranks of society investigated the Albion community in particular and the frontier in general. Adlard Welby of Lincolnshire journeyed westward in 1819 with his own carriage and valet. Welby explained that although some migrants returned to England, most were obliged to stay, "having spent their all to get there."[25] He further argued that Birkbeck's writings alone had caused immigration to the United States to increase tenfold.

William Faux, wishing to obtain positive evidence on the prospects for an English farmer, devoted about sixteen months to a survey of American opportunities, but reported conditions on the English Prairie to be most unattractive.[26] Thirty-nine farm families from Essex selected Henry Bradshaw Fearon, wine merchant of London, to investigate the Illinois settlement and study the general advisability of migration. His nine months' stay in the United States, from August, 1817, until May, 1818, left Fearon convinced that no clear-cut advantage could be secured by proceeding to the frontier.[27] The famous publicist William Cobbett, who in 1817 fled to the United States the second time, led the most vehement attack on the settlement and generally scorned the idea that Englishmen should go to the American backwoods. On the other hand, William Tell Harris, who traveled throughout the country between 1817 and 1819, concluded that when English farmers pushed into the interior, they found pleasant conditions and lands well suited for agriculture. Harris admitted, however, that thirty-seven migrants, mostly farmers, crowded on the ship as he sailed from Liverpool in May, 1817, and thirty returning Englishmen were on board as he left Philadelphia in July, 1819.[28]

25 Adlard Welby, *A Visit to North America and the English Settlements in Illinois, with a Winter Residence in Philadelphia*, 125.

26 Faux, *Memorable Days in America*, 268ff.

27 Henry Bradshaw Fearon, *Sketches of America*.

Although many of the colony's leaders, such as Edward Flower, Fordham, Lawrence, and Trimmer, refused to live in Illinois, the number of British migrants who returned from the Illinois prairies was not large. Nevertheless, the experiment was perhaps responsible for a major repatriation movement. Many reports indicate that during 1819, most ships leaving America for England were carrying disappointed immigrants. Morris Birkbeck's publications were blamed for having led hundreds to sink their entire fortune in worthless American land. Since many families had used all their resources to get to America or to buy a farm, they could return only through the generosity of friends and relatives in Britain.[29] English travelers and prospective settlers emphasized the return movement. The Yorkshireman William Savage, who had planned to settle in Kentucky in 1819, observed that "great numbers, who had the means and could bear to be ridiculed as being unsteady, and not knowing their own minds, have returned."[30]

John Pearson was one of the hundreds of British farmers captivated by the pro-American writings of Birkbeck and Flower. Although denied the opportunity of an advanced education, he was a clearheaded, self-sufficient farmer who produced one of the most charming and straightforward accounts of emigration and expatriation of the era. Dissatisfied with the economic opportunities in Ewell, Surrey, and with few personal or public obligations, he quickly resolved to heed Birkbeck's advice and sail for America.

Leaving London in May, 1821, with his wife and eighteen dogs, Pearson sailed to the Isle of Wight, where an assistant, Peter Price, and several farm families joined the party. After a hazardous voyage of nine weeks, they arrived in Philadelphia on July 20, 1821. Pearson's first reactions to America were unfavor-

28 William Tell Harris, *Remarks Made During a Tour Through the United States of America in the Years 1817, 1818, and 1819.*

29 *A Clear and Concise Statement of New York and the Surrounding Country,* 14ff.

30 William Savage, *Observations on Emigration to the United States of America,* 5.

able. Although he had once traveled in the East Indies, the Philadelphia temperature of "120 degrees in the sun" proved far more oppressive. Insects and thunderstorms disturbed his sleep, sixteen of his eighteen dogs died because of the heat, and he found it necessary to assist in legal action against the ship's captain and first mate for cruel treatment of the crew. Not wishing to remain in a seaboard city, he purchased a wagon and horse and, with his wife, the plowman Price, and the remaining two dogs, started for the home of a friend at Scrubgrass, near Butler, Pennsylvania, on August 17. Before leaving Philadelphia, Pearson bought a farm in Butler County, but he wisely refused to advance any money and even demanded that the farm be described in writing. He later brought an unsuccessful legal action against the land salesman for misrepresenting the estate.

Pearson became disheartened long before he reached Harrisburg. Mainly because of pride and a determination to accomplish what he had undertaken, he continued on toward western Pennsylvania. In crossing the Susquehanna River, he sensed that the toll woman was silently cautioning them to turn back. Some other homesick immigrant had scribbled on the bridge: "England with all thy faults, I love thee still." Pearson began to imagine himself an unthinking prodigal son fleeing from a compassionate mother country. While traveling toward Pittsburgh, the Pearsons were daily implored to turn back by Englishmen and Scotsmen who were themselves returning from the frontier. Their fellow countrymen informed them that not even the Devil could withstand the natural torments of the West and that the immigration propaganda of Birkbeck, Flower, and others should be burned. Despite the warnings, Pearson seems to have relished the novel experiences. As an observant traveler with a highly developed sense of humor, he was amused by revival meetings, flirted with good-looking young women, and even chuckled at his own deficiencies.

Upon their arrival at Pittsburgh after sixteen days of travel, the Pearsons found the city economically depressed, with more than one thousand persons destitute. Acquaintances, formerly from Derbyshire, Yorkshire, Scotland, and elsewhere, advised them to return home before they incurred further expense. Nevertheless, they pushed on nearly one hundred miles farther to the home of a Mr. Grant in the extreme northeast corner of Butler County. Pearson immediately became the center of attention in the remote community and found himself much sought after by the numerous persons trying to sell their farms so that they might move west to Ohio or Illinois. As he traveled throughout the area and delivered messages from friends in England to immigrants of the region, he observed a "wretchedness and poverty" so extensive that he "silently forgave" those who had written exaggerated accounts of their success, although such letters had led to much misdirected immigration, including his own. The land appeared less productive than the rockiest areas in southeastern England, and the remoteness and isolation of the western country greatly depressed him:

> *O solitude, where is the charm,*
> *That sages have seen in thy face*
> *Better dwell in the midst of alarm*
> *Than reign in this horrible place.*[31]

After exploring several other districts in western Pennsylvania and contacting many British settlers, the Pearsons made their way back to Philadelphia by way of Clearfield, Philipsburg, and Huntingdon. After visiting most of the city's places of interest and spending a total of 123 days in America, they sailed for England in late November, 1821. Peter Price remained at Scrubgrass, and the two dogs were left to make their way in the New World. Upon their arrival at Liverpool, the repatriates journeyed to Mrs. Pearson's home at Alton, Hampshire, and after a quick trip by Pearson to the Isle of Wight to carry messages from America, they rejoined the ranks of the British tenant farmers.

The popular belief that assimilation was easy and rapid for

31 John Pearson, *Notes Made During a Journey in 1821 in the United States of America . . . in Search of a Settlement*, 49.

immigrants who possessed a speech and culture akin to that of Americans requires careful analysis. Similarity of background obviously lessened the difficulty of adjustment; however, parallels between British and American institutions often encouraged or allowed the English to cling to old values more tenaciously than Continental migrants. While in search of economic improvement and political independence in the United States, the Briton often felt the customs, literature, and arts of his homeland to be superior. Consequently, full acceptance of new social patterns was difficult and slow. If, in addition, he experienced economic frustration or personal inadequacies, return seemed the natural solution.

A series of complex forces led hundreds of immigrants to cross and recross the Atlantic in a confused and contradictory search for success. Obviously, many had no clear understanding of why they sailed west in the first place. Life seemed unsatisfactory at home and the search for something better appeared promising, but when the New World failed to provide immediate improvement, they instinctively looked over their shoulder to the society left behind. The migrants fancied that their empty lives and idle hands would somehow be filled by friends and industry in their native land. Back in Britain, they found it impossible to fit into a niche created by fancy and imagination. The sentimental attachments bred of distance faded, and the opportunities for growth and happiness in America again overcame emotional fidelity to home and country. Within a few weeks or months, many again pursued the American dream. A few Britons continued the fruitless search for Elysium until physical infirmity, financial insolvency, or emotional satisfaction ended the quest.

Throughout the first half of the nineteenth century, scores of men sailed for America, scarcely conscious of whether they were British migrants or world travelers. Many were intent on spying out the land and determining for themselves, or for relatives or friends, whether it offered new or peculiar advantages. From 1818 to late 1820, the discriminating and intelligent Scotsman James Flint observed America from his vantage point at Jeffersonville, Indiana. Flint's celebrated book infuriated British journalists, who declared him an American apologist and "a millstone about our necks." *The Literary Gazette* suspected that he had suffered "every nuisance and abomination which man's stomach, entrals, blood, mind, or imagination can revolt at" and yet continued to project "the beam of transatlantic blessedness."[32] Flint never revealed the reason for his migration or the cause of his return. His shipmates out from Greenock were made up of families whose land leases had expired, and laborers and plowmen who could not support a family at home. While in America, he talked with Scots who thought themselves dissatisfied with American life. Upon recrossing the Atlantic, however, he observed scores of migrants who wished themselves back where provisions were cheap and land plentiful. Many did sail west for the second time.[33]

The extensive travels of Rich Short between October, 1828, and October, 1832, exemplify the indecision and uncertainty of many British immigrants. Short and a male companion sailed from London during the autumn of 1828. In the New York area they discovered neither satisfactory employment nor good farms; therefore, they traveled up the Hudson River to Albany and west by way of the Erie Canal. Sickness detained them in Buffalo until Christmas. During the winter of 1829, they moved around the south shore of Lake Erie to Perrysburg, Ohio. The winter was extremely cold, the food inferior, roads nonexistent, and the natives sickly.

The Englishmen settled near the Detroit Road, eighteen miles north of Perrysburg in Monroe County, Michigan. Three hundred pounds in cash allowed Short to purchase and to fence and stock an eighty-acre farm. The prospects for success at first appeared bright, but during the summer of 1829, the migrants were troubled by insects and fever, as well as by indolent laborers and poor crops. Still more annoying was the constant harassment by antagonistic neighbors. After a number of unpleasant incidents,

32 *The Literary Gazette* (1823), 692.
33 James Flint, *Letters from America.*

Short decided in the spring of 1830 to move west and locate on the St. Joseph River. No roads and the heavy rains made traveling extremely difficult. Short became discouraged, drove his livestock to market at Detroit, sold the farm, and retraced his course around the south shore of Lake Erie. In the early summer, 1830, he and his companion arrived back in New York City. Short visited the major cities on the eastern seaboard from Boston to Washington, but secured little employment. While traveling near Albany, he was seriously injured by a fall from a horse, and it was not until the autumn of 1830 that he was able to sail for home.

Much to Short's surprise, Britain presented an even more dismal economic picture than America. After a few weeks he and his colleague pooled their resources, purchased two tickets, and by the end of January, 1831, were again in the New World. Traveling alone, Short walked to Harrisburg, took a coach to Pittsburgh, and sailed down the Ohio River to Cincinnati. His original destination had been New Orleans, but insufficient funds forced him to interrupt the journey. Short worked in Cincinnati for a few weeks, walked south as far as Frankfort, Kentucky, then abruptly decided to return to England. Moving up the Ohio to Pittsburgh, he sold his watch and chain for five dollars with which to purchase food and walked to Philadelphia. Apparently, both he and his companion worked in Philadelphia throughout the summer of 1831, and when they had earned enough to pay their fare, they sailed for Liverpool.

From September, 1831, until the spring of 1832, Short had intermittent employment in London. In March, however, he borrowed money and again, with his partner, recrossed to America. After two brief and unsatisfactory jobs in New York, Short moved south to Philadelphia, Baltimore, Washington, Norfolk, Elizabeth City, and Raleigh. After a period of illness in Raleigh, he walked most of the way to New York, worked a few months for passage money, and arrived with his friend in London in October, 1833.

Within five years, Rich Short had migrated to America three

times, suffered two serious illnesses and an injury, spent his original £300 in addition to borrowing from friends, and yet he acquired neither position nor gain. In the migration to Michigan, he was unable to cope with the vexing pranks of crude backwoodsmen; in the migration to Ohio and Kentucky, he failed to secure employment or land; and in the migration to Virginia and North Carolina, he became a drifter, apparently making no concentrated effort to settle permanently anywhere.[34]

By the 1850's, the Middle West had matured into a flourishing agricultural region, its fertile lands providing a constant lure for British farmers. Perhaps few of the some 120,000 native-born English, Scots, and Welsh in the area in 1850 recrossed the Atlantic. Greater knowledge and understanding of American conditions had rendered settlement less uncertain, while the growing diversity of the American economy made absorption relatively easy for all qualified newcomers. Furthermore, agrarian conditions were improving in Britain, thereby allowing the prospective migrant an opportunity for a more rational evaluation of his actions before embarking for America.

But even under the best of conditions there was always a reverse movement of considerable proportions. After seven years in the United States, George Nettle returned to Devonshire convinced that a surplus of agricultural products would always depress prices in America. Patrick Shirreff of the East Lothian reported favorably on the Illinois prairies, but chose to live in Scotland. Charles Casey praised American life and pointed to middle western villages which were sure to become great cities, but he returned to England. Although he had developed a pleasant farm of three hundred acres near Princeton, Indiana, a Mr. Phillips, upon preparing for his return to Somersetshire, explained, "I hate the prairies, all of them; insomuch that I would not have any of them as a gift, if I must be compelled to live on them."[35]

34 Rich Short, *Travels in the United States of America . . . with Advice to Emigrants.*
35 Faux, *Memorable Days in America*, 221.

Although charmed by the opportunity of Illinois life, John Regan also decided to recross the Atlantic. As an Ayrshire schoolteacher, Regan, along with his wife, John Adams, and a Mrs. Wamsley and her children, landed at New Orleans in April, 1842. For Regan, the arrival in America was the realization of a lifelong dream. As a small boy walking along a village street in Ayrshire, Regan chanced upon a cobbler's awl blade wedged between the cobblestones. While he was giving the blade to a cobbler friend, a woman entered the shop and asked the proprietor to read a letter just received from America. The exciting life and promise of success held out by the letter haunted the youth "like a passion." When he sailed from Glasgow in early 1842, Regan experienced no sad impulses. The Old World had brought only "an unceasing round of vexatious conflicts" and had satisfied nothing beyond "the vulgar animal wants." Faced with a life of poverty, he had had no time to mature a love of home or country.[36]

From New Orleans the little party plied up the Mississippi to Fort Madison, Iowa, moved inland, and settled near the village of Virgil, Illinois. Utterly delighted with western democracy, Regan speculated that it would last "until the end of time." Thrilled with the anticipation of becoming a citizen, he informed home folks that he would be entitled to vote, serve on a jury, become a justice of the peace, and even serve in the state legislature. Somewhat overcome by the pride of ownership, he explained that his farm was small, but as a wedge it extended to the center of the earth. Disagreeing with Nettle, who told Britons that they would discover America "strange and unpleasant," Regan thought his neighbors friendly and hospitable. Indeed, the Scotsman deciphered the materialistic features and personal foibles of the new society with unique candor and insight. They were "free and affable in their manners—enthusiastically attached to liberty and free institutions—acquisitive and inquisitive ... brave and daring." Regan insisted that Englishmen often demanded respect without earning it. The Americans "have no

36 John Regan, *The Emigrants' Guide to the Western States of America,* 10ff.

patience with the moustached and scented dandies who make the tour of the States, and return full of wounded vanity, on finding that there they were looked upon as very small potatoes indeed."[37]

For years the Ayrshire schoolteacher had anticipated the glories of America. For half a decade, he appeared uniquely satisfied with what he found. Yet the disappointments slowly added up. Although he had taken precautions against disease, he contracted a fever during the first summer in Illinois and remained extremely ill for over six weeks. Between August and November of every year, the sickness reappeared. In addition to farming, Regan accepted the post of local schoolmaster only to discover an inferior educational system and a shocking lack of interest in true learning. In early autumn, 1847, he sold the farm and with his wife sailed for Scotland. They arrived in Liverpool in December and, like many other returning immigrants, were astonished and disappointed with the Britain to which they had returned. Plans were immediately formulated for a return to Illinois. Regan longed to enjoy again "the firm woof" of a great continent rather than be cast on a bleak and "raveled edge" of land.

The often quoted phrase of Crèvecoeur that "only the middling and poor emigrate" was an oversimplification when it was written in 1782 and a euphemism in the following century. By 1850, country gentry and even members of the aristocracy believed that America could offer significant rewards, both for themselves and, especially, for sons not provided for at home. Such migrants were generally cosmopolitan in outlook; many had served as officers in the military services, while others had resided in France or Italy. Few limited their interests exclusively to agriculture, but argued that any adult with a true claim to breeding or ripeness could not "admit belonging merely to one category of history."

The travel, inspection, and settlement program followed by

[37] *Ibid.*, 217–18.

Lieutenant Colonel Edward Money was typical of the migration experiences of many British gentlemen. After a lengthy tour of duty in India, Money became discouraged by the restrictions of English tradition. Therefore, he decided to use his limited capital to establish himself and his sons in western America. After purchasing a worthless tract of land in Antelope Valley, north of Los Angeles, he eventually settled on an attractive ranch near Colorado Springs. For a few months the outdoor life appealed to Money, but before long the isolation and boredom convinced him that he should give the ranch to his sons and retire to the more genteel world of a London club.[38]

Occasionally, wealthy English gentry attempted to establish baronies on the frontier. In the 1870's, Captain Alexander K. Barlow employed an English friend to build him a magnificent three-story brick mansion near Sioux City, Iowa. The structure was scarcely completed when the family decided that three thousand acres of rich Iowa land could not overcome the dearth of culture, the long winters, and the peculiarities of neighbors. The family moved to a smaller but more favorably located estate outside London.[39]

Scores of self-assertive and individualistic young Englishmen such as Horace Ansley Vachell made their way to America seeking excitement, fortune, and independence. Anxious to consider new ways and to be identified with new ideas, Vachell moved from Harrow and Sandhurst to hunter and cowboy in Colorado and Wyoming and then to ranch owner in California. Capital for the transformation was supplied by relatives in England. For almost two decades, Vachell contracted with English gentlemen for the training of their sons on his ranch. Virtually all of the young men, as well as Vachell and his two American-born children, returned to Britain. While in California, Vachell published his first novel, and later, in England, he picked up the western theme and became the author of more than one hundred books.

38 Edward Money, *The Truth About America.*
39 C. Addison Hickman, "Barlow Hall," *The Palimpsest,* October, 1941.

Motivated by many of the same inducements that aroused Money and Vachell, John Richard Beste traveled to the Wabash River in 1851 only to retreat quickly to the more prosaic life of rural Hampshire. Although a genuine English agriculturist, Beste was also a prolific writer. While he was equally at home in Italy or France, his broad estates of Botleigh Grange and Abbotsham Court always drew him back to southern England.

Richard Beste's father, Henry Digby Beste, was a famous Anglican divine who in May, 1798, joined the Roman Catholic church. After the break with the Establishment, he retired to one of his Lincolnshire properties. John Richard was born about 1805 and educated in a Lincoln school, but in 1818 the religious issue led Henry Beste to move with his family to southern France. In the late 1820's, Richard returned to England and as the result of a favorable marriage became master of attractive estates near Southampton. By virtue of his extensive holdings, he was made justice of the peace, deputy lieutenant of Hampshire, and on several occasions was seriously considered as the Liberal party nominee for Parliament.

Before returning to England, Richard Beste had published his first book, a travelogue entitled *Transalpine Memoirs*. After settling at Botleigh Grange, he established himself as a literate but conceited and over-ambitious historical and descriptive narrator. By 1851, Beste had produced eight books, many of them two and three volumes in length, and had fathered six boys and six girls, all still under nineteen years of age. In April, 1851, while Beste was temporarily residing in Bordeaux, France, a local physician prescribed a quiet sea voyage as a remedy for the ills of a sick child. The suggestion led Beste to attempt his "long contemplated plan" to sail for America:

> From the time of the birth of my second son, I had determined that emigration to the back woods would be the happiest lot for all of them during my life. . . . Fond of a country life myself, I had resolved that the chances of happiness were greater to young men who (first endowed with classical education such as is given in

Europe) should occupy lands of their own in the New World, and see their children grow up around them to a similar lot.[40]

In early May, Beste, along with his wife, 11 children, a lap dog, 6 canaries, an African parrot, 42 pieces of baggage, and 360 poor Germans, sailed from Le Havre. After spending a few days in New York City, the family traveled to Cincinnati by way of the Hudson River, Buffalo, Lake Erie, and Sandusky. Several days in the Queen City allowed Beste to check the Roman Catholic seminary as a possible school for his sons. He studied the social and political attitudes of the populace and investigated several farms that were for sale. The family had originally hoped to settle on fertile bottom land near St. Louis, but stories of cholera in the Mississippi River towns deterred their sailing down the Ohio. Instead, they traveled by train to Indianapolis, where they purchased wagons, horses, and supplies and started for the Illinois prairies.

On June 29, while resting at an inn in Terre Haute, Beste became ill, and the journey westward was discontinued. After they had been lodged at a local boardinghouse, one member of the family after another contracted dysentery and fever. One daughter died and was buried on the banks of the Wabash; the other children required weeks of care before they recovered. By late summer, the family was sufficiently active to push on, but with the exception of two of the older boys, all were disheartened and wished only to retrace their route to the East Coast. After inspecting several near-by estates and observing the farming methods of the region, Beste concluded that his agrarian program would not work in frontier America. Mrs. Beste, understandably bitter toward a climate which she blamed for the death of her daughter, argued that a year in the West could be divided into three parts. "Summer, when cholera and dysentery prevailed; autumn, when ague and fever was universal; and winter, when pulmonary consumption took its victims."[41]

40 J. Richard Beste, *The Wabash*, I, 27.
41 *Ibid.*, II, 177.

Beste theorized that America had reversed the order of European society, thereby lessening religious conflict, eliminating privilege, and facilitating human intercourse. He sensed that the universal ambition of Americans was to level all classes, and he readily granted the advantages of such action for the masses. But such a system offered little inducement for the cultured immigrant:

> To the mass of the population, such independence may be a blessing; but it mars the literary, scientific or luxurious leisure of those who would purchase the services of others to secure repose and seclusion to themselves. . . . In the United States there are no beggars; and the country is, therefore, much more enjoyable. In the United States there is no poverty; and the country is, therefore, much more disagreeable.[42]

After enrolling two sons in the Catholic seminary at Cincinnati, Beste, with the remainder of the family, left Terre Haute on August 12, 1851, They quickly made their way to New York City and sailed for Britain. The absence of accustomed amenities, an obvious case of homesickness, and a deep-seated pride in England hastened their return. Unfortunately, as with Rich Short and James Regan, anticipation was sweeter than realization. British customs officers were insolent and rude, whereas American officials, at least in retrospect, seemed polite and helpful. Liverpool harbor was foggy, the buildings seemed small and dirty, trains were cluttered and crowded, and negligence and inefficiency were evident everywhere. In an account of his immigration experiences, published as *The Wabash* in 1855, Beste explained that despite his personal loss, most Englishmen could succeed in America. As a Roman Catholic, he denied the existence of a nativist movement and suggested that ignorant Irish caused legitimate resentment. Alexis de Tocqueville's prediction that America would be converted to Roman Catholicism seemed to Beste unimportant nonsense. On the other hand, he warned his countrymen that American women were "whining, pining,

42 *Ibid.*, 277 and 279.

helpless, lack-a-daisical" creatures who could destroy a hard-working Englishman. American schools were inferior, and children were badly reared.

After failing to be selected as a nominee for Parliament, Beste sailed with his family for the Mediterranean in December, 1856. In Naples, he continued to write, but with ever decreasing effectiveness. By 1865, three of his daughters and four of his sons had died in a series of accidents. Returning to Botleigh Grange, Beste lived in retirement until his death in 1885.

Beste wrote over a dozen books during a long lifetime, but none received the high praise of *The Wabash*. A review in the *Sunday Times* typified the British reception: "There is a wholesome and enthusiastic spirit running through *The Wabash* which renders it extremely delightful as well as instructive."[43] Although an author, a contributor to magazines, a correspondent with leading men of the day, a trusted friend of Italian nobility and Catholic cardinals, and an interpreter of the religious ideas of his father, the highlight of John Richard Beste's career was the few months spent in America, climaxed by the publication of *The Wabash*. Beste, like many British farmers and rural laborers, was first induced to sail for America by a vague faith in the New World's inexplicable powers to promote growth and regeneration, and, like the majority of repatriates, he quit America after a series of flirtatious failures, none of which produced a deep-seated objection to the New World order.

Few British agriculturists returned for solely economic reasons, and an even smaller number left because of republican institutions. Nor did the unpleasant shocks attendant upon arrival and settlement in the United States seriously baffle or mystify British farmers. Even the most unsophisticated cotter was rarely unnerved by the immigration experience. Rather, the British encountered a medley of attitudes, influences, and conditions which they were forced to accept but often failed to interpret. Fidler, Fordham, Pearson, Barlow, Money, Beste, and

---

[43] J. Richard Beste, *Nowadays* (2 vols., London, Chapman and Hall, 1870), I, Preface.

scores of other returnees quickly perceived the frontier's immaturity and lack of amenities. Furthermore, America's devotion to change and expansion often engendered a feeling of apprehension rather than a sense of anticipation. With the past so close at hand, Americans intuitively sought the wide horizons of the future, but the British, not always electrified by a sense of destiny, were disturbed by a shallowness of tradition which seemed to border on the primitive. Nevertheless, few agriculturists allowed sentiment to misguide their intelligence, and not a single returnee claimed to have been bored by the American experience.

UNCERTAIN REWARD

$\mathbb{B}$y the end of the eighteenth century, new methods of scientific farming had captured the imagination of important men. Political economists like Colonel Robert Torrens, travelers like Arthur Young, and aristocrats like the Dukes of Bedford and even King George III were fascinated by the new agrarian techniques and discoveries. Most observers, however, failed to consider another facet of the changing milieu: they ignored the social transformation which forced thousands of peasants from the land and into the rising manufacturing towns. With neither soil to till nor a trade to follow, the displaced cotter had only his labor to sell to the factory masters. For more than forty years the American and French wars created a manpower shortage, but with peace in 1815, government contracts were canceled, impoverished Europe provided few markets, and America moved toward self-sufficiency and high tariffs. The dislocation was essentially economic; however, a government policy based on fear and suspicion prompted unemployed operatives to associate their personal distress with the need for political reform. If placemen, pluralists, fundholders, and princes were forced to give way to annual elections, universal suffrage, and pay for members of Parliament, prosperity would replace national exhaustion.

In this connection, the very existence and success of the United States, with its revolutionary and republican traditions, helped to determine the direction of British agitation. The American attack on privilege seemed to offer a precedent which Englishmen should follow. The reluctance of the Tories to accept a liberal program or tolerate agitation seemed to prove the necessity for reform. Disillusionment and suppression encouraged the radical extremists, yet the radicals disliked revolution as much as despotism. They believed in government under law and gave little support to willful men. Despite their aggressiveness, most were neither socialists nor communists. Nor were they vicarious critics or sophisticated cynics. Rather, they were craftsmen and mechanics who hoped in a very practical way to preserve and improve their lot, in Britain if possible, in republican America if necessary. Artisans had visions of owning their own shops, trained factory workers hoped to become foremen or independent journeymen, and laborers dreamed of moving up into skilled positions. As Marcus Hansen has explained, the bulk of such migrants were democrats, "but only in the sense that they believed the American brand of government would facilitate the acquisition of property and position and would protect them in what they had acquired."[1]

Although statistics on the occupation of emigrants were not compiled until the 1850's, perhaps half of the Britons sailing for the United States during the first years after 1815 were artisans or operatives. As seekers of employment, they crossed the Atlantic in the hope of finding a society that had need of their services. Hundreds failed to find such a society and returned bitterly disappointed. By midsummer, 1818, the British consul in New York City declared the distress and unemployment in America equal to that of England. Since the jobless would be worse off in a strange environment, he stressed the urgency of their remaining in Britain.

Politics and economics were entwined in the thinking of migrants. Consequently, many who chose to return emphasized America's inept political system, along with economic inade-

1 Marcus Hansen, *The Immigrant in American History* (Cambridge, Harvard University Press, 1948), 82.

quacies. William Clark's observations reflect such a mixture of political, economic, and social disappointment. Clark arrived in New York in midsummer, 1817, and quickly moved to Preakness, New Jersey. Bedeviled by the heat and mosquitoes, disgusted by the ignorance and braggadocio of the natives, and shocked by the forwardness of American women, Clark concluded that Americans enjoyed fewer bodily comforts and possessed less mental happiness than any people on earth. In advising a friend against emigration, Clark reaffirmed his faith in the superiority of republican institutions and stressed the "ignorance and imbecility of those who misrule" in Britain. Nevertheless, he pleaded:

> Stay! my good Sir, stay! never leave England. I am a daily witness of the wretchedness of hundreds of our countrymen and women, many of whom like yourself were in Europe, in respectable circumstances. Go to the docks in London, Liverpool, and Bristol, and enquire of those multitudes who came to this country with high, with sanguine expectations, and are now returned with broken spirits and empty pockets.[2]

Clark offered what was to become a familiar argument, namely, that American institutions had deteriorated since the days of Franklin, Washington, and Adams. Materialism had become a god, yet unemployment and poverty stalked the country; churches promoted "blue laws," yet gambling and immorality flourished. Indeed, America had ceased to be a true republic and should no longer be pictured by English reformers as an economic paradise or political democracy. Clearly, Clark did not possess a broad and supple adaptability, but his disappointment represented a recurring theme among artisan returnees.

About the time William Clark left America in early 1819, an anonymous artisan from Belper, Derbyshire, arrived. Like thousands of his countrymen, the Belper migrant landed during the depth of the 1819 business panic. Employment was unavailable. In August, the disillusioned Englishman declared:

> Almost every ship which returns to Europe from this and other

2 William Clark, *The Mania Of Emigrating to the United States*, 29.

ports, is carrying back many disappointed emigrants, who are fortunately able to raise the means of paying their passage; while many of such as are compelled by cruel necessity to remain here, look hag-ridden, broken-spirited, and daily [are] sinking into a premature grave.[3]

After explaining that only dirty and undesirable jobs were available, the writer suggested that British radicals would be welcome to assist Negroes with their wretched duties. The Belper returnee left New York in late summer, 1819, and arrived home on November 10, still condemning the mischievous reformers and propagandists who had misled so many hundreds into a barren cause.

A Manchester artisan who arrived in Baltimore in the spring of 1819 exhibited a similar disgust for American institutions. The anonymous Briton drifted to Philadelphia by July and, failing to find employment, sailed from New York in August. In a sixteen-page account, he argued that republican institutions and civil rights had failed to provide material prosperity. Every seaboard city offered a forbidding prospect, with no poor laws, a cold winter approaching, food, fuel, and rent expensive, and hundreds of unemployed in every city. The Englishman was not surprised to discover 164 fellow countrymen on board ship as he embarked for Liverpool.[4] The misery of America convinced the migrant that if Britain could rid herself of certain "tyrannical despots" and promote true monarchy, a salubrious climate and a talented populace would convert the land into a "noble paradise." Artisans often confused private gain with individual liberty, and material wealth with national greatness. If economically successful, they deemed the New World an inspiring achievement, but when unemployed, they reviled republicanism, materialism, and Americanism with equal vigor.

The changing attitudes of Andrew Bell typify the chastening

[3] *A Clear and Concise Statement of New York and the Surrounding Country Containing a Faithful Account of Many of Those Base Impositions which are so Constantly and Uniformly Practiced upon British Emigrants, by Crafty, Designing, and Unprincipled Adventurers* (New York, John Wilson, 1819), 3–4.

[4] *Things as They Are; or, America in 1819*, 16.

effect America exerted on many would-be radicals. Early in life, Bell embraced a Thomas Paine type of egalitarianism. Later, as an artisan and businessman, he advocated a Jeremy Bentham type of economic freedom, to be accompanied by easy divorce and Sunday recreation. After a sojourn in America, he gradually became more conservative and died a rigid traditionalist. Bell's grandfather had been a close friend of Thomas Muir and had helped to provide for the reformer's family when Muir was condemned to transportation and shipped to Botany Bay. As secretary for a correspondence society in 1794, Bell's father became a fugitive sought by the government. Andrew grew up a radical republican and, as a boy living near the sea, looked "with a longing, lingering eye at every American ship which sailed."[5]

Bell was apprenticed in the cloth trade, but by 1828 his failing health forced him to seek a change in climate and occupation. A liberal education, knowledge of the arts, and disgust for English conservatism led him to Paris and immediate employment in the textile business. With the July Revolution of 1830, his firm went bankrupt and he was forced to become a factory mechanic. By June, 1835, again with failing health and the conviction that neither British nor Continental workers enjoyed true freedom, he sailed for America. French anarchy on the one hand and British despotism on the other led Bell to speculate that man could never free himself from his own stupidity. Yet America, with its new and unique institutions, might be the "exception to break the rule."

After a leisurely trip down the Seine, Bell traveled overland to Le Havre and sailed as a cabin passenger aboard a ship crowded with German peasants. He arrived in New York in August, 1835. At first he maintained a calm objectivity and declared himself neither impressed nor discouraged by the city's external features. Surprised to find the workmen of his trade on strike and other groups feverishly organizing unions (Bell opposed all combinations), he attempted, without success, to secure a position teaching French or Italian. Nor did his six letters of introduction to

5 Andrew Bell, *Men and Things in America*, 2.

business firms and leading individuals in New York City give cause for optimism. In discussing the problem with other Britons, he was intrigued by a gentleman from Belfast who was preparing to return home after twenty years in the United States. The Irishman reiterated the almost monotonous opinion that hundreds of Britons would quit America if they but possessed the means to do so, "the Golden bridge of retreat, as it were, being broken down behind them."[6]

After finding no employment in Albany or western New York State, Bell moved to Philadelphia. However, the more he observed American labor, the more convinced he became that it represented the "latest edition improved" of the detested European unionism. American workmen were as confused and dissatisfied as any in the world. Instead of personal independence and complete freedom, the masses were surpassing the older European societies in mob action, riots, and combinations. Disturbance and movement, not peace and tranquility, seemed the rule of the day. Bell borrowed from Milton to explain the new order, or disorder, of American society. The people

> *Brawl for freedom in their senseless mood,*
> *And still revolt when truth would set them free:*
> *Licence they mean when they call Liberty!*[7]

Eventually securing a job in a Philadelphia factory, Bell determined to enlighten his colleagues through the publication of "A Few Short and Timely Addresses to the Artisans and Labourers of the United States by One of Themselves." The factory management requested that the manuscript not be printed, as it would lead to mistrust and further labor strife.

As an eighteenth-century rationalist, Bell favored amusements, not preaching, on Sunday. Separated from his wife, he advocated more lenient divorce laws. The many prostitutes led him to question Philadelphia's snobbish pietism. In search of social and individual independence, he resented both labor unions and the

6 *Ibid.,* 55.
7 *Ibid.,* 125.

"tyranny of domineering capitalists." Furthermore, "there is a positive want of stability in the prosperity of America which makes it very hazardous for any mechanic who has learnt but one trade to go thither."[8] As the homeward-bound Englishman sailed from Philadelphia in July, 1836, the steerage was crowded with returnees. Bell's denial of America, however, led him, not to immediate acceptance of Britain, but only to greater cynicism. Neither people knew how to cook, yet both ate too much. Both manufactured textiles, yet neither showed taste in dress. An inferiority in the arts, a false sense of morality, and a self-centered materialism characterized both countries. Britain and America lacked the good sense and cosmopolitan realism to follow the Latins and compromise ideals with human nature.

In late 1836, Bell accepted an assignment to help organize a newly formed company in Belgium. Back in England by 1838, he published *Men and Things in America*, a work designed for the intelligent man of the world. Over the next decade and a half, he returned to France on at least four occasions, and in the late 1850's, still dissatisfied with society, he migrated to Canada. During a three-year stay in British North America, Bell translated F. X. Garneau's massive two-volume *L'Historie du Canada*. Some years earlier, he had published the first edition of *Historical Sketches of Feudalism*, and in 1863 he revised the work so that it might be used as a textbook in British schools. Bell helped to compile an imperial dictionary, wrote on Canadian journalism, and contributed many articles to the *Leisure Hour*. Disappointed with Canada, he eventually settled in Southampton and took advantage of British interest in the Civil War by republishing *Men and Things in America*.

After his American residence, Bell grew steadily more conservative. In later life, he preached loyalty to queen, country, and empire and repeatedly apologized for his earlier heedlessness in ignoring the Sabbath and his libertarian tendency toward rationalism and agnosticism. Even as a Thomas Paine radical, Bell had

8 *Ibid.*, 276.

included the rights of property as one of the natural rights. He never suggested that the state control the means of production, and he always detested Owenite socialism. He, like hundreds of other disgruntled Britons, wanted a democracy of opportunity. They assumed that such a system existed in America, unrestricted by customs, religion, or labor organizations. Actually, their radicalism was little more than a clear-cut, ingenuous, and simplified type of self-interest. In a rational and tough-minded sense, they were looking for a political and economic order in which they could find rapid advancement.

Another example of a radical turning reactionary can be traced through the career of Thomas Brothers. As a boy of fifteen, Brothers was sent as a private courier to deliver a letter in Birmingham. The elderly recipient treated the youth with unusual kindness and in parting rewarded him with a copy of Paine's *Rights of Man*. Since Paine's effigy had been burned in Brothers' Warwickshire village only a few years before, the boy read the pamphlet with eagerness and, much to his surprise, found the doctrines fascinating. Determined to go to America, Brothers and a friend, William G. Lewis, made their way to Liverpool, only to discover that they possessed insufficient funds for passage.

Brothers apprenticed himself to a hatmaker and later returned to Southam in Warwickshire as a journeyman hatter. He married and became a successful artisan, but could not overcome the lure of America. In 1824, he sailed with his family for Philadelphia. For a number of years Brothers enjoyed considerable prosperity as a hatter, but after 1830 he found it more and more difficult to compete with machine manufactures. Unwilling to recognize the basic economic problem, the hatter turned to political pamphleteering. He railed against paper money, big business, and the "wretched school" of Adam Smith. His most famous work, *The Senator Unmasked*, was a twenty-five-page attack on Daniel Webster. *A Letter on Vested Rights*, *The Doctor Unmasked*, and many articles made Brothers a well-known pamphleteer of the 1830's. Stephen Girard was denounced as a selfish and spleenish republican, Matthew Carey was adjudged a confused and ineffectual leader, and the recurring recessions were assumed to presage the collapse of American society.

After fifteen years in the United States, Brothers returned to Bishops Itchington, near Southam, in 1839. The next year, William Lewis, the boyhood friend with whom he had once started to America, published *The United States of North America as They Are; Not as They Are Generally Described: Being a Cure for Radicalism*. While yet in Philadelphia, the Englishman apologetically explained, "I am now most reluctantly obliged to acknowledge the fallacy of self-government, believing that it has no existence in the nature of things."[9] American freedom led to lynchings, stabbings, shootings, cruelty to foreigners, inhumane prisons, and a complete breakdown of justice. When Captain Marryat suggested that American exuberance and youth fostered the violence, Brothers countered that it was a direct outgrowth of radicalism: "I only intend to hold up the United States of America as a beacon, hoping that all reformers will avoid it, whatever other way they steer."[10] The unrelenting extremism of the Brothers conversion was revealed in a note to the Chartists:

> For my part, I have discovered that we have already reformed too much; that there are too many alleviators, political economists, socialists, and all sorts of modern reformers, whose go-a-head propensities I should be very happy to see the end of; and, if it could be effected, instead of marching forward, to march backward, until we had passed the boundaries of the new era; and were once more safe in Old England.[11]

The Rights and Wrongs of the Poor, published in 1842, condemned paper money, banks, suffrage for all under thirty-five, and the cutting of women's hair. England should revert to the Roman Catholic faith of pre-Tudor times and abolitionists should discontinue their foolish efforts on behalf of Indians and Negroes.

[9] Thomas Brothers, *The United States of North America as They Are*, 2.
[10] *Ibid.*, 149.
[11] *Ibid.*, 260.

Basically, Thomas Brothers, like other Britons from Cobbett to Carlyle, was disturbed and confused by the factory absorption of artisans and agriculturists and the growth in industrialization. As a Philadelphia artisan, he had failed in the fight against modern trends and mechanization; therefore, he turned back in both time and spirit to an era when goods were aesthetically appealing to the consumer and psychologically satisfying to the artisan. Rather than attempt a different occupation or a strange job, he, like many another Briton, crossed and recrossed the Atlantic. The returnees were willing to seek new worlds to conquer, but lacked the flexibility to adjust to a rapidly changing society or the ability to seek new frontiers within themselves.

Thoroughgoing socialists and Chartists also sought American shores, only to return in disillusionment. George Julian Harney, onetime editor of the *Northern Star,* found American society monopolized by a "hoarde of brigands" far removed from the Chartist ideal. He, along with Peter McDouall, a violent Chartist leader of Manchester, eventually returned. Peter Bussey, a Chartist from Bradford who became a tavern operator in New York City, once explained that if "I could go back to England I would be as great a Tory as I formerly was a Chartist."[12]

In October, 1848, the English radical John Alexander sailed from London for the new state of Texas. The following spring, while living in Houston, he penned a series of letters which reflect his frustration with the Southwest and point up his disgust with New World institutions. A highly skilled joiner from Mauchline, Ayrshire, Alexander was caught up in the Chartist agitation of the 1830's and later moved to London, where he became a close friend and political associate of the gifted revolutionary James Bronterre O'Brien. Alexander also put much faith in the doctrines of Robert Owen and Étienne Cabet and in addition absorbed their utopian vision of Texas. His American letters published in *The Reformer* in May, 1849, reflect a baffling mixture of O'Brienite Chartism, Owenite socialism, and French communism.

12 William Brown, *America: A Four Years' Residence in the United States and Canada,* 34.

Obviously, the boisterous society of the American West could not provide Cabet and Alexander with their envisioned paradise; confusion and failure were perhaps inevitable. Nevertheless, Alexander's criticisms cast an interesting light on Texas society in 1849 and provide considerable insight into the character of an English radical. The divergence between American republicanism and European republican thought at mid-nineteenth century is clearly revealed in Alexander's reactions. Virtually nothing is known about the Scotsman's personal background, although the series of events which induced him to emigrate to Texas can be traced from the mid-1820's.

In a far-reaching attempt to encourage immigration, in August, 1824, the Mexican government approved a comprehensive colonization act, and in accordance with its provisions, the state of Coahuila-Texas promulgated a local settlement law in March, 1825. The English soldier of fortune Arthur G. Wavell was awarded an *empresario* grant in northeastern Texas on March 9, 1826.[13] Although personally unfamiliar with the Red River estates, Wavell's Mexico City associate, Benjamin Milam, knew the area well and quickly accepted the assignment as resident manager of the newly acquired tract. Wavell then returned to England and during the following two years attempted to honor the terms of the grant by encouraging Catholic migration to Texas. In the spring of 1828, Milam traveled to England to talk with his partner and while there decided to try his hand at emigration promotion.[14]

It was also in the spring of 1828 that the great experimenter Robert Owen concluded that the residents of New Harmony, Indiana, could "not acquire those moral qualities of forbearance and charity" which would allow his model community to succeed. Consequently, Owen disposed of his estates and returned to

[13] George P. Garrison, "Diplomatic Correspondence of the Republic of Texas," *Annual Report of the American Historical Association*, (Washington, Government Printing Office, 1908), II, Part 1, 293.

[14] Wavell's Texas ventures have been ably presented by Robert W. Amsler in "Life and Times of Arthur Goodall Wavell," a dissertation submitted at the University of Texas in June, 1950.

England, where he was immediately attracted by the emigration publicity of Benjamin Milam. Although Owen's American project had proved an intellectual and financial failure, Milam's glowing reports on Texas awakened a new optimism in the great visionary. Indeed, on August 30, 1828, Owen and Milam discussed an arrangement whereby the former would found a colony on the Wavell-Milam tract in Texas. After further consideration, however, Owen decided to secure an *empresario* grant for himself. Despite the discouragement of the Mexican minister in London, he prepared a memorial to the Mexican government in which he suggested Texas independence. He would accept the responsibility for forming a society in Texas with such a remarkable character that a fundamental change would be effected "in the conditions of the human race."[15] On November 22, 1828, Owen sailed for Mexico. Moving inland from Vera Cruz, he taught English to his Spanish-speaking guides, met Santa Anna, and eventually was received by President Guadalupe Victoria. Impressed by the Englishman's grandiose plans, the government seemed ready to grant him an enormous *empresario* contract, but before any action could be taken, the revolutionary party overthrew the Victoria regime. Owen returned to the United States in March, 1829. Although failing to correct "the fundamental errors" of the established order in Mexico, he remained optimistic over the chances to form a new society in Texas. During the thirties and forties, his faith in the Southwest excited the imagination of a close personal friend and fellow reformer, Étienne Cabet.

Perhaps no group of the period proclaimed a gospel of more complete socialism than the communist followers of Cabet. As a youthful member of the secret Carbonari, as a conspirator against Napoleon, and as a resistance leader after the restoration of the Bourbons, Cabet had been well trained in underground and revolutionary activities. By 1830, he, like other members of the secret leagues, had moved from political resistance to organized

15 Margaret Cole, *Robert Owen of New Lanark* (New York, Oxford University Press, 1953), 159.

socialism. Although at first he supported the revolution of 1830 and even accepted a governmental appointment and a seat in the Chamber of Deputies, Cabet's radical journal *Le Populaire* so angered the new regime that he eventually sought refuge in England.

Once in Britain, Cabet quickly fell under the sway of Robert Owen and was greatly influenced by the communistic elements in Sir Thomas More's *Utopia*. Cabet eventually agreed with Owen that environmental factors within the social structure formed man's character and that the proper institutions could produce goodness and decency in all men. Both agreed that only through argument, persuasion, and conviction could competition be eliminated and the truly free society realized. Before returning to France in 1839, Cabet absorbed much of Owen's fascination for the United States and became convinced that Texas, in particular, offered an unusual opportunity for a completely socialist colony.[16] In 1840, he published *Voyage en Icarie* and soon thereafter set up his society of Icarian communists. In September, 1847, he recrossed the Channel and again consulted with his English friend Robert Owen. Owen and a land agent persuaded Cabet that his community would work in the sparsely populated state of Texas. In January, 1848, the Frenchman purchased a tract of land estimated at one million acres from the famed William S. Peters interests.[17]

During the spring of 1848, the Icarian emigration appeal had spread to England. Many O'Brienites expressed interest in the Texas settlement, and plans for a semicommunal emigration society quickly matured. Although the association's motto was "each for all, and all for each," the program was scarcely launched when a cleavage appeared between the company's directors and several of the persons who had purchased emigration shares. Toward the end of 1848, John Ellis, a friend of Alexander and

[16] "The British Section of Icarian Communists," *Bulletin of the International Institute of Social History*, No. 2 (1937), 84–88.

[17] Peters was from Devonshire. He had been granted three *empresario* contracts by the Republic of Texas in the early forties and had returned to Britain to sell land and send out emigrants.

O'Brien, reorganized the group and became the head of the North Texas Colonization Company. As a member of Ellis' society, Alexander decided to precede his associates to Texas. He sailed on the *Henry*, along with 120 other English, German, and Dutch emigrants on October 20, 1848. O'Brien accompanied Alexander and his wife to the London docks and exacted a promise from him that as soon as convenient after landing in America, he would prepare a lengthy account of his impressions. In the spring of 1849, Alexander kept his promise by writing two letters to O'Brien, one to Ellis, and one to an unidentified friend. All were wrapped in a bundle and addressed to O'Brien, who, as publisher of *The Reformer*, printed them in the paper on May 26, 1849.[18]

Before leaving London, Alexander informed O'Brien that he was "anxious" about the fate of the socialist utopias planned for Texas and that he personally wished to investigate the merits of the region. According to O'Brien, "he went, therefore, determined to see and judge for himself, and according to what he saw and experienced, to report fairly and faithfully for the guidance of his friends in this country,—more especially of the Texas Colonization Society of which he was a member,—and of the friends of National Reform, to whose principles he is thoroughly wedded."[19]

Long before reaching New Orleans, Alexander became disenchanted by the ignorance and wild expectations of his radical shipmates. Ten days without employment in a "sickly and filthy" city and accounts of failure of Cabet's Red River settlement led him to push on to Texas in late December, 1848. But even in the expanding community of Houston, the Englishman found the

18 During the early thirties, O'Brien had edited *The Poor Man's Guardian* and later became proprietor of *The Operative*. *The Reformer* was a short-lived radical sheet founded by O'Brien after the Chartist fiasco of 1848. The publication ran through fifteen numbers between April 28 and August 4, 1849. With the failure of *The Reformer* as a two-penny weekly, O'Brien started a one-penny journal, *The Social Reformer*, which ran through eleven numbers between August 11 and October 20, 1849. On November 10, 1849, his more durable *Reynolds' Political Instructor* was begun.

19 *The Reformer*, No. 5 (May 26, 1849), p. 34.

conditions of labor peculiarly primitive. He was dumfounded when informed that workers often received part of their wages in land, and after being offered a job repairing a church, he was bewildered when told that it would be necessary to patronize his employer by attending religious services. Although a day's labor was from sunup to sundown, workingmen's organizations were viewed as not only unnecessary but un-American. Chartists and other radicals aboard the *Henry* had contended that the right to vote created a political democracy and thereby freedom, but their American experiences almost universally convinced them of their error. After four months in Texas, Alexander informed an English friend: "I have invariably found that those who boasted most of the advantages to be obtained in America, were soonest disheartened and the first to wish to return to England."[20] The peculiar intellectual contentment of Americans and their acceptance of the system, with its injustices, made improvement more difficult and more unlikely than in England. The press, the pulpit, the politicians, and most of the public constantly flattered themselves and the people by "boasting of the glorious institutions of America." They criticized the tariff, taxes, banks, or other nostrums, but no one admitted to any basic or fundamental inadequacies. "I expected to find America a few degrees better than England," wrote Alexander, "but it is not—it is worse; it is, in fact, in a hopeless condition, as regards either moral, political, or intellectual progression."[21]

There were many minor irritations, but the truly disturbing discovery for Alexander was American failure to understand the meaning of freedom. He and others who differed with the prevailing attitudes on slavery, religion, government, and social organization were not merely forced to remain silent, but were pressed into offering nominal approval of the offensive institutions. Five months in the United States convinced Alexander that neither the political "bobbles" of republicanism nor the economic wealth of the country had effected a true reformation.

20 *Ibid.*, 35.
21 *Ibid.*, 34.

America possessed what most radicals sought: manhood suffrage, no property qualification for voting, payment of members of Congress, and equal constituencies, yet the country was less free than Britain.

After his return to London in early summer, 1849, Alexander at times seemed to toy with George Julian Harney's more violent brand of revolution. Writing to O'Brien on July 17, 1849, he praised the purpose of *The Reformer*, but thought many of the reforms suggested were "tedious" and "of minor importance." Nevertheless, he thought the publication should be preserved and strengthened. Many trade-unions and other groups were beginning to realize that land "ought to be held in sacred trust by the state" for the benefit of all. He praised the "manifesto of the Red Republicans of Germany" and pointed to their demand for collectivized property and the assumption by the state of all financial and credit agencies. A greater following could be achieved and the elements of unrest in England mobilized through the widespread circulation of tracts and brochures. The landlords and money lords would be destroyed only by "a few choice spirits, leagued together for good." The "unthinking and apathetic" mass of society would follow competent leaders.[22]

Profoundly disturbed by the inadequacies of their society, artisans like Bell, Brothers, and Alexander embraced extremist doctrines: the radicalism of Tom Paine, the socialism of Robert Owen, or the utopianism of Étienne Cadet. All doctrines seemed to suggest that America was the most likely place to find or create the new freedom hitherto denied the toiling classes of Europe, but America often failed to measure up to her billing as a country of political democracy, material prosperity, and social equality. Rather than the ideal order, the migrants discovered a land of broken hopes and stunted imagination where even a discussion of deficiencies seemed impossible.

Clearly, the average level of competence and enthusiasm of most reforming migrants was commendably high, but, unfortunately, their index of economic and political conditions was

22 *The Reformer*, No. 14 (July 28, 1849), p. 107.

very low. They were neither tolerant nor consistent. The Bell-Brothers type returned home to become arch conservatives, whereas the Alexander type concluded that only through a communistic reorganization of society could the complete regeneration of human nature, so imperative for mankind, be achieved.

A foremost student of immigration once suggested that to the European migrant, America "was not New York but a distant crossroads village . . . not Boston but a forest clearing or a labor camp twenty miles from a post office."[23] Unfortunately, the migration of British artisans and mechanics was a more involved movement than the statement suggests. In 1850, the four largest Atlantic Coast cities claimed 60,000 persons of English, Scottish, and Welsh birth, while 200,000 Britons resided in the seaboard states. Furthermore, the urban immigrant was of paramount importance when studying British returnees. The process of assimilation was more difficult for the mechanic than for the farmer. The agriculturist, at least to a degree, could create his own "Little England," whereas the city worker was forced to seek employment, to conform to unfamiliar standards of labor, and to adjust to a new environment simultaneously. An immediate acceptance of, if not conversion to, the new system seemed mandatory.

Late in the century it became commonplace for young single men to seek temporary or specialized work at high wages in the United States, see the country, and return when the job was completed. British stonemasons, bricklayers, house painters, and similar tradesmen often became seasonal migrants, saving enough from their summer labor on the eastern seaboard to finance their round-trip steerage passage and sometimes support a family at home. Before the Civil War, however, Atlantic transportation was still too hazardous and time consuming to allow for a planned seasonal migration.[24] The majority of craftsmen and mechanics

23 Hansen, *The Immigrant in American History*, 70–71.
24 In 1860, the British merchant marine had a steam capacity of 400,000 tons as

who recrossed the Atlantic before 1865 did so because of a real or fancied dissatisfaction with America and not because they were migratory laborers.

No doubt a number of artisans reacted like the wheelwright who landed on Long Island a few days before Christmas in 1836. He ignored offers of unskilled employment and refused a job as carpenter. After a total of eight days in the New World, he embarked for home.[25] Typical of another type of returnee was the compositor who arrived in New York early in 1858. Well trained as a printer, the migrant assumed that Harper and Brothers or some other large publishing house would be eager to secure his services. Within a few months he was forced to agree with his English-born landlord, who observed that America was "flooded" with highly skilled job seekers. The compositor returned to London later the same year.[26] Few Britons maintained the chivalrous attitude of William Hancock, who, after five years in America, encouraged all who were ambitious to emigrate. Hancock argued that even failure could not destroy the psychological advantages derived from the spirit of adventure.

Experienced in both clerical and technical fields, Hancock sailed for the United States in June, 1852. He secured immediate employment in New York City but became fascinated by the reports coming out of the West. In late 1853, Hancock proceeded to Cleveland, Sandusky, and Detroit. He finally spent the winter at the village and lumber camp of St. Clair, Michigan. In the spring of 1854, he returned to Detroit and later removed to Chicago. Hancock finally took a job as surveyor with the Illinois Central Railroad. In 1856, he traveled along the Mississippi River and settled with a surveying party at Keokuk, Iowa. After suffering from ague, cholera, extreme heat, and intense cold, he moved east to Indianapolis and later to Cincinnati. Early in 1857, he arrived back in New York City and shortly thereafter received

compared with a sailing capacity of 4,000,000 tons. Steam tonnage did not equal sail tonnage until 1883.

25 Mrs. E. Felton, *American Life*, 123.

26 *The Real Experience of an Emigant.*

entreaties from his family to return to England. Confident and ambitious, Hancock was certain that he could succeed in America, but after a few weeks of indecision, he sailed for London.

Skilled, versatile, and willing to experiment, Hancock had worked at a lumber mill, a cement plant, in offices, and as a surveyor. As a perceptive young man, he quickly sensed that there was no room in America for "extravagant ideas on republican liberty." Concern was shown for equality, but more emphasis was placed on the "worship of the almighty dollar." The country was exciting but too crude for pleasant living. In the autumn of 1854, he had witnessed the lynching of an elderly Mormon at Janesville, Wisconsin. Although he was nauseated by the sight, it was the utter powerlessness of public officials to control the "brutal passion and blood-thirstiness [of the] maddened crowd" which frightened him. But despite the license of the people, the prevalence of disease, the thirst for quick gain, and primitive religiosity, it required the family call to dislodge Hancock from the "grand disorder" of America.[27]

James Burn was a drifter who left America for the same prosaic reason that stimulated his migration in the first place. Born of an unwed mother at an unknown place on an unknown date, Burn's first recollections centered on his mother carding hatter's wool in a rat-infested Dumfries garret. As he grew older, the boy begged and peddled items of cloth and hardware throughout Scotland. With the marriage of his mother, conditions grew worse. Five half-brothers and sisters were born into the family, and Burn's stepfather was both a drunkard and a thief. First apprenticed as a cowherd, James traveled with merchants and peddlers, worked in the harvest fields, was servant to a rich Indian, dug potatoes in Ireland, traveled as a stowaway back to Scotland, and finally apprenticed himself to a hatmaker. In 1826, he married; in 1827, he learned to read; and by 1833, he had five children. In the early thirties, Burn worked as a tavernkeeper and labor leader in Glasgow, but after the death of his wife, he moved to Greenock, where he became Grand Master of the Odd Fellow Lodge, leader

27 William Hancock, *An Emigrant's Five Years in the Free States of America.*

in the local Chartist movement, a political pamphleteer, and foreman of a small hat factory. Burn remarried in 1838, and about ten years later, after twenty years of relative prosperity in the Glasgow area, he again became a drifter; from Edinburgh to York to Leeds to Bradford to Liverpool, Burn moved with neither plan nor purpose. He published *Mercantile Enterprise* in London in 1845, *A Historical Sketch of the Independent Order of Odd Fellows of Manchester Unity* in 1846, and *Language of the Walls* in Leeds in 1853. He lectured on Robert Burns and attempted to sell political tracts. The older children helped to support the family by making hats while Burn wrote, lectured, worked at hard labor, sold magazines, and collected accounts. After failure in Dublin, Burn enjoyed a brief success in Edinburgh as manager of a London newspaper's branch office. But the venture was short lived, and in 1861 he moved to London for the fifth time.

At approximately sixty-one years of age, James Burn still possessed superhuman energy but exhibited the quixotic characteristic of snatching at phantoms. "I was not of a particularly excitable temperament, but I frequently had a good deal of trouble to keep my judgment on the whip-hand of my feelings."[28] In the spring of 1862, Burn received a letter and three pounds in currency from his son-in-law in New York City. He interpreted the communication as "a pressing invitation" to proceed to the United States "without delay." The sale of personal property barely provided passage money, but the family sailed from Liverpool in July, 1862. The son-in-law, dismayed by their arrival, could offer little assistance; however, a hat manufacturer formerly of Hexham provided the Scotsman with temporary employment.

Burn found his fellow employees tolerant and helpful, but they worked faster and had longer hours than their counterparts in Britain. Finally, a few days before Christmas, 1862, he was discharged. To return home had already become his great ambition:

[28] James Burn, *The Beggar Boy: An Autobiography*, 240.

When I left England it was with a certain idea of leaving my bones in the soil of the New World, yet, strange as it may seem, I had not been two months in New York before I became thoroughly impressed with the conviction that we should return home, although I could not see by the greatest possible stretch of imagination how the thing could be accomplished. . . .

I saw much in American society worthy of commendation, but I felt myself too stiff from age, and had been too long wedded to the social institutions of my own country, to allow me ever to become Americanized in any sense of the word.[29]

"Designing demagogues" often "made tools of the people," Yankee assumptions of superiority were exasperating, and success could be won only through hard work requiring the strength of youth.

In the winter and spring of 1863, Burn worked in Newark, but a strike forced him to seek still another job. In 1865, with failing strength, a mentally ill wife, and at least five of his sixteen children still dependent upon him for support, Burn accepted gifts and charity and sailed for Europe on a ship loaded with dissatisfied workers. But like other undecided migrants, before he reached England, he was eager to sail for America again. Indeed, he had seen one youth change his mind as they left New York harbor, leap overboard onto a steam tug, and return to shore. Still others had scarcely landed on British soil before they regretted their repatriation. Many again sailed for America over the following months, and a few returned on the same vessel that carried them to England. Burn estimated that "two-thirds of the emigrants who returned home, before having been naturalized, go back as soon as they are enabled to do so. They seem like the Jews under Moses to sigh for the flesh-pots they left behind."[30]

In retrospect, Burn emphasized that the American laborer was perhaps the only workingman in the world who enthusiastically supported the system of government under which he lived. Surely the Constitution of the United States was the most perfect docu-

29 *Ibid.*, 272, 300.
30 *Ibid.*, 349.

ment of its kind. Burn sensed that in America, "one of the most interesting social problems of this or any other age of the world's history" was in the course of being solved: "I mean self-government by the people. I could not help being agreeably impressed with the fact that a nation so young in years, and made up of a mass of such heterogeneous materials, should have arrived at a condition of such unrivalled greatness."[31]

Unable to find employment in London, his wife sick, and his purse reduced to ten pounds, Burn assembled his notes and sold *Three Years Among the Working-Classes in the United States During the War* for twenty pounds. In seeking employment, he drifted to Newcastle-upon-Tyne, worked on a newspaper in Hexham, and eventually, through the aid of a friend, secured a clerkship in the Salmon Fisheries Office at Westminster. Dismissed in 1868 after two years on the government sinecure, Burn did odd jobs until 1869, when he was awarded thirty pounds by the Royal Literary Fund. In 1871, he secured employment with the Great Eastern Railway and remained with the company for more than a decade. During those ten years, Burn sold a few articles to literary magazines and wrote *The Educational Places of Amusement in London* and *A History of Strikes*. Upon retirement from the railway, he received a second Royal Literary grant and in 1882, at approximately eighty-one years of age, moved to the home of a daughter in Hammersmith, London. He died a few months later.

As in the case of other British repatriates, it was James Burn's views on America which brought him public recognition, gifts, awards, and a government sinecure. He was perceptive in self-analysis and gloried in an elasticity of spirit. He did not claim to be the victim of either history or society, but, rather, of his own misdirected judgment. Emigration was sought as a refuge from his fears and conflicts, the product of his own weakness. He left home because flight proved easier than mastery of self. As the expressive and colorful prototype of thousands of British workmen, he found much to be admired and enjoyed in America. Yet

31 *Ibid.*, 335.

the Americans were also an uprooted people whose adolescent energy provided a distracting variety instead of the authority and direction which many immigrants craved.

A few self-made tradesmen and aspiring artisans discovered nothing in the new environment worthy of their energy. Some had sailed with great expectations only to find the "frontiers of industry" overextended and the "unexcelled opportunities" misrepresented. Others who had felt themselves stymied by class and custom at home declared that America's open society forced men to move out rather than allowing them to move up.

In 1817, Robert Horsfall, a Manchester merchant of considerable wealth, migrated to Philadelphia and, along with two English partners, Cheetham and Foster, invested in a business. After two years, all three had exhausted their finances and were anxiously preparing for the journey back to Manchester. In a letter of September, 1819, Horsfall avowed that some English migrants had committed suicide, many had died of yellow fever, and others had been enabled to return through the "humane assistance of British merchants." Horsfall's widely publicized letter declared that

England, with its heavy load of debt and taxes, and the misrule of its Government, is far, very far, superior, to this wretched country. Never was there as great a metamorphosis (from affluence to beggary) in the history of any country, as the last ten months have brought in America.[32]

Richard Weston "long cherished the desire" to better his condition through emigration, but it was not until his retirement as an Edinburgh bookseller that he found himself free to attempt the experiment. While a youth, Weston's brother had settled near Glens Falls, New York, and later in life had repeatedly asked his parents and brothers to follow him to America. Marriage, a

32 *The Times* (London), October 20, 1819, p. 2, col. 5.

family, and business prevented Richard from seriously considering the undertaking, but with the death of his wife and his own
retirement from business, he decided to launch a new life and a
new career in the New World. As a bookdealer, he was well
acquainted with immigration literature and American travel
accounts, yet the change in routine distracted him deeply and
from the very first his courage began to fail.[33]

Weston landed in New York in August, 1833. The confusion
and human misery at the debarkation port forced the Scotsman
to reconsider the wisdom of his action. In New York, he was less
disappointed by American business methods than perplexed and
irritated by American customs. He invariably opened the wrong
doors, sat in the wrong seats, entered ladies' compartments, and
received a jostling in the streets. Becoming confused and annoyed, he attacked one man with his umbrella, engaged another
in a fencing duel, and ordered a devout Methodist who shared
his hotel room to conduct all bedtime prayers in silence. After
contributing considerable money for the help of destitute Scotsmen, he moved to Philadelphia. Later, he traveled to Washington, west to Wheeling, and down the Ohio River to Cincinnati.
In returning to New York, he resided for several weeks with
nieces and nephews in the Glens Falls area, but he found rural
America as distasteful as the cities. Booksellers were nowhere in
demand. Noah Webster had the temerity to explain the English
language to Englishmen, and universal suffrage made the lower
orders unbearable. Clearly, the American people were dete-
riorating and would soon revert to a race of savages.

The provincial, puritanical, and pathetic Weston arrived back
in Scotland on January 15, 1834:

> I was once more at home and felt grateful to Providence for
> having delivered me from the snare which cold-blooded selfish-
> ness had spread for me, and which had proved, and alas! may yet
> prove, but too successful in ruining thousands of my country-
> men.[34]

[33] Richard Weston, *A Visit to the United States and Canada in 1833*, 5.
[34] *Ibid.*, 312.

Like Dr. Johnson, who could see nothing in Scotland but the road which led to England, Weston concluded, "Throughout my wanderings in America, I saw nothing to admire but the blue rolling ocean which was to waft me to my native shores."[35]

The year following Weston's rejection of America, a fellow townsman investigated mercantile opportunities along the Atlantic Coast and echoed the bookseller's findings. Leaving Edinburgh in March, 1834, the anonymous tradesman arrived in New York in May. Disappointed with business prospects, he pushed on to Canada, but returned to the United States within a few weeks and sailed for home later the same year. He, like Weston, believed the growing numbers of Irishmen a menace, he considered the violation of the Sabbath a crime, and he found Americans intemperate in all things.[36]

After failing in an American business venture, the Anglo-Irish landlord Francis Wyse, brother of Sir Thomas Wyse, returned to Rathcullin, Waterford, in the early forties to warn Irishmen against demanding America's federal principles of government and to advise Britons that only half of the Englishmen and not more than seven out of twelve Scotsmen succeeded in the United States.[37] The harsh but fair *Athenaeum* used Wyse's *America, Its Realities and Resources* as an example of the all too frequent "uncandid, illiberal, unfair" type of prejudice contained in accounts of transatlantic experiences. The reviewer suggested that disappointed and vengeful returnees were responsible for creating much of the ill feeling and smoldering resentment existing between England and America. Furthermore, personal invective neither provided penetrating analysis nor fell in the "legitimate province of literature." Wyse was accused of being unfair, "not occasionally, but systematically." Indeed, he was "unfair even when true, inasmuch as the statement of a fact, without allusion to the circumstances that qualify it, is almost as bad as direct falsehood."[38] Immigration, like literature, was a

35 *Ibid.*
36 *Journal of an Excursion of the United States and Canada in the Year 1834.*
37 Francis Wyse, *America, Its Realities and Resources,* I, 42.

sensitive and serious endeavor, and a returnee's "exhibition of spleen" provided no useful guide to either.

Some of the most prejudiced and vindictive immigrant reports of the period were compiled by middle-aged and middle-class Englishwomen. They discovered that America poisoned the human will and menaced the health and happiness of the new-comer. Frances Trollope's ineffectual mate quickly returned to London, while Mrs. Felton's husband grew sickly and eventually returned to Lancashire. Only Mrs. Ritson, however, commem-orated the death of her spouse by writing anti-American poetry.

In 1799, Anne Ritson ignored the advice of her genteel friends and sailed for Alexandria, Virginia, where she was to join her husband. Overbearing and class conscious, she insisted that the ship's captain clear the deck of steerage passengers so that she might enjoy the special comforts to which her ticket entitled her. Greatly disturbed by the poverty in Alexandria, Mrs. Ritson per-suaded her husband to move to Norfolk, where he became an active and prosperous merchant. Although she was accepted in the best social circles, American customs and living conditions greatly annoyed the English lady. In 1802, Ritson became seriously ill with yellow fever; five years later, he died. Mrs. Rit-son returned to England and immediately began the composition of a 177-page poetical lament in which the fateful steps of her emigration were dolefully recounted. In the last pages of the poem, Mrs. Ritson's "rapt'ious joy" upon arriving in England and again becoming the subject of His Gracious Majesty not only overshadowed but seemed to provide meaning for her husband's death.[39]

If William Brown could have afforded Francis Wyse's three volumes or had bothered to read Richard Weston's *A Visit to the United States and Canada*, he might have been able to overcome the "mysterious and irrational compulsion" to emigrate. Forced to enter a Yorkshire textile mill while yet a boy, Brown worked his way through the various grades to become a skilled finisher of

[38] *The Athenaeum*, 1846, p. 884.
[39] Anne Ritson, *A Poetical Picture of America.*

woolen cloth and finally a Leeds clothier. Always in search of the more independent life, he, along with his wife and teen-age children, sailed for New York in August, 1841. Moving inland, Brown located at Cleveland, where he became tavernkeeper and manager of a boardinghouse. Immediately disturbed by the American educational and judicial systems and intemperate toward Irish and Yankee Anglophobes, Brown argued with his customers and alienated his friends. Vocal support of all things British and carping criticism of all things American resulted in his being censured by the local press and the ruin of his business. As a participant in the Underground Railroad, he hid at least one runaway Negro in his home and later helped to smuggle him into Canada. After two years in Cleveland, the Brown family came to the conclusion that they should seek more hospitable surroundings among Her Majesty's subjects in Canada.

Living alternately at Toronto and Scarborough, Brown operated a sawmill and engaged in the lumber trade, but after two years in British North America, the Englishman decided that the superior political advantages of the provinces were more than offset by their limited economic opportunities. Brown suggested that the United States would soon seize all of the North American continent and with the assistance of the Irish might well sing "Hail Columbia" at Hyde Park Corner or in Trafalgar Square. Both in America and after his return to Yorkshire, Brown talked with many Englishmen who had tried immigration, only to become politically irritated with Yankee democracy and economically "reduced to selling trinkets from a wheelborrow" in American streets.[40]

Certainly not all business-class returnees were steeped in temperament and crammed with bias like Horsfall, Weston, and Brown. Several tradesmen recrossed the Atlantic with little or no animosity toward the Western world. Indeed, they proclaimed the economic advantages of America and indicated dissatisfaction only with living conditions or social customs. In 1835, a merchant

40 Brown, *America*, 42ff.

who had recently arrived back in Britain informed his countrymen that a small amount of capital could reap great profits and
a properly managed business would insure a good return in the
United States. Unfortunately, the country was not a pleasant
place in which to live and "nothing but want, or the dread of
approaching poverty and destitution" could drive "an Englishman to seek a permanent home in a foreign land."[41] J. G. Woollam traded along the Missouri River above St. Louis for many
years before returning to England. In the forties, he published
Manchester and Missouri and an emigrant guide to the western
states in which he emphasized the economic opportunities of the
Mississippi Valley but pointed up the crude aspects of frontier
society.[42]

Well versed in immigration literature and a student of North
American life, Edward Hepple Hall sailed from Newcastle-upon-
Tyne in 1848. After a brief residency in Canada, he pushed on to
Chicago, where he accepted a post as editor of official guides and
directories for the city and surrounding area. In addition, he
wrote pamphlets and designed maps for migrants traveling to
Canada or the western states. In 1856, Hall returned to New-
castle, but after the publication of *The Traveller and Emigrant's
Handbook to Canada and the Northwest States of America*, he
again crossed the Atlantic and for some time did editorial work
in both Chicago and New York. During the Civil War, Hall
headed the advertising department of D. Appleton and Company,
but in 1870, he again returned to England. He settled in Herefordshire and in the following years produced over a dozen
brochures, most of which depicted the growth and opportunity
of the American West.[43]

[41] *Letter from a Tradesman, Recently Arrived from America to His Brethren in
Trade,* 5.

[42] J. G. Woollam, *Useful Information for Emigrants to the Western States of
America.*

[43] Edward H. Hall, *Ho! For the West!!! The Traveller and Emigrant's Handbook to Canada and the Northwest States of America* (London, Algar & Street,
1856). See also Edward Hepple Hall, *Lands of Plenty: British North America for
Health, Sport, and Profit* (London, W. H. Allen and Co., 1879).

Thomas Dixon and Edward Sanderson typify the American success story and yet both returned to England. In 1816, at the age of twenty-four, Dixon arrived in New York City. He worked at odd jobs, became a storekeeper, and eventually was the owner of a prosperous dry-goods trade. Later, he expanded into banking and became a dealer in foreign exchange. After he had lived in New York City for forty-six years, the confusion of the Civil War led Dixon to retire to Eastbourn, Sussex in late 1862.[44]

Edward Sanderson also arrived in New York at the age of twenty-four. Within a few years, he had become the senior member of Sanderson Brothers and Company of Sheffield and New York. Later, as director of the Merchants' Bank and of several insurance companies in New York City, he retired from business and devoted his time to the study of scientific literature, mineralogy, and philanthropy. Although his wife was American born, his fortune American made, and his social and business position unquestioned after thirty-three years in the United States, Sanderson decided to retire to Eastbourn in 1856.[45]

A slightly different type of business repatriate can be seen by following the early career of David Mitchell. As a young man of twenty-five, Mitchell resigned from a London financial firm to go in search of adventure and wealth. After ten years in America, he had succeeded in the first instance but failed in the latter and therefore returned to Britain:

> I was one day sitting at my small desk, in a little dark cage of a room, with no other business than to look out on the crowded thoroughfare. I had just finished *The Last of the Mohicans*. The mildness, the freshness, the freedom of the New World, its abundance of land and scope for enterprise and adventure, all delighted and tempted me. I gazed almost with disgust and disdain on the anxious hurrying streams of people. "Yes," I said to myself, descending from my three-legged stool, and buttoning my coat, "I will get out of this artificial state of things; I will go and dwell with nature herself, her works and her children.". . .

[44] *A History of St. George's Society of New York*, 116.
[45] *Ibid.*, 125.

I was too comfortable perhaps; things went on too easily and prosperously, and life was becoming monotonously pleasant. At any rate, I wanted a change, and to see the world. England seemed to me to have seen her best days, to be overdone, overcrowded. What sort of a career had she to offer to her sons?[46]

In midsummer, 1848, Mitchell's ship arrived at the mouth of the James River. As the vessel moved upstream, the young Englishman reflected upon the delightful aspects of the country and contrasted it to the revolutionary chaos and gloom which had overtaken Europe. After a few weeks, Mitchell settled in Richmond and, although employed in an office, never allowed business matters to interfere with travel and observation. The practical sense of the people rather than any philosophical theories impressed him. Slavery was distasteful, yet it was no more reprehensible than the actions of British mill owners. The newspapers were rash and immoderate, the Irish loud and annoying, and the repeated epidemics disturbing, but better a society that is bizarre, baroque, and funny than one that is dull, conventional, and without movement. Mitchell often visited the seaboard cities, attended band concerts on the White House lawn, and cultivated the acquaintance of the leading men of the day.

While earning a comfortable living, Mitchell did not grow wealthy; furthermore, as time passed, the hazards to health seemed to become graver. In 1858, "to escape from the national scourge, dyspepsia," Mitchell sailed for London. After living and working in Richmond for ten years, he had come to the conclusion that democracy was inevitable and unavoidable in the United States, but that as an effective system of government, it could in no way remedy the evils with which mankind was beset. Although indulgent of the South, Mitchell showed a unique penetration of the real problems and issues. He sincerely respected what America was attempting to do but, sensing the coming conflict, doubted its ability to do it.

46 D. W. Mitchell, *Ten Years in the United States*, 1–2.

The younger, more cosmopolitan, and less firmly attached migrants like Mitchell, Woollam, and Hall found adjustment to American life and institutions less irritating than did the older, more provincial, or more firmly rooted Britons like Weston, Wyse, and Brown. Basically, however, when Mitchell scolded England, it was to some extent a self-flagellation. The careful reader cannot fail to see that he, like many other returnees, loved his country and never really left it: "I did not know how much I loved poor old England until, on the deck of the parting ship, I saw her white cliffs and green fields flitting away."[47]

As the Industrial Revolution gained momentum, Britain built a world-wide economic empire based on her ability to produce inexpensive goods in mass and her readiness to transport them to purchasers on six continents. Lancashire textile operatives could manufacture cloth cheaper than the underpaid handicraft workers of India. With a monopoly on modern machinery, with labor flowing in from agricultural enclosures, and with Whitney's gin providing a new supply of raw cotton, British manufacturers were ready to clothe the world.

Even before the War of 1812, cotton began to replace tobacco, indigo, and rice on the eastern plantations, and after the war, American frontiersmen quickly cleared the lands of the Gulf Plains and the Lower Mississippi Valley. Farm products of the Old Northwest, along with the commercial activity of New England, supplemented the cotton of the South in creating dollar credits in Britain which allowed Americans to import more of the Old World's finished products. The dependency of Lanarkshire and Lancashire mills on southern cotton and the American purchase of overseas goods led hundreds of British business representatives to travel to America. The majority of such agents conducted their business in eastern-seaboard cities, took a quick tour into the South or West, and returned home. Some established businesses and remained permanently in the new land, while several attempted American enterprise but later recrossed the Atlantic.

47 *Ibid.*, 2.

A Liverpool cotton merchant, Isaac Holmes, settled in New Jersey in 1817. He purchased raw cotton in Virginia and the Carolinas and on several occasions traveled west across Alabama and Mississippi to New Orleans. Both during his journeys in the South and while conducting business in Philadelphia and New York, Holmes encountered many English immigrants who were acutely dissatisfied with their condition and opportunities. Some were disturbed by the prevalence of disease and sickness, others had been swindled by Yankee land salesmen, while the largest number could not find satisfactory employment.

At first, Holmes was little impressed by his countrymen's complaints, but with repeated tours into the South, he began to abhor slavery. Despite his need for cheap cotton, he became more and more convinced that the institution of slavery induced immorality and cruelty within the white population. Slavery in the South and financial panics in the North led Holmes to publish *Advice to Emigrants* in early 1821. He emphasized that America could not provide employment for skilled Englishmen, that republican leaders did not welcome radical migrants, and that professional men, clerks, and cotton merchants should stay in Britain. In May, 1821, Holmes sailed for Liverpool, but, like many another immigrant, he found upon returning that conditions at home were far less attractive and prosperous than pictured in his memory:

> I have discouraged emigration; but had I been so well acquainted as at present, with the great distress of the British agriculturists, I certainly must have allowed, that the American cultivator, was in an enviable situation, when compared with many English farmers.[48]

The shock and surprise of return led Holmes to retract his *Advice to Emigrants*. In *An Account of the United States*, published in 1823, he explained that despite its republicanism, America was not radical; despite the social pressures and a hyper-

[48] Isaac Holmes, *An Account of the United States of America, Derived from Actual Observation During a Residence of Four Years in that Republic*, Preface.

93

sensitive nationalism, the country possessed real freedom; despite the hard work, mechanics and laborers could earn three times the English wage; and despite the recessions, an unexcelled mercantile expansion could bring success to industrious businessmen.

Peter Neilson was a product of the age. He possessed a positive enthusiasm for both material progress and the contemporary doctrine of *laissez faire*, yet he never outgrew a love for restraint and tradition or a faith in the supernatural. In 1828, after a prosperous career in America, the practical and the romantic blended to draw him back to a contemplative Scottish life.

Born in 1795 as the ninth child and seventh son of George Neilson, a successful cloth calendar of Stirlingshire, Peter made an excellent showing in both the arts and the sciences at Glasgow Grammar School and the University of Glasgow. Family influence led him to enter his father's expanding export business, and, in the spring of 1817, he sailed for the United States to arrange for the purchase of raw material and at the same time to advertise the company's cambrics, cottons, and other manufactured goods. Neilson became active in both New York and Charleston, but returned to Britain within a few months. He sailed the second time for America in 1820, but soon returned to Glasgow and married his cousin, Elizabeth Robertson, later the same year.

The Neilsons eventually came to the conclusion that if cotton could be bought in the South, transported to Scotland, manufactured into cloth, and sold in American cities, surely an American factory would be doubly lucrative. In 1822, Peter, accompanied by his wife and infant daughter, sailed for New York. After careful study and investigation of labor and market conditions, they moved to Bristol, Pennsylvania, and opened a textile factory in late 1823. The new industry prospered. Peter regularly visited Charleston as a cotton drummer and in 1827 made an extended tour throughout the South. After a study of New England industry, he almost opened a second factory in the mountains of Vermont. While the Neilsons were living at Bristol, two more children were born. Peter's sister traveled from Glasgow to live with the family, and his father made lengthy and frequent visits to America. On one of the visits, the elder Neilson died and was buried in Charleston. Many friends, relatives, and employees also followed the industry to the United States. Peter even came to think of himself as a native American. When composing a poem for a Fourth of July celebration, he wrote:

> *O'er the green mountains of my native home,*
> *With liberty, fair goddess! let me roam.*[49]

It came as a surprise to many of Neilson's American friends when in early 1828 he announced that the plant at Bristol was to be sold and that he planned to return permanently to Scotland. But, as was true in the case of many other repatriates, Neilson's American experiences greatly influenced his later life. Soon after arriving in Glasgow, his wife died, and over the following years he lost all interest in business affairs. In 1841, he moved to Kirkintilloch to live with an unmarried sister who for several years cared for his four children.

Two years after returning to Scotland, Neilson published his first literary work, *Recollections of a Six Years' Residence in the United States of America*. It was followed in 1834 by "The Millennium," a religious poem suffused with mystical suggestions for emigrants and an abstruse description of the coming of the Messiah. *The Wanderer*, a story about America, appeared in 1835. *The Adventures of Zamba, An African Negro King, and His Experiences of Slavery in South Carolina* was Neilson's last major work. Designed to be a "practical Uncle Tom's Cabin" which would bring about the freeing of the slaves, the book received little acceptance. Neilson wrote on the cotton-import business for the *Glasgow Herald*, composed poems for the *New York Journal of Commerce*, and published a controversial pamphlet entitled *Remarks on Iron-built Ships of War, and Iron-*

49 William Whitelaw, *Poems by the Late Peter Neilson of Kirkintilloch* (Glasgow, Robert Forrester, 1870), 167.

plated Ships of War. Although it led to a dispute with Parliament, he later claimed to have been the inventor of ironclads. Peter Neilson died at Kirkintilloch in May, 1861.

Despite his full life as businessman, author, and inventor, Neilson's enduring contribution was an outgrowth of his six years in the United States. His view of America, however, was confused by a strange mixture of idealism, pragmatism, and humanitarianism. He would have preferred a static world. Although not deterred by the unfamiliar, he sought comfort in the warmth of memory. Americans were friendly, honest, and imaginative, but they were caught up "in the pursuit of gain." They desired immediate and tangible profits and pursued honesty because it was the best policy. They seldom sought truth for the noble purpose of overcoming ignorance. Women were generally abstemious, but boys drank, smoked, and gambled, the Sabbath was seldom sincerely observed, and sickness threatened everyone.

Neilson's entire family suffered a severe attack of fever in 1825, and other illnesses constantly plagued the Scottish workers. The failure of the United States to place a high tariff on British imports, the problems growing out of slavery, the crass materialism and lack of refinement, and an "inextinguishable love of sweet home" led Neilson, when only thirty-three, to retire to a more contemplative life in Scotland. Yet, even when returning, he emphasized that Americans held no "malice and hatred toward Britons" and that men with industry and perseverance should emigrate "without hesitation."[50]

Uprooted persons have been the despair of all those who try to categorize man, his actions, or his motives. They change their environment more quickly than they can change themselves. They often become eccentric. Of course, every movement has its deviationists, but immigrants—and certainly repatriated immigrants—are all deviationists. The return movement is filled with countless instances of human inconsistency and even absurdity.

[50] Peter Neilson, *Recollections of a Six Years' Residence in the United States of America*, 79.

Clearly, the most significant issue is individual behavior; the object of study must always be the figure and not the garment.

But the life of hundreds of returning mechanics, artisans, clerks, and businessmen was managed, not by their intelligence, but from behind the scenes. An American recession, difficulty in finding suitable employment, or the failure of a business sparked the return of the majority of urban workers. The influence of intelligence appears to have been secondary to accident and the subsconcious. While uncertainties influenced the lives of all immigrants, city workers were more subject to economic chance than were farmers or professional people. Nevertheless, many craftsmen and tradesmen dealt deliberately with the decision to return. Since they had substituted purpose for tradition before leaving England, they often reversed themselves in America and upheld attachment over substance and continuity over perspective.

4

THE SEARCH THAT FAILED

Nineteenth-century Americans were not-
ed for their externalized criteria of happiness. As an outward-
looking people they were caught up in a headlong rush to improve their physical environment. Possessed of a vast potential
and given a unique prestige throughout Europe, the New World
seemed to promise rewards commensurate with effort. Indeed,
the earlier doctrine of social and individual perfectibility again
emerged as an accepted faith. If man's everlasting challenge were
met by hard work, sound reason, and unswerving virtue, he could
achieve material comfort and leisure for intellectual improvement. Persons from every phase of British life were attracted by
the restless ingenuity and utopian worldliness of America. Artists
and performers, adventurers and travelers, reformers and experimenters, naturalists and explorers sought the promise of emigration.

To many Britons a clear statement of national loyalty or
governmental preference seemed meaningless. Fanny Kemble
crossed and recrossed the Atlantic eighteen times, and only during the excitement of the Civil War did she consciously consider
patriotism or official attachment. William Bullock casually took
out Mexican citizenship, helped establish his son in Philadelphia,
and eventually retired to England without reflecting on his
national loyalty. Thomas Nuttall, when requesting a passport
from the American government, indicated uncertainty about

whether he was British or American. Granted the passport by United States authorities, Nuttall decided that he was a British subject and conducted his research on the American-Canadian frontier without benefit of official documents.

British actors were particularly casual in their movement between Britain and America. Many resided for years in the United States, never quite sure whether they had immigrated or merely taken an extended leave to perform on the American stage. The romanticism of the age tended to make the theater a vehicle for the display of deep emotion. Although the period yielded few great playwrights, the demand for passion and sentiment produced great actors. A dearth of art in the young republic allowed a large number of British performers to occupy the American stage, organize theatrical companies, and design theaters in American cities. When Archibald Prentice, a former editor of the *Manchester Times,* returned to England, he assured all artists that they would discover new possibilities and be well paid in the Western world. "Bad actors are so much in the majority that one of average merit stands a fair chance of becoming a trans-Atlantic star of the first magnitude."[1] English critics indeed often contended that the American theater was staffed by persons of less than average talent.

> *Can you place poet Barlow above poet Pope?*
> *Can you wash at an inn, without towel or soap? . . .*
> *Can you sit out the second-hand tragical fury*
> *Of emigrant players, discarded from Drury?*[2]

Few British actors sailed as outright discards from Drury Lane; however, many undertook the journey only after financial embarrassment at home, and nearly all viewed the experience as an unpleasant necessity.

As something of an adventure, William Charles Macready re-

[1] Archibald Prentice, *A Tour in the United States* (London, Charles Gilpin, 1848); *Chambers Edinburgh Journal,* Vol. XI, No. 272 (March 17, 1849), 171–73.

[2] *The Colonial Magazine and Commercial-Maritime Journal,* Vol. VIII (May–June, 1842), 82.

sided a few years in America during the 1820's. Two decades later, after an unsuccessful season and feeling himself "on the downward path of life," Macready resolved to return to the United States. The idea proved so distasteful to his family that they refused to accompany him.[3] Macready played the circuit from Savannah and Mobile to St. Louis and Saratoga. In New York, however, the Astor House riots of May, 1849 demonstrated the resentment which cultivated Englishmen often faced in America. On May 7, Macready's performance of *Macbeth* at the Astor House Theater was broken up by ruffians who had been encouraged by a jealous American actor. Embarrassed citizens persuaded Macready to continue the engagement, but on the evening of May 10, when the performance was repeated, a full-scale riot led to the death of over twenty persons and the injury of many more. The actor fled New York disguised as a soldier while crowds estimated as high as thirty thousand persons cheered the inflammatory, anti-British speakers. Placards calling on Americans to arise and overthrow English aristocrats were posted throughout the city, and mobs were informed that the English might well sweep to control in the metropolis. Macready continued the program in Boston, and only after recouping his fortune did he beat a hasty retreat to London.

While touring the country, the Yorkshire comedian and writer John Bray married an American lady and settled in the rising city of Washington. The aging actor returned to Leeds in 1822 upon the death of his wife, but his son, John Francis Bray, crossed and recrossed the Atlantic, never quite certain whether he preferred England or America.[4] Edmund Kean, Junius Booth, Elizabeth Whitlock, Charles Mathews, Tyrone Power, James Fennell, Thomas Cooper, the singing Cowells, and many others

[3] *The Diaries of William Charles Macready, 1833–1851*, ed. by William Toynbee (2 vols., London, Chapman and Hall, Ltd., 1912), II, 197–98.

[4] G. D. H. Cole, *Socialist Thought: The Forerunners, 1789–1850* (London, Macmillan and Co., Ltd., 1955; volume I of *A History of Socialist Thought*, 5 vols. in 7, London, Macmillan, 1953–60), 132ff. As a devoted follower of Robert Owen and a precursor of Karl Marx, Bray's son, John Francis Bray, re-immigrated to the United States.

traveled to and departed from the United States more intent upon seeking profits than upon becoming permanent residents.

On the other hand, success was never assured, and occasionally a prospective immigrant returned for financial reasons. William Priest sailed in August, 1793, only to find New England cold to his talents. Philadelphia and Baltimore were more receptive; nevertheless, he embarked for England in April, 1797 because of "a plentiful lack of money."[5] The famous actress, Miss Mary George, discovered herself stranded in America. Soon after her arrival in Philadelphia in 1793, she became estranged from her husband, Sir John Oldmixon. The support of a large family made return impossible. Miss Gorge did enlist three of her sons in the British Navy, however, so that they might serve their country during the Napoleonic Wars and the British-American engagement of 1812.[6]

The musician Joseph Parry portrayed another kind of emotional and intellectual involvement. Born in Merthyr Tydfil in 1841 the seventh of eight children, Parry went to work in a coal mine at ten and joined his father as an employee in the Cyfarthfa Iron Works at twelve. Daniel Parry had become disturbed by the meager economic opportunities of South Wales. He suggested emigration but found his wife reluctant to leave Welsh institutions. She relented after the Merthyr cholera epidemic of 1849, but emphasized that in America the family must hold to the Welsh tongue and the children marry into Welsh-speaking families.[7] Migrating piecemeal as passage money could be earned, the last members of the family arrived in Pennsylvania in late 1854. At thirteen Joseph had absorbed his mother's feeling for Welsh culture, and along with her bitterly opposed the move.

Joseph worked in the iron rolling mills of Danville, Pennsylvania, studied music, won eisteddfodic competitions, and in 1868

---

5 William Priest, *Travels in the United States of America: Commencing in the Year 1793, and ending in 1797* (London, J. Johnson, 1802), 214.

6 William R. O'Byrne, *Biographical Dictionary* (London, 1849), II, see Oldmixon.

7 Jack Jones, *Off to Philadelphia in the Morning.* Also see *Dictionary of Welsh Biography.*

secured sufficient financial aid to sail for Britain to attend the Royal Academy of Music. Parry returned to Pennsylvania by 1871, but he was subsequently offered a professorship in music at the college in Abrystwyth and settled permanently in Wales. He received a doctor's degree from Cambridge in 1878, and went on to become one of the leading figures in Welsh music. Although primarily a teacher and performer, he also enjoyed wide acclaim as a composer of operas, oratorios, and hymns.

Joseph Parry exemplifies the not uncommon type of contemplative and sensitive Briton who, while outwardly adjusted to the new life, always had his roots firmly anchored in the Old World. American opportunity for growth and training allowed Parry to become a fruitful contributor to Welsh society. His native institutions became more meaningful because of an early separation from them. If Parry had remained in Merthyr's ironworks, would he have become a great leader in Welsh music or merely another contributor to the local church choir? Although America could not capture the migrant, it provided the catalytic agent which stimulated and transformed.

Basic and material needs, not artistic or intellectual curiosity, led John Bernard to emigrate in 1797. Unable to continue the convivial life as secretary of the Beefsteak Club, member of Buck's Lodge, friend of the Prince Regent, and connoisseur of fine wines, the performer prepared himself to face the "perils of swamps, snakes, tomahawks, and Yankees."[8] Bernard, as a relative of Sir Francis Bernard, the royal governor of Massachusetts during the hectic 1760's, was led into expensive speculations by the royal family and other fashionable patrons. He became so deeply involved financially that it appeared that only retreat could save his honor. Consequently, when Thomas Whignell, the English actor turned American director, offered Bernard one thousand pounds for a year's contract in Philadelphia, the bankrupt performer accepted. "I was the slave of a despot, of whom despots are slaves—necessity. . . . I went abroad to improve the future, but not to forget the past."[9]

8 John Bernard, *Retrospections of America, 1797–1811*, 23.

Bernard was born in Plymouth in 1756, the son of a navy lieutenant. He attended Latin grammar school at Chichester and, for a few months, was articled to a solicitor. An overpowering love for the theater led him to join a strolling troupe in 1773. His talents carried him to Bath, to Ireland, and eventually to London in 1787. Success in London allowed Bernard's extravagant tastes to grow more rapidly than his income. He boasted that his friends were the best judges in the world "of port wine, mock-turtle, coats, guns, dogs or horses."[10] In 1791, Bernard began his career as a stage manager. He moved rapidly from Guernsey to Plymouth and finally to Brighton, where he anticipated that crowds drawn by members of the royal family would fill his theater. But the tourists went to Margate instead, and Bernard, after borrowing five hundred pounds from the Beefsteak Club, again took over the direction of the Guernsey theater. Failing as a manager, he returned to London and, rather than suffer the humiliation of a reduced standard of living, decided to emigrate.

A yellow fever epidemic in Philadelphia forced Bernard to make his first American appearance in New York in August, 1797. The critics agreed that as a comedian he was discriminating but not dazzling; "his, if not the pencil of Titian, was at least that of Hogarth."[11] London acquaintances in America informed the Englishman that he had arrived a few years too late, the period of great opportunity had passed. Others called him a "fool" for sailing at all. "A third [group declared] that as I looked 'a florid habit, there was every chance of my being packed in a black box before spring.' The better tempered cheered me in a way an army agent does a cadet in war time. 'The yellow fever,' said they, 'thins the Green Room of at least twenty every summer, so that in a short time the field will be your own.'"[12] Despite this assurance of openings, employment in America proved uncertain, and in

9 John Bernard, *Retrospections of the Stage* (2 vols., London, Henry Colburn & Richard Bentley, 1830), II, 336.

10 Bernard, *Retrospections of America, 1797–1811*, 23.

11 William Clapp, *A Record of the Boston Stage* (Boston, James Munroe, 1853), 80.

12 Bernard, *Retrospections of the Stage*, II, 25–26.

1802 Bernard returned to Europe. After he had spent a few months in England and Ireland, a new offer from Philadelphia again drew him across the Atlantic. In 1803 the local "blue laws" led the actor to join a Boston company, in which, at $1,050 a year, he became the second-highest-paid performer on the Boston stage.

In 1806, Bernard accepted the position as joint manager of Boston's Federal Street Theater and returned to England in search of talent. He married his third wife while in London. (His first wife had died before he sailed for the United States and his second in 1805.) Bernard returned to Boston in October, 1806, finding his wife a valuable addition to the company; nevertheless, the endeavor failed some three years later. He toured Canada in 1810 and in the autumn of 1811 formed a small company at Albany, New York. In 1812, the Green Street Theater was completed, and Bernard took over its management. The Albany venture proved disappointing, and, in 1816, Bernard toured the United States, but eventually he suffered a complete financial collapse and returned to Boston in 1817. After offering a final performance on the Boston stage in April, 1819, the ever popular but destitute and aging comedian sailed for England a few days later.[13]

Dire necessity led Bernard to write a multi-volume biography, from which he hoped to realize some income. Although it was completed in 1827, the publishers considered the work too voluminous for printing, and before a revision could be attempted, the author died, on November 29, 1828. In 1830, Bayle Bernard, a son born in Boston in 1808, published part of his father's work.[14] The sections of the biography dealing with America, however, did not appear until 1887. *Retrospections of*

[13] Bayle Bernard, "Early Days of the American Stage," *Tallis's Dramatic Magazine and General Theatrical and Musical Review*, six articles, December, 1850, through May, 1851; *The Gentleman's Magazine*, Vol. C (December, 1830), Part II, 526–28; *Notes and Queries*, No. 156 (December 23, 1876), 513; *The Literary World*, Vol. XVIII (March 5, 1887), 69–70.

[14] Additional Manuscripts, British Museum, 33,964, letter of William Bayle Bernard to R. Bentley, 1830.

America was perhaps overly sanguine in evaluating the New World's strengths and weaknesses. Nevertheless, Bernard was a keen observer and deeply impressed by American life. He studied it, he participated in it, he understood it, and he enjoyed it. The *Gentleman's Magazine* found that he "was obliged more than once to return home to avoid starvation,"[15] yet to Bernard, America represented progress whether "in invention or adaptation, in expansion or clarity." The Americans had devised a new standard for movement: when the British set a fast pace, the Americans rushed; when the Old World galloped, the New World flew. Despite a hatred of slavery and its accompanying evils of indulgence and libertinism, Bernard praised the South because of its active role in the Revolution. It "had at least never lost this one purifying influence—a love of liberty."[16] He suggested that returning immigrants, travelers, and British writers underrated American morals and overrated the country's scenic wonders. Migrants settled on a plot of land, failed financially, and returned without really understanding America. Visitors flitted like swallows from region to region "always on the wing," but learned little. Unsuccessful immigrant adventurers often tried to recoup their losses and justify their failures by hastily writing disparaging books about the country. American governmental procedures particularly impressed and pleased Bernard, and, despite his earlier acquaintance with the royal family, experience in the United States convinced him that people could live pleasantly without either aristocracy or royalty. The republican principle was like a "block of ice, too massive to be broken and too pure to defile."[17] Always the optimist, Bernard predicted a great material and cultural interchange within the English-speaking world.

As a robust, balanced, and self-sufficient personality, John Bernard saw defeat as promise and failure as fulfillment. He learned to prefer "the humble subjects of a republic" to the

15 Vol. C (1830), Part II, 527.
16 Bernard, *Retrospections of America, 1797–1811*, 6–7.
17 *Ibid.*, 14.

"glories of saturn," and yet a sentimental urge and personal compulsion led him to seek a British stage for his final performance. "I am an Englishman: after twenty-three years absence, and nearly fifty years wandering in a profession which has made me appear the veriest citizen of the world, I have returned to die in my native land with unaltered feelings. I love my country, its people, and its institutions."[18]

Less than four years after John Bernard's death, in 1828, the already famous twenty-two-year-old Frances Kemble arrived in America. Born late in 1809 while her actor family was playing at the Covent Garden Theatre, schooled on the Continent and in the tradition of the stage, Fanny received wide acclaim as an actress while yet in her teens. The year 1832 found Britain split over the reform issue, frightened by foreign revolution, and in the throes of a severe business panic, with London facing a cholera epidemic. Theater attendance was sporadic, the Kembles were near bankruptcy, and Charles was broken in health and spirit. John Howard Payne and Washington Irving, both close friends of the family, suggested that a tour in the United States generally proved lucrative; and Stephen Price, the American who replaced Charles Kemble as manager of Covent Garden, offered to arrange the itinerary. Any action which could provide economic solvency had to be considered, and even the inconveniences of a theatrical tour through the United States seemed justified. After lengthy preparations and affectionate farewells, Charles, Fanny, and Aunt Dall (Adelaid Decamp) sailed for New York in August, 1832.

As anticipated, the Empire City appeared crude and boring, but later the same year the more restrained and dignified atmosphere of Philadelphia rather favorably impressed the English troupe. Of the city's many gentlemen who attempted to entertain the actors, Pierce Butler emerged as the most persistent. After receiving the fulsome praise of critics in Philadelphia, Baltimore, Washington, and New York, the Kembles traveled to Canada in 1833. Aunt Dall died in early 1834 and was buried in Boston.

[18] *Ibid.*, 21.

Charles, who was emotionally unable to cope with emergencies, tended to vacate his position of responsibility and authority, and Pierce Butler stepped into the void. Fanny was embittered by the family's failures and argued that her aunt and chaperon had died because of the demands of the stage. With a sudden desire to begin anew, she accepted Pierce Butler's standing proposal, and in June, 1834, they were married at Philadelphia.

Fanny had always found American society staid and dull, and her husband's family seemed especially narrow and unimaginative. In turn, she demonstrated little tact or discretion, even printing a personal *Journal* in 1835, which depicted her experiences in America from August 1, 1832, to July 17, 1833. Since Fanny's chief object in publishing the *Journal* was to make money and gain attention, she deliberately set out to "abuse" her adopted country. Washington Irving had warned her not to follow the example of her countrymen and complain so much that she become a "creaking door." But Fanny was less anti-American and pro-Tory than supercilious and egocentric. Friends advised against the venture and were assured that Pierce Butler would read the manuscript; however, his insistence upon editing the work led to a family embroilment. Only Harriet Martineau, visiting in Philadelphia while on her American tour, was able to persuade Fanny to suppress some thirty pages of the most offensive material. Fanny Butler was a vain, caustic, spoiled and tormented, albeit passionate and gifted Englishwoman who found herself anchored in an unsympathetic, pompous, and restrained Philadelphia. She neither wished to be attached to the society nor accepted her position in it. Nevertheless, her intimate and contemptuous depiction of American friends was clearly a bold attempt to regain the attention once accorded her. She reflected a pathetic lack of understanding of either her problem or America's. The *Journal* created the sensation which Fanny craved, but few were favorably impressed. Her parents found it disgusting and vulgar, Edgar Allen Poe thought it less a foreign libel on America than coarse and indelicate, and *The Athenaeum* typified British journals in declaring it "one of the most deplorable exhibitions of vulgar thinking and vulgar expression that it was ever our misfortune to encounter."[19]

In an attempt to escape boredom and to study slavery firsthand, Fanny accompanied Pierce to his Georgia plantation in December, 1838. Although she kept a journal on this occasion, she refrained from publishing her extreme dislike of southern institutions. After a lengthy visit to England during the early forties, the Butlers grew steadily more incompatible. Charges of his infidelity were matched by examples of her intemperate speech and unorthodox social behavior. When they became estranged, he tried to remove their two children from her supervision. They separated in late 1844, and in the autumn of 1845 Fanny returned to England. Confused, depressed, and for the first time in her life a little uncertain, she accompanied other members of the family to Italy, where in 1846 she compiled *Year of Consolation* in diary form. Vivid, expressive, mature, and occasionally sad, Fanny Kemble's thoughts were constantly drawn to America, to her children, and to her personal failure. She readily admitted that the unpleasant peculiarities of the New World resulted in part from her insular background. While traveling in France, she recalled

> the honor and security in which a woman might traverse alone from Georgia to Maine, that vast country, certain of assistance, attention, the most respectful civility, the most humane protection, from every man she meets, without the fear of injury or insult, screened by the most sacred and universal care from even the appearance of neglect or impertinence,—travelling alone with as much safety and comfort as though she were the sister or the daughter of every man she meets.[20]

The wretched pauperism of Italy made her thank God that she was born in England and would live in America. Even the me-

[19] *The Athenaeum*, 1835, p. 404.

[20] James Pylsted Wood (ed.), *One Hundred Years Ago* (New York, Funk and Wagnalls, 1947), 35.

chanical wonders of New York City were far finer than the antiquities of Rome. Despite propensities for wealth, excitement, and contest America was the hope for the poor of Europe.

> A few years of industry and economy may convert the poorest emigrant into a lord of the soil in the great fertile wilderness . . . where the unfettered action of human activity resembles the healthful coursing of the blood through the veins of a child, unimpeded by ligaments and compressions, and left to move and grow as God has ordained.[21]

A brilliant and impetuous actress had come to feel the lure of America. When she sailed again for the United States in 1848 to contest her husband's suit for divorce, she had already made up her mind to settle in New England, "the noblest country in the world." Forced to accept the divorce decree, she purchased "The Perch," a home at Lenox, Massachusetts, in the summer of 1849.

Catherine Sedgwick assisted in the reordering of Fanny's life, and the readings from Shakespeare again brought her before enthusiastic audiences, but in a way that was considered less daring than theatrical performances. Hawthorne lived only a short walk from "The Perch," and she visited the Longfellows when they were in Pittsfield. The Lenox community attracted leading literary figures like William Ellery Channing, Herman Melville, William Cullen Bryant, Ralph Waldo Emerson, and Oliver Wendell Holmes. Fanny gave the village a clock and assisted in organizing a public library, and in appreciation Lenox named a street for her. Fanny added spirit to the discussions of the literary lions. However, she was the child of Europe as well as of America. Street fairs, Christmas trees, itinerant bands, dancing dogs, barrel organs, jugglers, Maypoles, and processions were all missing. In the same decade, Dickens complained of the lack of cheerfulness and sociability and of the unique quiet of American streets at night. To sensitive immigrants, the gay patterns of the Old World did much to offset economic privations. Nor could the dreary

21 *Ibid.*, 81.

sameness of America always be overcome by the gratification of basic material needs. Fanny found America's open society with its much-touted frontier democracy stodgy and prudish. When she suggested giving a performance with the proceeds to be distributed to the poor, she was informed that America had no poor. When she produced a keg of beer for the workers on her farm, she found they embraced the temperance movement. When, with marked agility, she rode horseback through the countryside, she gained the reputation of being immodest and garish.[22]

An enemy of slavery even when married to a slaveowner, Fanny thought the North's absorption in making money as disgusting as the South's selfish egotism. After the Civil War started, she saw the conflict as an outgrowth of faults, not virtues, and equated defeats with justified punishment. Fanny had been disturbed during the Prince of Wales' tour in 1859 by what she considered the vulgar familiarity of his hosts. With Captain Wilkes' seizure of the British steamer *Trent*, her English sympathies were thoroughly aroused. Furthermore, the demand for Shakespearean actors had declined; therefore, Fanny and her daughter Frances sailed for England in the summer of 1862.

In 1863, Fanny Kemble published in both England and America her long-suppressed *Journal of a Residence on a Georgian Plantation, 1838–1839*. Actually the work was neither romantic nor melodramatic, but rather blunt, ugly, and depressing. Although she had written several plays, a book of verse, the autobiographical account of a year in Italy, and the *Journal* of 1835, it was the Georgia journal which brought British reviewers to suggest that Mrs. Kemble should be honored "by all who honour genius." With the death of Pierce Butler in 1867, Fanny for the third time decided to move permanently to the United States. She occupied their old home near Philadelphia and planned to retire and enjoy the association of her children and grandchildren. In 1868, despite the entreaties of relatives and friends, Fanny's younger daughter, the twenty-nine-year-old Frances

22 Margaret Armstrong, *Fanny Kemble: A Passionate Victorian* (New York, Macmillan, 1938), 325–26.

Butler, moved from Philadelphia to the old plantation in Georgia and undertook an ambitious project of restoration.

In 1870, the Reverend James W. Leigh, brother-in-law of Lord Saye and Sele, toured the United States. He met Miss Frances at Philadelphia and later visited Butler Island and found her "a fair queen . . . [who] resided amongst her sable subjects and entertained strangers with royal grace."[23] When Frances and her mother traveled to England later the same year, they visited Leigh at his home at Stoneleigh Abbey, near Warwick. James Leigh and Frances Butler were married in June, 1871, and Fanny settled in London. In 1873, after months of indecision, the Leighs decided to emigrate to Georgia and assume the management of the Butler plantations. Although critical of the idea, Fanny decided to accompany her daughter and son-in-law to America. She again bade good-bye to the gay refinement of London. Upon arrival at Philadelphia, she purchased York Farm and contented herself with entertaining English travelers and the publishing of letters and memoirs. In Georgia, James Leigh ruled the old plantation with a successful blend of efficiency and paternalism. But an influenza epidemic spread along the eastern seaboard in late 1876, and in Georgia yellow fever added further names to the list of fatalities. The Leighs became frightened for the health of their children and resolved to return to Britain. Fanny Kemble was delighted with their decision. She sold York Farm and revisited New England. Then, as the Leighs traveled north, she joined them, and in January, 1877, embarked from New York on her eighteenth and last voyage across the Atlantic.

Perhaps few observers were less qualified to judge the prospects of a new nation or to evaluate the advantages of immigration than Fanny Kemble in 1832. She carried the glory and the status of a century of Kemble acting; she had been accepted socially beyond the usual limits of her guild. Her early acquaintance with Americans had been highly selective. Washington and Peter Irving, John Howard Payne, and Stephen Price did not provide a reliable index of the American temperament.

23 J. W. Leigh, *Other Days,* 114.

Family tradition, careful training, natural wit, and fortuitous circumstances had allowed her to become a success too quickly. As a girl of twenty-two she had been presented to the royal family, had dined with William Thackeray and Sir Walter Scott, had received the compliments of Alfred Tennyson, Arthur Hallam, Richard Mockton Milnes, and Edward Fitzgerald, and had known Lord Byron. After a tiresome Atlantic crossing with uncongenial associates, she performed before mainly male audiences in cramped and stifling theaters and accepted the self-conscious hospitality of fawning hosts. Her husband was handsome and talented, but ineffectual and unimaginative. She longed for stimulation, romance, and excitement, and instead was asked to submit to Philadelphia priggishness.

After the flight to England in the mid-forties and the residence on the Continent, Fanny returned to the United States determined to seek out the excellent and contribute to the mainstream of cultural development. Turning to New England, she enjoyed the counsel, the friendship, and the acclaim of the most literate Americans of the age. She had never believed that the preservation of critical values required social insulation, and she accepted the democratic notion of freedom which stressed minimizing social control and removing most external restraints. But New England's dearth of healthy satire produced a sober air and a strange "intellectual complacency." In time of national tragedy it was neither North nor South, but rather Great Britain which captured her sympathy. In 1867 and again in 1873, Fanny Kemble made the United States her home, but it never quite became a satisfactory replacement for London. Upon final exit from the stage upon which for over four decades she had captured love and tasted despair, Fanny reflected upon the forces which had transformed America from "some remote part of England" in 1832 to a culturally and ethnologically independent nation in 1877.[24] As America came of age, it lost the congenial traces of British tutelage. As its uncouth traits were overcome, a heterogeneous culture sprang up. For Fanny Kemble, as for many sensitive British

[24] Armstrong, *Fanny Kemble*, 365.

immigrants, it was comforting to retire to the select association and sheltered permanence of English life.

The varied forces of war, depression, industrialization, and an awakening humanitarianism produced a veritable avalanche of experiments in and proposals for planned living during the nineteenth century. Emerson's observation that everyone in America seemed to have a prospectus in his pocket also applied to Great Britain. Even during the rapid growth and economic rivalry of the last half of the century, many semi-co-operative British communities were formed on the western frontier. The most popular regions were Iowa and Kansas. Perhaps a dozen settlements were attempted in the two states between 1850 and 1880. Most were inclined more towards a sophisticated social organization than an economic integration.

In 1867, a party of Anglo-Indian army officers and English country gentlemen settled near Decorah, Iowa. Limited knowledge of American farming, an uncertain labor supply, and cold winters rendered the frontier "distressing in the extreme." One of the party's leaders, Colonel William T. Baker, along with his brother, Captain Charles G. Baker, moved into the village of Decorah and became merchants. Harcourt Horn and some five other English families followed the Bakers to Decorah. Horn declared that ten years after the colony's founding only one of the original English families remained on the land. Many had drifted back to the more congenial British society.[25] Despite the return, however, by 1880 other English families had arrived and were resettling northern Winneshiek County.[26]

The poor Scottish boy George Grant made a fortune in the London mercantile world and lost it, as well as his life, while trying to manage a spirited colony near Fort Hays, Kansas. After nearly a decade at the Victoria, Kansas, settlement, the Maxwells,

---

[25] Horn, *An English Colony in Iowa*, 35ff.

[26] Edwin C. Bailey, *Past and Present of Winneshiek County, Iowa* (Chicago, The J. J. Clark Publishing Co., 1913), 66. Also see Winneshiek County, Iowa, 1880 Census. Note Bloomfield, Bluffton, Lincoln, Hesper, and Decorah townships.

Fultons, Rawlinses, Ainslies, Petries, Smithies, and many others recrossed the Atlantic. Mrs. Henry Smithie resumed her career on the London stage, and Walter Maxwell became a member of the Queen's Bodyguard, but the majority returned to their pleasant rural life.[27]

The English colony of Runnymede in Harper County, Kansas, enjoyed an even gaudier, albeit shorter, life than Victoria. At its height, the town boasted a three-story hotel, several stores, two stage lines, and a population of over five hundred. Bad crops, the panic of 1893, and the burning to death of an intoxicated English gentleman along with fifty prize ponies broke up the gay settlement. Upon learning of the drunkenness and dissolute habits at Runnymede, most English fathers ordered their sons home. Two of the colony's founders, Herbert Seppings and Edward Turley, returned to Britain along with the other young adventurers.[28] In his "Reminiscence of Runnymede," Captain Charles Seton, once of the British Army in India, explained that they were a "jolly lot of men and women . . . [who] expected to grow rich in a day then return to England and enjoy life."[29] At least six British army officers in the Boer War were formerly of Runnymede.

The grandiose experiments of James, William, and Frederick Close may have resulted in as many as five hundred Britons recrossing the Atlantic. The Closes hoped to settle much of northwestern Iowa as well as parts of Minnesota and Kansas. Members of the aristocracy like Lord Hobart, later the seventh Earl of Buckinghamshire; Almeric Paget, the future Lord Queenborough; two of Lord St. Vincent's sons; Captain Reynolds Moreton, R. N.; and numerous sons of bishops, knights, and gentlemen were among the emigrants. Over three hundred young

27 Marjorie Gamet Raish, *Victoria: The Story of a Western Kansas Town*, 80ff. See Kansas State Historical Society, "Ellis County Clippings," for the extensive newspaper and pamphlet literature on Victoria.

28 Nell Blythe Walden, "Colonization in Kansas from 1861–1890," Northwestern University Ph. D. Dissertation (1923), 70.

29 Kansas State Historical *Collections*, XII, 468. Also see Kansas State Historical Society, "Harper County Clippings," for the extensive newspaper and periodical literature on Runnymede.

men paid tuition to study agriculture under a single English farmer at the Le Mars, Iowa, settlement, but very few of them remained in America.[30]

The spectacular and celebrated community of Thomas Hughes at Rugby, Tennessee, resulted in many more British gentlemen's learning to their sorrow that the "Edens of America" were frequented by "playful cyclones" and plagued by floods and droughts.[31] H. F. Sherman's settlement near Fairmont, Minnesota, proved only slightly more successful. Reginald Moro, the organizer of the local cheese factory and founder of the public library, returned home after a few years. Young men from Oxford and Cambridge, like John Thirwell, nephew of the famous Bishop, and Maurice Farrar, a Fairmont justice of the peace turned London writer, spoke favorably of the country, but found the outlet for their talents too limited.[32]

Certainly not all British colonies of the era were founded by gentlemen or peopled by aristocrats. However, the less colorful settlements often left scanty records and no doubt produced fewer returnees. Typical of the more commonplace experiments were Kansas groups like the Welsh colony at Arvonia in Osage County, the Powis colony at Bala in Riley County, and Llewellyn Castle in Nemaha County. All were founded about 1870, and all quickly dissolved because of grasshoppers, inexperience, and internal friction.[33] A dozen English settlements like those at Weeping Water and Albion, Nebraska, suffered a similar fate. However, if Richard Wake's colony at Palmyra, Nebraska, can be accepted as representative of the middle-class groups who mi-

[30] Jacob Van Der Zee, *The British in Iowa*, 166ff.

[31] Edward C. Mack and W. H. G. Armytage, *Thomas Hughes: The Life of the Author of Tom Brown's Schooldays* (London, Ernest Benn, Ltd., 1952).

[32] Arthur Reginald Moro, "The English Colony at Fairmont in the Seventies," *Minnesota History*, Vol. VIII, No. 2 (June, 1927), 140–49. Maurice Farrar, *Five Years in Minnesota*.

[33] W. Weston, *Weston's Guide to the Kansas Pacific Railway* (Kansas City, Mo., Bulletin Steam Printing and Engraving House, 1872), 49, 55; Kansas State Historical Society, "Riley County Clippings," I, 59; John T. Bristow, *Memory's Storehouse Unlocked*, 192.

grated to the Middle West, only about 10 per cent of the farmers and artisans returned.

The Reverend Richard Wake arrived in New York in 1854. After occupying several Methodist pulpits in New York State, he moved to southern Illinois in the late fifties. Through a series of letters published in the *Christian World* of London, Wake became widely known as a proponent of emigration. In the spring of 1866, he traveled across Iowa and inspected several tracts of land in Missouri, Kansas, and Nebraska. He then hastened to the East Coast and sailed for England. Wake organized a party of 115 men, women, and children, who embarked at Liverpool in August, 1866. Several of the group located in eastern states, but at least nineteen families proceeded to Otoe County, Nebraska, and in 1870 participated in the founding of the town of Palmyra. Of the original nineteen families, some fourteen homesteaded or otherwise settled permanently in the immediate area. Three migrants became businessmen in adjoining counties, but J. Johnson and R. Sears moved their families back to Bedfordshire about 1873.[34]

After locating the one party of Englishmen in Nebraska in 1866, Wake became affiliated with London interests and in 1869 founded Wakefield, Kansas. Several Welsh families migrated to Wakefield in 1870, and a third group, the famous Sparrowhawk party, arrived from Oxfordshire in 1871. The experiment collapsed in 1874. Several of the investors who had spent thousands of dollars buying land, constructing a bridge across the Republican River, building a town, and founding the newspaper *Star of Empire* deserted the prairies to return to Britain.[35]

Before the Crimean and Civil wars, many of the English programs for group settlement in America tended to be socialistic or utopian in nature. Fortunately, communication, transportation,

34 Albert Hatkins (ed.), *Collections of the Nebraska State Historical Society*, XVI, (1911), 224; *History of the State of Nebraska* (Chicago, The Western Historical Co., 1882), 1235.

35 W. G. Chapman, "The Wakefield Colony," *Transactions of the Kansas State Historical Society*, X, (1907–1908), 485; Kansas State Historical Society, "Clay County Clippings," I and II.

and financial difficulties prohibited the launching of the more quixotic schemes. Nevertheless, several projects were actually put into operation and generally resulted in the return of their British organizers.[36]

One of the most bizarre experiments of the century grew out of the combined sophistry of Bronson Alcott and Charles Lane. In May, 1842, Ralph Waldo Emerson advanced Alcott funds which allowed the reformer to undertake a trip to Europe. The chief object of the mission was to visit Alcott House, a school founded in Britain by admirers of the American educator. While in England, Alcott preached his idea of escape to primitive nature; man should leave "alone much that he is in the habit of doing." Carlyle explained that the venerable Don Quixote was "all bent on saving the world by a return to acorns and the golden age."[37] With encouragement from English experimenters like Robert Owen, Alcott convinced three of the school's founders that their hatred of industrialism and overspecialization could best be proclaimed by organizing a rural "Fruitlands." When Alcott returned to New England in October, 1842, Charles and William Lane along with Henry Wright accompanied him to his poverty-stricken home at Concord. They immediately set to work on details of the projected colony.

The forty-two-year-old Lane and his son William were spiritual descendants of Gerard Winstanley and the seventeenth-century Diggers and Levelers. They tended to enhance rather than diminish Alcott's eccentricities. In January, 1843, Alcott was arrested and for a time incarcerated for nonpayment of taxes. Lane continued with the enterprise and, during the spring of 1843, invested his entire savings in a ninety-acre farm at Harvard

---

[36] One of the more ephemeral plans was devised by James Silk Buckingham. In 1842 he suggested that England, France, Austria, Prussia, and the United States contribute four million pounds to a fund which would be used to transport Europeans to America. England was to provide a fleet of five hundred ships for the transport of emigrants. James Silk Buckingham, *Canada, Nova Scotia, New Brunswick, and the Other British Provinces in North America* (London, Fisher, Son and Co., 1849), 437–39.

[37] See Amos Bronson Alcott in *D. A. B.*

Village, thirty miles south of Boston. Founded during the early summer of 1843, the community attracted eleven persons before it collapsed some seven months later.

The colony was to be transcendentalist, vegetarian, and self-sufficient. Fish, fowl, milk, eggs, cheese, and butter, as well as tea, coffee, molasses, and rice, were forbidden. All "degraded vegetables" which produced food underground were to be shunned. Horses could not be used for domestic purposes, and only pine knots should light the houses. Lane and Alcott devoted most of their efforts to various reform meetings, while Mrs. Alcott and her daughters performed the menial farm duties. With the collapse of the project, Lane accused the Alcott women of weakening Bronson's determination and of generating dissension. "Constancy to his wife and inconstancy to the Spirit have blurred over his life forever."[38]

With the failure of the experiment, Lane and his son joined the Harvard Shakers, but later moved to New Jersey. Charles returned to England in 1846, and William followed him two years later. The Lanes argued that they had been lured to Massachusetts only to lose $2,000 at Fruitlands Farm because of Alcott's capricious loyalty to the cause. They were answered in kind by Louisa's *Transcendental Wild Oats*, in which she characterized her father as "Able Lamb" and Charles Lane as "Timon Lion."

The fascinating career of Robert Owen and his socialistic catechisms are well known. His suggestion that the government employ and train the poor in agricultural and industrial co-operatives was never seriously considered by British authorities. Not only did the officials ignore his pleas, but they became more apprehensive as they grew to understand his beliefs. Owen decided, therefore, to initiate the program on a private basis and chose for his area of operations the congenial atmosphere of North America. He arrived in the United States in 1824 and quickly launched the "practical social utopia" at New Harmony, Indiana. Persons of every description flocked to the banks of the Wabash to champion equality, democracy, socialism, atheism,

38 F. B. Sanborn, *Bronson Alcott*, 67.

temperance, abolition, free love, and the good life without work. As the society split into at least a dozen different communities, Owen traveled on into the Southwest and in 1828–29 attempted to convince the Mexican government of the feasibility of founding a British settlement in Coahuila-Texas.

Few of the British colonists at New Harmony became repatriates. Robert Owen's greatest significance from the standpoint of returning immigrants was his indirect influence on Texas settlement. As a close friend of and intellectual mentor for Étienne Cabet, he helped influence the British Section of Icarian Communists as well as members of the North Texas Association and the North Texas Colonization Company to settle in Texas in the late 1840's. Many of the migrants going out under the auspices of these and similarly motivated societies returned to their homeland.[39] Owen was convinced that the world would be socially revolutionized through rapid industrial growth and that the United States would lead in such material progress. At the same time he perceived a primitive pureness in American capitalism, which would force Americans to be the first people to renounce unearned incomes and insist upon all enjoying the fruits of their labor. Socialistically or communistically inclined migrants who embraced the Owenite principles were almost universally disappointed in the New World.

Abundance of land, high wages, and republican institutions provided nineteenth-century America with an unusual magnet for attracting imaginative immigrants. It was only natural that venturesome Europeans should develop schemes whereby entire communities would be organized around the central design of land, freedom, and health. Unfortunately, William Bullock's vision of a happy and prosperous settlement on the banks of the Ohio proved as disappointing as Fruitlands or New Harmony.

As a businessman and showman, Bullock enjoyed a singular distinction in England. He began his career as a jeweler and silversmith in Liverpool about 1795, but later in the nineties, the

[39] "The British Section of Icarian Communist," *Bulletin of the International Institute of Social History*, No. 2 (1937), 84–88.

hobby of collecting native and foreign curiosities began to over-shadow his vocation. Soon after the turn of the century, he fashioned his home workshop into a series of apartments in which were displayed a heterogeneous assemblage of oddities ranging from lizards, shells, and gourds to medieval armour, flying squirrels, and Oriental art. First known as Bullock's Museum or the Liverpool Museum, the establishment later took the impressive title of Liverpool Museum of Natural History. The display became immediately popular, and a brochure describing the collections received wide circulation; editions were printed in Hull and Bath as well as in Liverpool and London. In 1811, Bullock moved to the heart of London, where he augmented his collection through the acquisition of other museums and gifts from the royal family. In 1812 he constructed Egyptian Hall, one of the city's most curious edifices. London and soon all Britain were astonished and delighted by the displays housed in the hall. Occasionally, Piccadilly thoroughfare was closed for hours to permit a whale or some other specimen to be carted into the museum. By way of contrast, Bullock also collected humming-birds; in one instance, he mounted ninety species in a single case. Indeed, the catholicity of the exhibits led Foreign Secretary George Canning to express the hope that ministers sent abroad "might possess half the information Bullock's Museum could afford them."[40]

In 1813 the collector sought to exhibit Cromwell's well-preserved head, but the Prime Minister dissuaded him.[41] Two years later he purchased Napoleon's military carriage from the Prince Regent. Subsequently, he hired Napoleon's valet and coachman to provide an added touch of authenticity to the exhibition and delighted the government by showing the carriage and the Napoleonic entourage throughout Britain so that all might see the completeness of the British victory over the French.[42] In

40 *The Leisure Hour*, No. 611 (September 12, 1863), 582.

41 Additional Manuscripts, British Museum, 38,252, Liverpool Papers, LXIII, Letter 265 (April 24, 1813).

42 William Bullock (ed.), *The Narrative of Jean Hornn, Military Coachman to Napoleon Bonaparte* (London, London Museum, 1816), Preface.

a period of four years, Bullock purportedly made over £25,000 from this single display.[43] Competition created by the official opening of the British Museum led Bullock to sell his collection of over 32,000 items in 1819. But ever the showman, he quickly arranged a display of trees and animals in an adjoining building and converted Egyptian Hall into a bazaar. In the meantime, he made frequent excursions to the Continent and began to accumulate another equally diverse collection of foreign specimens. He also became interested in stocking English parks and forests with foreign game. In 1821 he introduced the Wapiti deer from the Baltic, and the next year displayed reindeer and Laplanders in London. In 1822, after being intrigued by the specimens collected by the celebrated Captain Cook, Bullock decided to visit the New World for a firsthand look; on December 11, accompanied by his son, he set sail for Vera Cruz, Mexico.

Although Bullock had written little, he was already regarded as one of England's leading naturalists. His productions and exhibitions in conchology, ornithology, and horticulture were said to be without rival in Europe. As a Fellow of the renowned Linnean Society of London, he delivered learned treatises on the birds of England. Bullock was also an honorary member of the Dublin Society, a Fellow of the Wernerian Natural History Society of Edinburgh, the Royal Horticultural Society of London, and the Geological Society of London.[44]

Bullock returned from Mexico in November, 1823, and fitted out Egyptian Hall with the most elaborate display of his career. The exhibit was entitled "Ancient and Modern Mexico" and proved to be a resounding financial success. In addition, he published a work on Mexico which was widely circulated. Editions were printed in Dresden, Jena, Brussels, and Delft. In Paris alone, three editions were printed between 1823 and 1831.[45] The exhibition, coupled with the sale of his publications on Mexico, made the showman wealthy.

43 *The Enquirer* (Cincinnati), April 12, 1903, sec. 3, 7.

44 *The Monthly Magazine*, Vol. XLVII (1819), Part I, 159; *The Transactions of the Linnean Society of London*, XI (1815), 175. See *D. N. B.*

45 See British Museum and National Union Catalogues.

During a second trip to Mexico in 1826, Bullock and his wife decided to return to Europe by way of the United States. They landed in New Orleans, ascended the Mississippi and Ohio rivers, and arrived at Cincinnati on Easter Sunday, 1827. They were instantly electrified by the beauty of the landscape, the vitality of western society, and the many varieties and species of plants and animals. They were delighted to observe that food was carefully prepared, and, unlike other English visitors, were only slightly annoyed by the table manners of the Americans. As Roman Catholics, they were gratified to learn that it was not necessary to "disguise or conceal" their faith.

After a few days in Cincinnati, the Bullocks received an invitation to visit Elmwood Hall, the home of Thomas D. Corneal, which was situated on a Kentucky hillside overlooking the Ohio River and Cincinnati. Bullock's attention first had been called to the homesite while traveling up the Ohio. If he was impressed by the estate from below, he was dazzled beyond belief when he actually set foot on it. The river winding through the fertile valley, the steamboats passing with colors waving, and the city "with domes, pinnacles, public buildings and manufactories" formed a view that for the artist was irresistible:

> It is scarcely possible to find a more beautiful, fertile, or healthy spot. A ride round its boundaries, embraces every variety of landscape. Its general feature is level, gently rising from the river into undulatory hill and valley, resembling the finest part of the country of Devon, excepting, that the portion farthest from the river is clothed with woods, to which, from the size of the trees, their beauty, and variety, nothing in Europe can compare.[46]

The classical Elmwood with its European furnishings seemed to Bullock to be surrounded by a rich multiplicity of wild birds, animals, and plants scarcely equaled in Egyptian Hall. At Elmwood, Bullock's great appreciation for art, his deep interest in nature, his romantic spirit, and his acquisitiveness were all

[46] William Bullock, *Sketch of a Journey through the Western States of North America*, xix–xx.

joined. He determined to establish a new community—"a small town of retirement"—for Britons of modest means. At the new Elmwood, his countrymen could participate in the "good life"; they could amble through horticultural gardens, browse in libraries, worship in the church of their choice, and enjoy the fellowship of their countrymen. It would be a "bit of Old England" in the wilds of Kentucky. The settlement would be christened Hygeia in honor of the goddess of health.

Hygeia differed from New Harmony in that no social revolution or rebirth of human character was visualized. It was little influenced by the Birkbeck-Flower settlement of Albion, Illinois, and it borrowed nothing from the Frances Wright experiment in free love and free Negroes at Nashoba, Tennessee. Yet, the founder of Hygeia, like his contemporary British colonizers, believed that a kind of uncorrupted, primitive pureness existed in the New World. He, as had they, fastened his eyes on frontier America as a region where a man's intellect and will could be usefully and pleasantly projected, and where the very harmony and richness of nature would help meet the challenges and crises of life.

After a few days of feverish thinking and planning, Bullock purchased the estate from Corneal, and on June 2, 1827, he began the long journey to England to set his plan in motion. Soon after his arrival in London, he published *Sketch of a Journey Through the Western States of North America*. To it he attached a plat of a three hundred-home village which he proposed to establish. He further publicized his project through a lecture tour of England. Bullock convinced himself that Englishmen would soon be crossing the Atlantic to enjoy his utopia. In the early spring of 1828, he returned to Elmwood with his family.

Over the months and years that followed, the estate became a social center for the genteel society of Cincinnati. English immigrants like Frances Trollope were regular guests at Bullock's sumptuous dinner parties. Indeed, after Mrs. Trollope left Cincinnati, she exclaimed, "There is more taste and art lavished on one of their beautiful saloons, than all Western America can show elsewhere." Nevertheless, she felt Bullock's efforts were in vain. "Mr. Bullock is rather out of his element in this remote spot, and the gems of art he has brought with him, shew as strangely there, as would a bower of roses in Siberia, or a Cincinnati fashionable at Almack's." His "truly English hospitality, and his enlightened and enquiring mind, seemed sadly wasted there."[47]

After three years, Hygeia was still a dream on paper, a vision in the mind of its founder. In April, 1831, Bullock made a partial concession to reality by selling Elmwood Hall and 710 acres of his property for $31,000. He retired to a small cottage on another section of the estate. For five more years, the aging Englishman strode his Kentucky hillside, pursuing the elusive utopia. By 1836, with immigrants failing to appear, the ardor of his ambition was finally dampened. He sold the remainder of the property and terminated an eight-year residence in the United States. The disappointed promoter returned to England and retired into an obscurity from which he emerged only once. In 1843, when Madam Tussaud and Sons purchased Napoleon's military carriage, they called upon Bullock to substantiate the authenticity of the vehicle.[48]

The failure of Hygeia marked the end of Bullock's career. Although he returned to England as a man of means, the bold and daring enterpriser, with his unique blend of the businessman, showman, and humanist, had failed. The American experience was his only significant undertaking which proved unsuccessful. For William Bullock, as for many other European promoters who became bewitched by the physical grandeur and unrivaled opportunity of the New World, the great American success story unfolded in reverse.

Obviously not all of the English communities in America were perfectionist or transcendental in character. Indeed, emigrants more often joined together for the practical purposes of assisting

[47] *Domestic Manners of the Americans*, I, 71–72.
[48] Madam Tussaud and Sons, *The Military Carriage of Napoleon Bonaparte* (London, 1843); Acknowledgment.

one another while traveling and settling in the new land. The mid-century was particularly prolific in producing such economically orientated associations. Well over a dozen British groups attempted to locate in Texas and the Upper Mississippi Valley in the forties and fifties. The Rowed-Makery Devonshire party, which arrived at Galveston in 1849, and the Lieutenant Charles McKenzie party, which founded the City of Kent in Bosque County in 1851, were typical of the English failures in Texas. George Sheppard's 1850 arrival at Welton in Clinton County, Iowa, the founding of English Settlement in Racine County, Wisconsin, and the migration to Jacksonville and Peoria, Illinois, were indicative of the group migration to the Middle West.

J. Gray Smith's plans for an English settlement in East Tennessee in the late thirties, Richard Keily's advertisement of southwestern Georgia in 1849, and Thomas Lake Harris' hope for a Garden of Eden in Virginia in 1851 resulted in disappointment and return for many, including the British promoters. Although distinctly Welsh in character, the small colony founded by Samuel Roberts at Brynyffynon, Tennessee, in 1857 fits into the general pattern of group migration.

Welshmen first participated in American settlement under the benevolent auspices of William Penn. For a hundred years after the initial Quaker arrivals in the seventeenth century, few Welshmen traveled to the New World, and the Welsh Tract near Philadelphia became thoroughly Anglicized. A second wave of Welshmen began to make their way to Pennsylvania during the 1790's. By the 1830's and 1840's, a major wave of migration was flowing into New York, Pennsylvania, Ohio, and Wisconsin.

The opening up of America's hinterland coincided with a national reawakening and social transformation within Wales. The stimulus of Calvinistic Methodism and a general growth in nonconformity led Welsh leaders to revive their vanishing tongue and to cultivate Celtic literary traditions. Some Welshmen began to think of themselves as a national minority suffering under the heavy hand of the English. Naturally, many of the young, impetuous, and romantic crossed the Atlantic. Welshmen had long debated the feasibility of founding a Welsh community in America. William Bebb, the Whig governor of Ohio during the late 1840's, had often suggested the idea to relatives in northern Wales. In the early fifties, while an immigrant in Cincinnati, Michael D. Jones carefully studied the possibility of a settlement in Wisconsin. Within a few years, however, Jones returned to his Methodist pulpit in Bala, Meryoniethshire, with the firm conviction that Welshmen could never withstand the inroads of Americanization, whereas they might survive Anglicization.[49] Samuel Roberts, a friend of Jones and a Congregational clergyman, for years assessed the difficulties connected with emigration. At last, when fifty-seven years of age, he decided to lead his harassed followers to the land of promise.

Roberts was born in 1800, the son of John Roberts, a Congregational preacher from the parish of Llanbrynmair, Montgomeryshire. Samuel also became a clergyman and in 1826 accepted a post as his father's assistant. He taught in the local school, prepared wills, wrote letters for the parishioners and was the itinerant preacher for ten chapels. As he assumed more of his father's activities, he led a movement to secure a local post office, campaigned for a railway, entreated with the local landlords on behalf of the tenants, and, in general, became the social guardian and intellectual counselor for the isolated community. In 1843, Roberts introduced his own journal, *Y Chronicl*.

Y Chronicl not only championed reforms, but, from the first, warned landlords of the feasibility of mass rural emigration. Gradually growing more impatient with the economic domination from England, Roberts in 1850 prepared the pamphlet *Farmer Carefull of Cil-Haul Uchaf*. The work detailed the many wrongs done his family, as well as all hard-working tenant farmers. In July, 1852, he used *Y Chronicl* to publicize the extent of the local exodus and concluded with a terse listing of the facts

[49] In 1865, Michael D. Jones sent out the first shipload of Welshmen to the valley of the Chubut River in Patagonia. Many misfortunes befell the first party; however, with the assistance of the Argentine government, the colony ultimately succeeded.

showing the effectiveness of emigration. Later the same year appeared *Letters on Improvement, Addressed to Landlords and Road Commissioners* . . . . After referring to the landowners and stewards as thieves, Russian barons, and barefaced robbers, Roberts concluded:

> I love my country, and am aware that most of my neighbours are strongly attached to their native land: but when I think of the promises of sure and ample reward to industrious agriculturists so temptingly held out by the rich loam-soil of the boundless prairie and forest territories of Western America . . . and when I think of the rapid multiplication of travelling facilities; and when I think of the vast numbers that have already gone; and especially when I think of the heartless blackguard manner in which some industrious tenant-farmers have been treated, I am fully persuaded that we shall soon see a clean Exodus from large districts of our old country.[50]

The 1854 publication of *Diosg Farm: A Sketch of Its History During the Tenancy of John Roberts and His Widow* further stressed the advantages of America. At the end of the first edition of *Diosg Farm,* Roberts attached a letter or postscript which revealed both his method of agitation and his emigration psychology. "Husbandmen and herdsmen of Wales!—cheer up. The New Western World, extending its right hand of fellowship towards you, bids high for your services and offers you a full and quiet home."[51]

In the summer of 1855, former Governor William Bebb and a Welsh-American land agent, E. B. Jones, visited Llanbrynmair. Bebb informed his cousin, Samuel Roberts, that inexpensive yet fertile estates could be purchased in Scott County, Tennessee. Samuel Roberts, his brother Richard, an associate, Guilliam Williams, and two of Roberts' nephews, John R. and William Jones,

[50] Samuel Roberts, *Letters on Improvement, Addressed to Landlords and Road Commissioners, with a Petition to Parliament, for a Cheap Ocean Postage; and a Memorial to the Prime Minister for Franchise Reforms* (Llanbrynmair, Montgomeryshire, the author, 1852), 32.

[51] Page 46.

bought what they believed to be 100,000 acres of land and immediately set about forming a colony to settle the tract. Nearly three dozen families purchased plots, but before the date of departure many withdrew from the project. During 1856 and 1857, the five original land purchasers plus one additional family made their way to the new settlement of Brynyffynon, some eight miles northwest of Huntsville, Tennessee.

The Welsh suffered multiple hardships. William Bebb had failed to complete the construction of log cabins for the migrants. Despite a geographical nearness to centers of population, East Tennessee proved isolated and inaccessible. From the first the little party was harassed by vagrant squatters, plagued by inaccurate land surveys, and confronted by a dilatory system of justice. Most of the party quickly withdrew to the more fertile soil of Ohio, leaving the brothers Samuel and Richard Roberts to work out their destinies in the American backwoods.

Although the Robertses were no longer young, they were made of stern fiber, stubborn and proud. They resolved to remain in Tennessee. Lectures and preaching tours were undertaken in Welsh communities to provide a source of income, lengthy legal battles were fought to maintain their property, a railway was promoted to open up the region, a plan was devised to settle New Yorkers on the near-by lands, and a request for a post office at Brynyffynon was carried to President Lincoln. Throughout 1863 and 1864, both Union and Confederate troops used the primitive facilities and requisitioned considerable property at the Welsh settlement. Physically and intellectually torn between North and South, Roberts, during the last months of the war, rather unwittingly criticized certain aspects of Union policy. In early 1865, he published *Pregethau a Darlithiau (Sermons and Lectures)*,[52] which included a 117-page article entitled "The Great Rebellion in America." The article censured Northern leaders and warned against the "sheer madness" and unchristian policy of force. He registered disgust for the Celtic Anglophobia shown by Welsh

[52] Utica, printed by T. J. Griffiths.

Americans and for the chauvinistic imperialism so apparent in Union policy.

With the cessation of hostilities, Roberts found that he was *persona non grata* in the Welsh communities of Pennsylvania, New York, and Ohio. His plans for a railway near Brynyffynon collapsed, as did his hopes for the development of a great mining and lumber business in Scott County. Beset by economic failure and humiliated where he was once revered, in 1867 he quietly left the United States and in 1870 was followed by his brother Richard.

Roberts lived for eighteen years after his return to Europe, during which time he maintained his active interest in America. Throughout the entire period, he was plagued by disputes growing out of the failure of the Tennessee experiment. Many who had purchased lands as well as partners who had settled in Ohio demanded the return of their entire investment. Denunciations, recriminations, and threats of public exposure were hurled between Roberts and former friends. Of the medley of American-related issues which plagued the repatriated Welshman, the question of a government refund for losses allegedly sustained when Northern forces seized property at Brynyffynon concerned him the most. Roberts' claim was disallowed in 1873, but he never gave up the fight against the United States government.

After the return to Wales, Roberts became less a harbinger of Americanism and more a defender of an aggressive British policy. Late in life, he entered into correspondence with members of the royal family. When eighty-four years of age, he wrote to Queen Victoria and, while conducting religious services, often moved a resolution of patriotism and loyalty to the Crown and to the Prince of Wales. Roberts insisted that the United States follow England's lead in free trade and the enunciation of an international economic policy. As a man of peace, he welcomed the 1871 Treaty of Washington which amicably settled the *Alabama* controversy, but readily admitted his fears for the future. A decade after leaving America, he wrote, "I hope Europe is never again to see a general war—or the Great Western World will at once 'dash ahead' of us; and leave the poor old Kingdoms of Europe in the background."[53]

As the sage of Llanbrynmair, Roberts had counseled two generations of Welshmen to seek the advantages of a new life in the New World, yet his own migration had resulted in criticism and frustration. Although the post-American years brought numerous personal accolades and many positive accomplishments, Roberts was not able to dissociate himself from the humiliation and defeat of the Brynyffynon experiment. Samuel Roberts' lifelong involvement with American immigration demonstrates the unique spell the New World often cast over nineteenth-century British experimenters and reformers.

As American expatriates have sought fulfillment in Europe during the twentieth century, so did British expatriates seek self-realization in America in the nineteenth. The New World exerted an uncommon attraction for ambitious youth with background and banknotes. By his eighteenth birthday, John G. Taylor had decided that "suitable openings" were unavailable in England, whereas his American relatives could provide "abundant means" for his improvement. While he was traveling first class, eating at the captain's table, vacationing with Philadelphia kinsmen, and talking with President Tyler, the American experience proved delightful. Even the employment extended to him by relatives seemed exciting. But when his job as a mine inspector was concluded, Taylor's view of America quickly clouded. He later admitted that "the fatal eagerness with which I clutched at every chance the least likely to lead to any employment seems almost unaccountable."[54] Consequently, when in the spring of 1842 a ship arrived from Cuba with news that gold had been discovered, Taylor eagerly accepted a second assignment from his

[53] National Library of Wales Manuscripts, 13,195D, Samuel Roberts to David Howell, February 13, 1877.

[54] *The United States and Cuba: Eight Years of Change and Travel,* 72.

Philadelphia relatives and left for the island to investigate the rumor. Although the mines proved to be worthless, Taylor made three trips to Cuba before abandoning his promotional schemes. In the meantime, he had observed the smuggling of slaves, contracted typhus fever, and completely failed in his hopes for lucrative adventure. He sailed for Liverpool in October, 1843, after two and one-half years in the United States.

Taylor admitted that American independence had proved successful; the country's farms were clean and prosperous and her wealth and expansion unquestioned. Yet, the United States had been oversold. British exaggeration of republican accomplishments and official fear of a colonial precedent encouraged disgruntled and unemployed Englishmen to turn to America as the cure for all their ills. Young Taylor admitted that even he had listened to "voices which whispered 'never fear' in a country like America there are always abundant means."[55] Intelligent, alert, adventuresome, and yet somewhat irresponsible, Taylor preferred the luxuries of home to hard work, deprivation, and exhaustion in America.[56]

Charles Augustus Murray was the antithesis of Taylor. Murray sailed from Britain as a traveler, but became so much impressed with America that he decided to become an immigrant and settle permanently on the Wisconsin frontier. Murray's family commissioned him, as the grandson of the Earl of Dunmore, the royal governor of Virginia at the outbreak of the Revolution, to investigate the legal status of the family lands in Virginia. The affable Scotsman arrived in New York in July, 1834, and spent several months touring New England and New York before proceeding on his mission. While at Geneseo, New York, as a guest of James Wadsworth, he fell in love with his host's daughter, Elsie, and planned to visit her again on his return to the state.

After inspecting the Virginia lands during the winter of 1834–35, Murray made arrangements to travel to the Far West with

55 *Ibid.*, 6.

56 While on a tour in the Far East, Taylor died at Battacola, Ceylon, in January, 1851, a few months before his work on America was published.

Colonel Henry Dodge and a party of explorers. Although missing Dodge at Fort Leavenworth, Murray nevertheless visited a number of Indian tribes, becoming a student of Indian lore and a master of Pawnee and other Indian languages. Returning to St. Louis, he proceeded up the Mississippi River as far as Wisconsin, then trekked overland to Geneseo.[57] Murray asked for Elsie Wadsworth's hand in marriage in the spring of 1836, with the stipulation that after the ceremony she would accompany him to England. Apparently James Wadsworth agreed to the marriage, but refused to allow his daughter to leave the country. Thereupon Murray changed his plans. He would purchase a baronial estate in Wisconsin and with his wife reign over the district with the supremacy that Wadsworth held in the Geneseo Valley. On August 6 and 8, 1836, Murray bought lands totaling twenty thousand acres in Grant County, Wisconsin, listing New York City as his permanent address. When he apprised the Murray family of his intentions, however, the young traveler was ordered to return to Britain at once.[58]

On the death of Elsie's father in 1850, Murray returned to the United States, and fourteen years after his original proposal he claimed his bride. Charles had served as Master of the Queen's Household and showed himself to be a talented writer, linguist, and diplomat. After the marriage, the Murrays decided to reside in England rather than on their Wisconsin estates.[59]

Seldom did the purported opportunities, glories, and excitement of the Western world prove more thoroughly illusory than in the multiple failures of the Oldmixon family. No other figure in Bath during the 1780's enjoyed the notoriety of Sir John Oldmixon. He was as familiar to the inhabitants as "the Mayor of the Pump-room."[60] He reached both the zenith and the nadir in

57 Joseph Schafer, *The Wisconsin Lead Region* (Madison, State Historical Society, 1932), 148.

58 Charles Augustus Murray, *Travels in North America During the Years 1834, 1835, and 1836*, II, 365.

59 Joseph Schafer, "Lands Across the Sea," *The Wisconsin Magazine of History*, Vol. XIII, No. 4 (June, 1930), 417–29.

60 Bernard, *Retrospections of the Stage*, II, 21.

social intercourse. Spectacularly attired in old clothes, with one black and one white stocking, the "Bath beau" drank much, yet employed his private chaplain; read much, yet disfigured books by tearing out favorite passages and stuffing them in his pockets. Overly generous to the poor, something of an artist and playwright, Oldmixon could be found in the theater four nights of the week.

Sir John had been knighted while a lieutenant of Dragoons at Dublin Castle in 1782. After the return to Bath, he showed none of the methodical application that had made his grandfather into the famous Whig historian.[61] After marrying the talented Miss Mary George about 1787, Oldmixon found his economic problems growing particularly pressing. Consequently, when his wife was offered an attractive salary with a Philadelphia theatrical troupe in 1794, they embarked for America to escape further financial embarrassment. Settling on a small farm near Philadelphia, Miss George supported a large family while Sir John, sinking into miserable obscurity, hawked vegetables in the city streets. Eventually they separated. Sir John died at Sag Harbor, Long Island, in 1816 "neglected and forgotten," while Miss George, assisted by her two daughters, ran a finishing school in Philadelphia until her death in February, 1835.[62]

John W. Oldmixon, born in England in 1788, was six years of age when his parents moved to the United States. Their failure led him to cultivate a love for England, and, when but fifteen, he returned home to enlist in the Royal Navy. Two younger brothers followed his example, while a fourth joined the American cause and fought against his kinsmen during the War of 1812. John W. applied for a further appointment in the navy, but was discharged as a lieutenant in 1816.[63] After a visit to France in the early 1820's, Oldmixon wrote *A Lounge in the Tuileries* in 1824, but soon thereafter recrossed the Atlantic to live again in the

[61] William A. Shaw, *The Knights of England* (2 vols., London, Central Chancery of the Orders of Knighthood, 1906), II, 297.

[62] *The Gentleman's Magazine*, Vol. LXXXVIII, (November 1818), 478.

[63] Additional Manuscripts, British Museum, 38,049, John William Oldmixon, not dated.

United States. Always eager to succeed, he consistently failed. Years later he wrote of America, "In her woods and fields there is no thing I have not turned my hand to."[64]

Back in England, in 1830, Oldmixon married the moderately wealthy Anne Barrington and some two years later for the third time migrated to Pennsylvania. He hoped to become a gentleman farmer, but within a few months recrossed the Atlantic to England. In 1851, after the death of his wife and only child, Oldmixon decided to revisit the New World. He toured the country from September, 1851, to May, 1852, but made no further attempt to settle permanently. The more than fifty immigrants aboard the ship upon which he returned convinced him, however, that his earlier misfortune was merely part of a mass disappointment.

After the fourth trip to America, Oldmixon tried to evaluate the reasons for his multiple failures. He readily agreed that the people of the United States were more ambitious, their cities better kept, and their arts and crafts more flourishing than those of Europe. North America was a great, vast, rich, and growing continent, yet it was devoid of physical health and mental happiness. In England, men might go to bed hungry, but they retained a felicity of spirit. In America, though the table was well supplied, the immigrant had no appetite. In rural districts "men rather vegetate than enjoy life." They led a sullen and monotonous rather than a social and stimulating existence. In the cities the laboring man worked "ten times as hard . . . and grows surly in a kind of lonely independence."[65] Children were rude and undisciplined, older people received little respect, and sensitive Englishmen could find neither suitable employment nor a pleasant environment.

The failures of his own family exemplified the inability of sophisticated Englishmen to achieve the status, stimulus, and success which would have bound them to republican institutions. John's father, Sir John, passed from the "Bath beau" into a Long

64 Capt. J. W. Oldmixon, *Transatlantic Wanderings*, 2.
65 *Ibid.*, 3.

Island derelict; his mother, the renowned Miss George, suffered a poverty and humiliation which barred her from return; two brothers found their way back to become officers in the Royal Navy. Nevertheless, when he balanced opportunities against annoyances, the elderly Englishman admitted that if he were young and could seek his fortune with "rifle and axe," he would again choose the naked life of America. Despite the many failures in the land of promise, John William Oldmixon always envisioned the United States as "life's young dream."[66]

Many intelligent and capable Britons were drawn to North America through curiosity and an innate desire to roam. Most professed no philosophy except adventure, no ambition save discovery. Arriving in 1768, John Long quickly became an expert explorer, authority on native life, frontier guide, and Indian interpreter. Long's fascination with the New World failed to provide him with economic security, and in 1788, he returned to England to face action by his creditors. Other Britons found stimulus in the natural wonders and relished the physical challenge of America. John Bradbury once escaped death by disassembling his watch and distributing the pieces among his Indian captors. As a representative of the Liverpool Botanical Society, the Scottish ethnologist became so much intrigued with western plains, plants, and Indians that he lingered in the United States for years before returning to Liverpool with his collection of rare specimens.

Bradbury's assistant on a journey up the Missouri River in 1810 and 1811 was a young English immigrant by the name of Thumas Nuttall. Born at Settle in the West Riding of Yorkshire in 1786, Nuttall became a journeyman printer in his uncle's shop at Blackburn and later accompanied the organization when it moved to Liverpool and reorganized as Nuttall, Fisher and Dixon. A disagreement forced young Thomas to leave the firm,

[66] *Ibid.*, 84. After forty-five years of naval inactivity Oldmixon was recalled to active reserve status in 1861 and retired with the rank of commander in 1865. He died at his home overlooking Hyde Park in 1869. See the *Navy Lists* for pertinent information concerning Oldmixon's promotions and retirement.

and, after spending several months in London, he decided to sail for America in the spring of 1808. Nuttall, although only twenty-two years of age and boasting little formal education, possessed an unusually sound knowledge of Latin, Greek, mineralogy, history, and a peculiarly intense fascination with nature. Upon arrival in the Delaware River on April 23, Nuttall recorded his delight with the verdant shores in surprisingly similar spirit to William Bullock's later description of the countryside as seen from the Ohio River below Cincinnati. "As we sailed up the Delaware, my eyes were rivited on the landscape with intense admiration. All was new, and lifelike, that season was full of hope and enthusiasm. The forests, apparently unbroken in their primeval solitude and repose, spread themselves on either hand as we passed placidly along."[67]

Within a few days after landing at Philadelphia, Nuttall's interest in plants led him to the home of Benjamin S. Barton. The great naturalist's assistant had recently resigned, and Nuttall was soon employed as a replacement. Barton became the youthful immigrant's friend, colleague, and patron. He first outlined and financed local trips into Maryland and Delaware, later into Virginia and North Carolina, and by 1809 extensive studies were undertaken in the Great Lakes region. In 1810, Nuttall traveled up the Missouri River with the Bradbury party as far as the Mandan Indian country, but was back in St. Louis by early 1811. Perhaps he anticipated the outbreak of the British-American war or perhaps he wished to capitalize on his manifold discoveries; at any rate, for some reason, he disobeyed his mentor's instructions to return to Philadelphia and instead drifted down the Mississippi and sailed for England in early 1812.[68]

Seeds taken during the expedition were grown by the Fraser Nursery of London while Nuttall prepared a catalog in which

[67] *Proceedings of the American Philosophical Society*, Vol. VII, No. 63 (1860), 298.

[68] Francis W. Pennell, "Travels and Scientific Collections of Thomas Nuttall," *Bartonia*, No. 18 (1936), 7ff.

the plants were advertised. Research at the British Museum and election to membership in the Linnean Society established the young naturalist's reputation in Britain. But with the cessation of the war, Nuttall again sailed for Philadelphia. The two decades that followed were crowded with discovery. In 1815, he undertook an expedition into the southeastern United States. Between 1818 and 1820, he explored the Arkansas River valley. In 1821, he turned to mineralogy and chemical analysis and reported the discovery of two new minerals. In the early 1820's, he lectured at Yale and at the Philadelphia Academy of Natural Science, and in 1824, he became lecturer on natural history and curator of the Botanical Gardens at Harvard. Nuttall made scientific trips to the Azores, to England, and to many parts of the United States and Canada. In 1834, he joined the Nathaniel Wyth expedition to the Pacific and, after two visits to Hawaii and much research in California, returned to Philadelphia by way of Cape Horn. Richard Henry Dana, a shipmate on the return voyage, declared the naturalist eager to be put ashore among the icebergs of the Cape so that he might study spring flowers.[69]

By 1840, Nuttall had published books on North American plants, rocks, trees, birds, shells, and Indians. While becoming a famous ornithologist, mineralogist, conchologist, ethnologist, and "father of Western American botany," he had also attracted the favorable attention of literary and political figures like Washington Irving, Richard Henry Dana, Thomas Jefferson, and William Henry Harrison. Even English journals like *The Literary Gazette*, which criticized him for living in America, praised his "industry, love of liberty and intelligence." Nuttall was not pleased with the reception of his efforts, however. When one of his most significant studies, *The Genera of North America*, was indifferently received, he denied any wish for personal emolument but contended: "I had a right, however, reasonably to expect from Americans a degree of candour, at least equal to that which my labours had met with in Europe. But I have found,

[69] *Popular Science Monthly*, Vol. XLVI, No. 5, (March 1895), 689–96.

what indeed, I might have reason to expect from human nature, often, instead of gratitude, detraction and envy."[70] Furthermore, few of Nuttall's American acquaintances ever became warm personal friends. Nuttall was an assiduous worker, regularly refusing to eat and often forgetting to sleep, and his peculiarities tended to isolate him from the world. Melvina Lawson, an assistant in the preparation of one of his books, found him "dirty and disorderly," with manners that were "rough and abrupt." He was "the least attractive of the *genus homo* I ever met."[71]

Despite personal irritations, it was with sadness and misgivings that Nuttall, during the autumn of 1841, decided to return permanently to England. The will of Jonas Nuttall of Liverpool bequeathed the estate of Nutgrove, near Blackburn, to his nephew Thomas, with the stipulation that the recipient reside on it at least nine months of each year. At first, Nuttall refused to accept the inheritance, but, out of consideration for his sisters, he eventually agreed to return. In a moment of reminiscence, Nuttall revealed his spiritual kinship with William Bullock, Samuel Roberts, and others who loved America for her natural beauty and diversity. Upon leaving Philadelphia, he explained that thirty-four years earlier, upon viewing America for the first time, he had riveted his eyes "on the landscape with intense admiration." Any privation was a cheap price if it provided the privilege of roaming "over the wild domain of primeval nature":

> How often have I realized the poet's buoyant hopes amid these solitary rambles through interminable forest . . . . But the oft-told tale approaches its close, and I must now bid a long adieu to the New World, its sylvan scenes, its mountains, wilds, and plains, and henceforth, in the evening of my career, I return, almost an exile, to the land of my nativity.[72]

[70] Thomas Nuttall, *A Journal of Travels into the Arkansas Territory, During the Year 1819, with Occasional Observations on the Manners of the Aborigines* (Philadelphia, Thomas H. Palmer, 1821), Preface.

[71] Frank L. Burns, "Miss Lawson's Recollections of Ornithologist," *The Auk*, No. 3, (July, 1917), 282.

[72] Andrew Michaux and Thomas Nuttall, *The North American Sylvia, or, a*

The last eighteen years of Nuttall's life were strangely unproductive. He published a few articles and experimented with rhododendrons, but his career as a productive scientist ended at Christmastime, 1841, when he embarked for England. Once at Nutgrove, he neglected to catalog and even to unwrap part of his treasured American collection. Nuttall's death in September, 1859, received considerable notice in British, French, German, and American journals. The 1883 unveiling of his marble bust at the Botanical Gardens in St. Louis provided a fitting memorial, as did the founding of the *Quarterly Bulletin of the Nuttall Ornithological Club*. However, a dozen North American plants named in honor of the first naturalist to cross the Mississippi River represented a more significant remembrance. Nuttall differed from many repatriated Britons in that he returned more as a victim of circumstance than from personal choice. Nevertheless, his life parallels others in that his American experience carried him to the peak of expectation and excitement, in contrast to which his last eighteen years in Europe were but a pale and faded anticlimax.

The concepts of artists, showmen, aristocrats, naturalists, and community planners tend to highlight the repatriation story. Determined and often eccentric men, they were inclined to misjudge America, and at the same time, they not uncommonly overestimated their own ability to fashion a new life out of a raw environment. Such immigrants were rarely pious, moralizing, or hypocritical. They seldom confused politics with polemics and only infrequently demanded ironclad absolutes. Sensitive and conscientious, they sought self-realization through discovery, social improvement through creativity. They were exhilarated by the opportunity for both vertical and horizontal mobility. They often possessed a faith in America that survived reality. Colonizers in particular enjoyed the conviction that European ideas grafted to the American experience could form the near-perfect society.

Description of the Forest Trees of the United States, Canada, and Nova Scotia (5 vols., Philadelphia, D. Rice and A. N. Hart, 1857), IV, Preface.

Yet, the abundant energy failed to shape historic circumstances, and the honest concern failed to produce dramatic events. All too often their plans proved futile and unproductive. They could not translate a vision into a practical program. Although they sought a new meaning in America in which all could freely place their faith, as individuals they failed to transcend their very personal concerns. Most performers who returned were men and women of action. They favored a positive and direct approach to their needs; and therefore, rationally but often impractically, they sought to improve their status in America. Some lacked discipline, others had no clear-cut understanding of their own aims, and many returned merely as a result of a series of fortuitous events. The sons of aristocrats and gentlemen were usually mere onlookers rather than participants. They received the confidences of many, but seldom wished to exchange their British inheritance for trans-Atlantic equalitarianism. Not being able to mold their American environment, they in turn refused to be molded by it.

Nevertheless, relatively few false notes appear in the character of the actors, the experimenters, and the adventurers who returned. Perhaps man the thinker and dreamer was as significant and basic to the development of the New World as man the maker and taker. If the story can be told in terms of beliefs and imagination as well as in terms of expansion and production, then it was America's loss that men like Bernard, Lane, Oldmixon, Roberts, Bullock, and scores of others ended their lives outside the land to which they had been joined by an inner emotional harmony.

UNSEVERED TIES

In pre-Civil War America, as in most frontier societies, youth and brawn were in greater demand than culture and maturity. The New World had less need for trained and experienced professionals than for mechanics, artisans, laborers, and farmers. Nevertheless, the large number of British-born professional people in America attest to a migration of quality as well as of quantity. In evaluating either the immigration or the re-immigration of lawyers, teachers, physicians, writers, or clergymen, the greatest hazard is individual uniqueness. The educated returnees frustrate economic categorization and defy broad generalization. The elite of any migratory group tend to be encumbered with more mental and physical baggage than their compatriots. They more often become the symbol of traditions left behind. But at the same time their reactions to the new society are inclined to be more sophisticated and circumspect.

There was little question regarding the reception of the professional class. Since they possessed essentially the same qualities as the receiving society, they experienced little social prejudice and were seldom viewed as progenitors of a new or alien race. Indeed, the unusually close relationship between many Anglo-American intellectual, religious, and humanitarian groups tended to erase nationality in favor of a common Atlantic community of interest. From John Wesley and George Whitefield to

George Thompson and Joseph Sturge, revivalists and reformers ignored national boundaries to write and lecture for the English-speaking world. Antislavery advocates, proponents of the temperance movement, and supporters of world peace organizations represented a unified purpose, although they came from both sides of the Atlantic. The movement for women's rights, educational reform, and religious evangelism bound persons in England and America to a common goal. Extensive travel and frequent conferences further cemented trans-Atlantic connections.

Although there was a major British-American interchange in many fields, it was missionaries and clergymen who actually migrated to the United States in largest numbers. Most English denominations contributed to the creation and support of related American bodies. Methodists, Congregationalists, Presbyterians, Quakers, and Anglicans forwarded literature, sent money, and promoted the migration of their clergy and missionaries. By the end of the nineteenth century over 15 per cent of the Protestant Episcopal clergymen of the United States were natives of the United Kingdom, while 11 per cent of the Northern Presbyterian ministers were British born.[1] British clerics made their way to all corners of the Union. For example, in 1870, every clergyman, Protestant and Roman Catholic, who ministered to the more than seven thousand residents of Virginia City, Nevada, was born in the United Kingdom.[2]

American churches were multiplying much faster than those in Britain, and religious leaders saw in the new and robust society an opportunity to build a profitable, intellectual, and moral community often difficult to envisage at home. Furthermore, many writers believed Americans to be more active churchgoers than the British. Archibald Prentice explained that in 1848 New York City was provided with 215 places of worship, while his home town of Manchester with a comparable population supported only 114.[3] The close personal ties maintained by many of

1 Rowland Tappan Berthoff, *British Immigrants in Industrial America* (Cambridge, Harvard University Press, 1953), 21.

2 *The United States Census*, Storey County, Nevada, 1870.

the Anglo-American denominations further paved the way for the migration and repatriation of clergymen. The assembly of twenty-eight Congregational ministers meeting at Monmouth, Wales, in 1846 had no hesitation in asking the Congregational ministers of the United States to preach against the Oregon expansionists. The southern Welshmen emphasized that, since the two churches professed the same beliefs, grew from identical racial stock, and were led by ministers who had been trained in the same academies, war was unthinkable.[4] The Congregational preachers, like most nonconformist leaders, emphasized the bonds of race and human brotherhood and excluded national antipathies or political antagonisms. National and patriotic motives were relatively insignificant in fostering either the migration or the return of nonconformist clergymen.

Welsh preachers in particular were caught up in the immigration movement. A very high proportion of the migrating Welsh ministers crossed the Atlantic several times. Much of the revitalization and even preservation of the Welsh language and culture can be credited to the eloquence of a school of mighty pulpit orators who were at the height of their influence during the first part of the nineteenth century. As Welsh settlements in Pennsylvania, New York, Ohio, and Wisconsin multiplied, a steady stream of Welsh-speaking preachers sailed for America to minister to the expanding congregations. Often they returned in order to refresh their knowledge of the language or to retire to a romanticized Welsh valley.

The life of John T. Griffiths demonstrates the unique duality of many Welsh ministers.[5] Griffiths was born at Penyparc in the Vale of Glamorgan in 1845. His mother died when he was three years of age and his father when he was fifteen. As a boy he worked in the local coal mines, but after marriage in early 1865,

3 Archibald Prentice, *A Tour in the United States* (London, Charles Gilpin, 1848), 19.

4 National Library of Wales, Manuscript 2719C.

5 For a brief biography of Griffiths, see T. Valentine, "Y Parch John T. Griffith, D. D." ["The Reverend John T. Griffith, D. D."], *Seren Gomer* [*Gomer's Star*], January, 1918, pp. 1–6. Late in life Griffith changed his name to Griffiths.

he decided to enter the ministry. Convinced that Pennsylvania held out greater professional opportunities than Glamorganshire, Griffiths and his bride sailed from Liverpool in 1865. They settled in the Welsh community at Scranton, where Griffiths preached on Sunday and worked in the mines during the week. In 1868, he enrolled as a member of the first class at Crozer Theological Seminary. Within a year, Griffiths had perfected his English and was ordained a Baptist minister.

Over the decades that followed, Griffiths established a score of congregations, built a dozen church buildings, reorganized many Baptist societies, and preached nearly two hundred sermons annually. Invited back to Wales in 1883, he accepted a pulpit in the Rhondda Valley, but within a few months returned to the United States. His wife died in 1905, and soon thereafter he sailed for Britain a second time. Several months of preaching in South Wales again terminated in a return to Pennsylvania. Finally, in 1908, after living and working in the mountains of Pennsylvania and Ohio for forty-three years, John T. Griffiths reluctantly decided to retire permanently in his homeland. At his final service in America, a Welsh deacon attempted to explain Griffiths' reasons for leaving: "There is a magnet that is drawing him away from this community, and that is his native land. The flowers bloom more brightly and the birds sing more sweetly there."[6] A fellow Welsh-American preacher carried the theme further:

> I have been thinking that the people who come from the Old Country here after all have no country. . . . They belong here and they belong there, and they hardly know where they do belong.
> We feel that the other side has a grip on us, and this side has a grip on us. One would think that after so many years in this country Dr. Griffiths would be the last man in the world to have any desire to go to the other side, but you see that after all these years of service, of all these years of fellowship, after gathering around his life so many traditions and memories that bind him to this state, he still feels that he has to go to the other side.[7]

6 John T. Griffiths, *Reminiscence: Forty-Three Years in America*, 128.
7 *Ibid.*, 130.

Limited opportunity at home and encouraging reports from abroad led Griffiths to the New World. Years of activity as a preacher Americanized him. During the Pennsylvania decades, he published at least ten books and pamphlets, accepted an honorary doctorate, and became a leader in the Baptist church. Yet, like scores of other professionals, he failed to discover positive values or sentimental moorings equal to those of Britain. Forty-three years in America intensified rather than dulled the thrill of singing *"Mae nghalon yn Nghymru"* ("My Heart Is in Wales"). After the return, Griffiths continued to write, but he never quite captured the spirit which he sought. He again returned to the United States in 1914, but died in Wales in June, 1917. A Welsh biographer accounted for Griffiths' restless buoyancy by suggesting, "The spirit of freedom and the go of America has entered into his constitution."[8]

While less clannish than the Welsh in their settlement patterns, English and Scottish nonconformist preachers were also drawn to America in large numbers. William O'Bryan, founder of the Bryanites or Bible Christian Connexion, arrived in the United States in 1831 and helped build the newly formed Methodist Protestant church. Although responsible for the migration of scores of Primitive Methodists, O'Bryan eventually returned to Cornwall to guide the destinies of the Bible Christians in southwestern England. Late in life, he recrossed the Atlantic and died in the United States in 1868.[9]

As one of a party of forty steerage passengers, the Reverend D. Griffiths landed in New York in May, 1832. As a self-educated Presbyterian preacher from the village of Long Buckby, Northamptonshire, Griffiths decided to seek employment in the rapidly growing rural communities of the West. He settled in the Western Reserve of Ohio, became a farmer-preacher, an organizer of revival meetings, and an emotional advocate of tem-

8 T. Valentine, "Y Parch John T. Griffith, D. D.", *Seren Gomer*, January, 1918, pp. 1–6.

9 S. L. Thorne, *Obedience to the Call of God: A Funeral Sermon on the Death of William O'Bryan* (Plymouth, S. L. Thorne, 1868).

perance, repentance, and education. Griffiths was delighted to find that the outpouring of the spirit went hand in hand with honest labor. "The good people of Ohio never dream that the word of God is less worthy of credit, because it is dispensed on the Sabbath day by a clergyman whom they have seen milking his cows, or driving his corn to mill during the week."[10] Although delighted with American society, Griffiths refused pulpits in some of Ohio's larger towns so that he might further his education in England and carry the excitement of the West's protracted meetings to the lukewarm Presbyterians of Northamptonshire.

The American Revolution only temporarily interrupted the close ties maintained between the Church of England and its New World counterpart. But in the following century, Anglican clergymen who hoped to be transformed into Episcopalian ministers often recoiled at the process of republicanization. Ten years in the diocese of London with only temporary appointments led Isaac Fidler to resent the British social and aristocratic order. Fidler was a man of broad training and unquestioned intellectual ability, yet he had become destitute in the service of a wealthy and powerful church. As dissatisfaction with Anglicanism deepened, a misconceived admiration for America matured. He later wrote "Whenever, therefore, any real or fancied evil oppressed me, my imagination and my hopes took refuge among the free, wild and rising communities of the great republic."[11]

With a vague faith in American patronage, Fidler sailed from London in late October, 1831. He was accompanied by his wife, two children, and a servant, but failed to carry either records or recommendations. Arriving in New York in December, the family found the climate disagreeable and the society repugnant. The servant deserted the Fidlers for a more lucrative position, but just as quickly left the second post to return to England.

[10] D. Griffiths, Jun., *Two Years' Residence in the New Settlements of Ohio, North America*, 79–80.

[11] Isaac Fidler, *Observations on Professions, Literature, Manners, and Emigration in the United States and Canada*, 2.

Fidler's landlord proved to be an avowed radical and atheist from Liverpool who was eager to return if the Reform Bill should become law. More congenial English acquaintances also talked of return, while an Episcopal clergyman explained that British immigrants trained in a profession commonly found America unreceptive to their learning. Neither the Episcopal authorities, the Roman Catholic Bishop, nor printers of classical manuscripts offered encouragement.

During the years of waiting for a permanent assignment, Fidler had taught school and mastered the classical as well as several Asiatic languages. Nevertheless, prospective employers suggested that he forget his training and undertake yet another profession. Fidler informed English friends that "it is no unusual thing for a person to have been schoolmaster, doctor, lawyer, clergyman, and to have been engaged also in other professions; and in the business classes of society, to have followed almost all the circle of trades."[12] Few persons appeared interested in his linguistic abilities. Even Harvard College could find no opening for a master of Sanscrit or Persian. The Englishman stood flabbergasted when informed that Americans had "more need of being taught how to handle the axe or spade, than how to read Hindoostani." Disgust replaced astonishment when he was told that "strong, active, hardy ploughmen" were worth encouraging while Episcopal divines were not. Further search for professional employment led Fidler to conclude, "Americans possess, in an eminent degree, talent and energy; but these are exerted, almost exclusively in other than sedentary studies."[13]

As Fidler's anxiety increased, his manners deteriorated. After arguing with those who tried to befriend him, he steadfastly refused to concede any quality of refinement or intellect to the Americans. He informed Dr. Francis Lieber of Boston that he knew of no first-rate professional men in the New World and that remote villages in England possessed residents of greater academic ability than university cities in America. He declined

12 *Ibid.*, 29.
13 *Ibid.*, 32, 46.

an offer of employment in Ohio because of the bears and Indians, quarreled with his host when invited for dinner, humiliated his few students, and stressed the conflict of '76. Indeed, Fidler's English manners and speech, his irritability and temper, and his impractical and prejudiced disposition converted him into an amusing yet plaintive figure. *The North American Review* dismissed his *Observations* as "another specimen of the class of books with which John Bull is now regularly humbugged three or four times a year."[14] He typified the misguided Briton who "came out to the United States a thorough-going radical" but who was quickly converted "into as thorough-going a Tory."

Fidler was ultimately reduced to applying for a post in a nonconformist pulpit, but the service became so repugnant to him that he withdrew the application. Soon thereafter he determined to flee to Canada. With the assistance of the British consul in New York, in the spring of 1832, he secured an appointment in the village of Thornhill. The region proved to be remote and primitive, servants were difficult to find, and the impenetrable forests depressing. After spending the summer in Thornhill, the clergyman's wife demanded that they return to civilization. Arriving back in New York City in the autumn of 1832, Fidler deemed it futile to make further attempts to search for employment. In late 1832, the family sailed for England.

Despite Fidler's scholarly and intellectual achievements, American institutions of the 1830's could not absorb his brand of erudition. He preferred nineteenth-century romantic traditionalism to American experimental realism. He resisted social mutations demanded by the American environment and strove to maintain an aristocratic spirit rather than to seek a democratic camaraderie.

Any investigation of human motives and purposes must try to encompass dozens of disparate facts, trends, and tendencies. A discussion of the reasons which led educated Britons to seek a

14 *The North American Review*, Vol. XXXVII (1833), 273.

new life in America adds up to a composite biography, not to a body of easily classified data. Re-immigration was prompted by inner tensions, basic disagreements, and limited vision as well as by the more obvious inadequacies of America. Since professional and intellectual people enjoyed a preferred social position at home and possessed less occupational mobility than farmers, laborers, or artisans, fewer considered immigration. Yet once in America, absorption into the new environment sometimes proved more difficult for the educated Briton than for his untrained compatriot. In the new land, culture was mobile, secular interests dominated the professions, ranks were blurred, and practices were dictated by local needs.

Educated Britons, like other migrants, were often undecided in their evaluation of America. The indecision of Henry Pellew typified the uncertainty of many. Pellew was born at Canterbury in 1828, the son of the Dean of Norwich and grandson of the first Viscount Exmouth. After Eton and Trinity College, Cambridge, he became a justice of the peace in Middlesex. Dissatisfied with England and intent upon adventure, he sailed for America about 1850. New York failed to provide Pellew with the cultural and intellectual stimulus which he sought. It did furnish him with a wife, however, and after marrying a granddaughter of John Jay, he returned to Britain in 1859. In England, the young devotee to humanism spent much time promoting educational reform, and in 1870 he helped to found Keble College, Oxford, for students of limited financial means. In 1873, Pellew returned to America and became commissioner of education for New York City. He was an active member of the St. George's Society and other British-American organizations. Toward the end of the century, he settled in England, but after a few years again recrossed the Atlantic and retired in Washington, D. C.[15]

Teachers and educators were often attracted to America. As an advocate of a practical and scientific system of education, the Scottish phrenologist and experimenter George Combe became so enamored with the pragmatic approach to learning that in

15 *A History of the St. George's Society of New York,* 145.

1837 he traveled to Massachusetts to assist Horace Mann, the state's secretary of education. Two years of propagating the "rational" as opposed to the "traditional" approach to learning convinced Combs that America was well on the road to universal education and moral excellence. He, like the Reverend D. Griffiths, returned to Britain to preach the New World's spirit of innovation to the old. Immigrant educators like Patrick O'Kelly, a teacher in Roman Catholic schools in Kentucky and Maryland, envisioned an equally bright future for American learning. Nevertheless, when it came time to educate his own children, O'Kelly deserted his "flourishing academy" to return to Europe's "classical pattern" of study.[16]

As a wife of a schoolteacher from Bolton Percy, Lancashire, Mrs. E. Felton only grudgingly accepted her husband's plan to migrate. Once underway she "grew melancholy" and even before embarking at Liverpool was certain that the venture would end in failure. Although they were accompanied by a servant, the voyage proved disagreeable. She thought the crew incompetent and the captain rude. However, quite to her surprise, New York, with its bright October weather and pleasant boardinghouses, seemed an amiable city. Within a few days, Felton was offered profitable employment as a teacher in a private school and the immigration venture seemed a complete success. During the first winter, several members of the family became seriously ill. Felton failed to recover quickly and was forced to resign his teaching post. While recuperating, in the spring of 1836, he moved with the family to a fifty-acre estate on Long Island. A few delightful weeks on the land led Felton to desert his profession and take up farming. Again the move seemed propitious, but Mrs. Felton and two of their three children contracted bilious fever. Throughout the summer the family was plagued by clouds of mosquitoes, annoyed by myriads of flies, and frightened by thunderstorms. To Mrs. Felton, the torrid summers were surpassed in discomfort

16 Patrick O'Kelly, *Advice and Guide to Emigrants Going to the United States of America* (Dublin, William Folds, 1834).

only by the frigid winters. Every season seemed to bring some new malady.

In addition to the hazards to health, the Feltons were irritated by American provincialism and by an indifference to European culture. A peculiar admiration for the "false and fallacious" doctrines of Paine, Jefferson, and Jackson particularly irked Mrs. Felton. At the same time, she was gratified to observe that English political radicals who crossed the Atlantic found neither moral nor financial support in the United States. They were not received with rejoicing, but rather "were met with aversion and contempt." The "free-born citizens of the new world" offered no "fraternal affection" for British malcontents, most of whom returned home utterly disillusioned with the United States.

It was neither the political philosophy nor a lack of professional opportunities which prompted the Feltons to leave America. For almost two years the family suffered repeated attacks of ague and typhoid fever.

> Unfortunately the climate of the United States was found to be so very prejudiced to the health of my husband and family, that we were compelled to relinquish all thought of remaining. . . . Were it not for the climate, I could have spent my days there with a fair proportion of comfort, for I met with much kindness.[17]

John Davis was a more successful pedagogue. However, his experiences in a Virginia schoolroom were cut short by a driving ambition. Davis was born into a cultivated and moderately wealthy Salisbury family. In 1787, at eleven years of age, he went to sea. Four years in Asiatic waters introduced him to the languages and literature of the Orient, and he returned to Salisbury at fifteen to pursue a more formal course of study. During the mid-1790's, he again enlisted in the Royal Navy, but soon resigned, and on January 7, 1798, sailed from Bristol for the United States. Extensive reading and travel rendered Davis fluent in several modern languages as well as a master of Latin and Greek.

[17] Mrs. E. Felton, *American Life,* 135–36.

First employed in New York to translate contemporary French publications, he later tutored and taught school throughout the Middle Atlantic and Southern States. Davis witnessed Jefferson's inauguration, and upon the recommendation of Aaron Burr was seriously considered for an appointment in the Treasury Department. Failing to procure the government post and sincerely eager to gain a deeper understanding of the American people, Davis founded Pokoke Academy near Occoquan, Virginia.

The young Englishman taught male and female students the excitement of language and the art of Gray, Goldsmith, Addison, and Shakespeare. He scrupuously ignored "mediocre scribblers" like Noah Webster and Caleb Alexander and pointed up the error of radical doctrines found in Voltaire and Rousseau. As a voracious reader and careful observer, Davis became disturbed by the many feeble and naïve travel accounts on the United States. At length, he decided to produce a book with taste and literary merit that would reveal the "true spirit" of the Republic. As the months passed, however, Davis slowly succumbed to the mellow grace of Virginia, and when he fell in love with one of his more mature students, he almost surrendered ambition to romance. But purpose overcame emotion. He secured a teacher replacement and sadly but stubbornly turned from Virginian pleasures to the practical task of preparing a narrative about America. When the book was completed, Davis traveled to England to get it published, but soon thereafter returned to the United States. *Travels of Four Years and a Half in the United States of America* received favorable reviews and quickly brought the author notice in the best literary circles. In 1806, Davis was offered a lucrative position with a London publishing firm and returned to England to accept the post.

As an alert, intelligent, and traveled Englishman, Davis saw the great promise and enjoyed the natural romanticism of America. He was tolerant as an observer and sensitive when describing Pokoke Academy and portraying his life as a pedagogue. He dedicated his first and only good book to Thomas Jefferson and added a subtitle for its second edition, "Travels in

Search of Independence and Settlement." Yet Davis remained a conservative English gentleman. Eighteenth-century French thinkers were to him a "fanatic crew of Deists," and he assured English readers, "I am no Republican! No Federalist! I have learned to estimate rightly the value of the British Constitution; and I think no system of government so perfect as that of Kings, Lords, and Commons."[18] Despite John Davis' "search for independence" and his love of teaching, when respect and place were offered in England, the enchantment of Virginia was exchanged for cosmopolitan London.

Not all Britons were as sympathetic toward American education as Combe, O'Kelly, Felton, and Davis. Isaac Fidler was horrified to learn that no Harvard professor could read Sanskrit, Persian, or Hindoostani. Andrew Bell found few families in New York interested in employing private tutors in French or Italian. William Cobbett gained employment in Philadelphia as a language instructor, but it was to teach English to French *émigrés*, not French to native Americans. Fidler, Bell, and Cobbett all returned to England bitter critics of American educational standards. In the case of all three, however, the teachings of language was a secondary occupation undertaken as a result of financial necessity.

Although successful in the teaching profession, Elizabeth Blackwell became famous because of her prolonged fight to be accepted as an American physician. Elizabeth migrated to New York with her parents and six brothers and sisters in 1832. Six years later, when she was seventeen, the family moved to Cincinnati; soon thereafter her father died. Financial necessity led her to accept employment as a schoolteacher. She first taught in Cincinnati and later became a school principal in Kentucky and North Carolina. Miss Blackwell read medicine in her spare time and worked as an assistant to several physicians. Refused admittance by leading medical schools, she was eventually accepted at Geneva, New York. She graduated in 1849 as the first woman doctor of medicine.

18 *Travels of Four Years and a Half in the United States*, 7.

Almost universal disapproval in the United States prompted Dr. Blackwell to travel to England, but British indifference brought about her return to America within a few months. After numerous futile attempts to win admittance to American hospitals, she sailed for England a second time in the late 1850's, but news of the Civil War again drew her back to the United States. During the war, she organized the Ladies' Sanitary Aid Institute and the National Sanitary Aid Association and actively participated in setting up Union hospitals. Once the war was concluded, however, the country she had served so selflessly again refused Dr. Blackwell equal professional privileges. Returning to Britain in 1875, she accepted the chair of gynecology at the London School of Medicine for Women and remained an active medical practitioner until a short time before her death in 1910.

As an abolitionist, transcendentalist, and nonconformist, Elizabeth Blackwell found northern institutions strangely orthodox and inflexible. The small medical college at Geneva, New York, granted her a degree, but it was London which accepted her as a physician and valued member of her profession. In the fight against prejudice, restrictive mores, and unenlightened convention, Victorian Britain, not republican America, provided Dr. Blackwell with a new frontier.[19]

Some two years in the Illinois country convinced the English engineer Elias Fordham that digging wells and surveying the prairies was less exciting than designing steam engines for George Stephenson. A generation later the engineer for the Illinois and Michigan Canal, Joseph Trutch, also became dissatisfied with Illinois; however, he tarried thirty-nine years in North America before retiring in his beloved England. Born in Jamaica in 1826, Trutch was enrolled by his solicitor father in Mount Radford College, Devonshire, when he was eight years of age. Trained as a civil engineer, Trutch was employed by the Great Western Railway when news of the gold discoveries in California reached England. He quickly entered into an agreement with a British

[19] Ishbel Ross, *Child of Destiny: The Life Story of the First Woman Doctor* (London, Victor Gollancz, Ltd., 1950).

firm to construct a warehouse in San Francisco and sailed from Gravesend in July, 1849. Although confident and ambitious, Trutch found San Francisco in "perfect pandemonium" and bubbling with "vice and iniquity."[20] Within six months, he moved to Oregon and devoted the next five years to a survey of the Columbia River and the layout of townsites. In 1852, Trutch became assistant to the territory's surveyor-general and in 1855 married his employer's sister-in-law. Soon after marriage, the young couple moved to Chicago, where he became a superintendent on the Illinois and Michigan Canal and later the surveyor for the Illinois River.

Trutch found Illinois an ideal place to make money, but reasoned that life was "nothing without sentiment" and the United States could never command his devotion. In late 1857, he sailed for Britain, but after consultation with and encouragement from governmental officials, he traveled to British Columbia in 1859. As a road surveyor, engineer for the Alexandria Suspension Bridge across the Fraser River, chief commissioner of lands and works, lieutenant-governor of British Columbia, and supervisor of construction on the Canadian Pacific Railway, the masterful Englishman became a vital force in the new province. In 1889, Trutch received a knighthood, and in 1890, after a total of almost forty years in North America, he returned permanently to England. Whether in California, Oregon, Illinois, or British Columbia, Sir Joseph Trutch steadfastly resisted all forces that might have assisted his assimilation. Yankees remained a "disagreeable and vulgar lot"; and even as an important Canadian official, he consistently demonstrated that his first loyalty was to the imperial government.[21]

To sensitive and literate educators like George Combe and John Davis, America offered a dramatization and heightening of normal life. For the aggressive type like Elizabeth Blackwell and Joseph Trutch, the new society provided adequate motivation,

---

[20] Hollis R. Lynch, "Sir Joseph William Trutch, a British-American Pioneer on the Pacific Coast," *Pacific Historical Review*, Vol. XXX, No. 3 (August, 1961), 244.
[21] *Ibid.*, 243–55.

but showed a peculiar reluctance to radical innovation. But to the self-conscious attorney, Charles Janson, the Western world presented only a vexatious display of vulgar superstition.

Charles William I'Anson (later Janson) is a classic example of a Briton who could not overcome one thousand years of family tradition. Janson was a descendant of the historic Forbes family which dated its Scottish lineage back to the year 870. In the early 1300's, one member of the clan moved to France. A descendant, Janson de Forbin, joined Henry VII and fought at Bosworth Field. John I'Anson became a sea captain for Henry VIII and later retired to a large estate in Yorkshire.[22] Charles's father, William I'Anson, was born at Leyburn, Yorkshire, in 1741, married the beautiful and wealthy Miss Hutchinson, moved to Bedford Row, Bloomsbury, and became an eminent attorney in the Court of the King's Bench.[23] William I'Anson's only daughter, Frances, gracefully accepted her position in life and became the subject for a romantic song, "Sweet Lass of Richmond Hill." But the eldest son, Charles William, flouted the family's dignified reserve. While serving as an ensign in the Middlesex Militia, he became "inflamed" with revolutionary ideas, a desire to see foreign lands, and a determination to create his own dynasty.

In the early 1790's young I'Anson proceeded to France and fell under the spell of several French officers who had fought in the American Revolution. Assured of the rising prosperity and political liberality of the New World, he returned to London and invested heavily in American stocks. Parental reproof made him doubly anxious to be near the scene of his success. In the summer of 1793, at thirty-one years of age, he migrated to the United States. Intent upon establishing himself as a new man in a new land, I'Anson changed his name to "Janson," but from the first found it impossible to divorce himself from his background. Neither the captain, the crew, nor the passengers on board the

22 Jessie C. I'Anson, *The I'Anson Family* (Adelaid, Australia, Pioneers Association, 1949).

23 *The Gentleman's Magazine*, Vol. CCXVI, No. 2079 (March, 1904), 259ff. Bryan I'Anson. *The History of the I'Anson Family* (London, Henry Good and Son, 1915).

lumber vessel on which he sailed showed him especial courtesy. The food, the service, and the equipment was improper or inadequate. And when he attempted to point up the deficiencies, he was branded "the grumbler." Janson landed in Boston on July 3, and was immediately confronted with Independence Day, which he considered an affront to his intelligence; by young ladies whose temerity shocked his sense of propriety; and by the hot weather, which destroyed his purpose and initiative.

Not too proud to accept repeated financial grants from his family, Janson made a number of bad investments. He traveled throughout the seaboard states, but appeared to be an intruder everywhere. Overly anxious for quick profits, he attempted farming in the Carolinas, failed at commercial enterprises in New York and New England, invested large sums in a highly speculative land venture, and then foolishly tried to recoup his losses by a second and equally injudicious land scheme. Cash for the purchase of forty thousand acres from the New England and Mississippi Land Company as well as money for his other investments was advanced by his father. The excessive and unwise spending led William I'Anson to deny his son further capital. Later Charles was disinherited.

After failing in the fatuous business ventures, Janson fell back upon his early legal training and was admitted to the Rhode Island Bar. Although possessing superior talents, he was only moderately successful. Janson, like other British elite, found that the historical depth and meaningfulness of his traditions strengthened his pride in race and national sentiment. The longer he remained in the adopted land, the more intense became the feeling of strangeness. After thirteen years in the United States, Janson admitted defeat and returned to England in the autumn of 1806.

Charles Janson settled in London and took up the practice of law in Westminster. At the same time, he attempted a literary career. *The Stranger in America* appeared in 1807. A massive four-volume autobiographical novel, *Edward Fitz-Yorke* was published in 1810. An analysis of British policies in North

Africa, entitled *A View of the Present Conditions of the State of Barbary,* came out in 1816. With his marriage in 1810 to the wealthy Maria Walker, the Janson home became a center for London social life and famous for elaborate dinner parties. Janson died in March, 1819.

Charles William Janson's experiences in and his impressions of America were neither new, novel, nor valid, yet he was unique in the claim that in thirteen years he failed "to form a true friendship" in the United States.[24] The physical discomforts and daily inconveniences became irksome. The crudities, inquisitiveness, and acquisitiveness of the populace led to a resentment of the society; and American criticism of Britain provoked an abhorrence of both Jacobinism and Jeffersonianism. To Janson, it was incomprehensible for men to lead physically miserable lives in unpainted shacks in the backwoods and yet argue that republicanism had brought them untold blessings. He agreed that British agriculturists and mechanics could find employment in the United States, but contended that no opportunity existed for academically trained or professional people. What encouragement could there be for architects when most of the populace lived in log cabins? What progress in the arts or education could be expected when a deficiency of taste left beauty neither sought nor appreciated? Of what value were expertly trained lawyers when railsplitters were elected to Congress and when storekeepers dispensed justice?

The Stranger in America received generally unfavorable notice on both sides of the Atlantic. *The Electic Review* agreed with Janson's claim that Americans were conspicuous and ostentatious in proclaiming their freedom and it readily granted that license and rudeness were often in evidence. But the *Electic,* along with *The European Magazine and London Review,* suspected that Janson helped to provoke the faults about which he complained. Most English publications suggested that Janson tried to justify his personal failure by berating the New World. *The Edinburgh*

[24] *The Stranger in America: Containing Observations Made During a Long Residence in that Country* (London, Albion Press, 1807), Preface.

Review thought him an unsophisticated bore. The journal pointed to many intellectual absurdities. He chastised Philadelphia for naming a thoroughfare Arch Street when no arch appeared on it. New London, Connecticut, appeared vainglorious because it was smaller than old London. North Carolinians were declared sacrilegious because an old log church had been converted into a cow shed.[25] Certainly Janson introduced rather than treated issues. He could not accept a philosophy that used success as the test for truth, that discarded irrelevant ideas in favor of practical tools. He deserted family and friends, but never forgot his background and never forgave Americans for failing to acknowledge his birthright. As a scion of an old family with an impressive tradition, he refused to overcome the past or to establish a new frame of reference.

The books, diaries, letters, and newspaper reports of the professional literati who immigrated require careful interpretation, for they describe more often than they analyze. Nevertheless, such records are generally more sophisticated, their range of observation more encompassing, and their comments more penetrating than the remarks of most returnees. With the end of the Napoleonic Wars, the famed Continental tour often gave way to the more boisterous American tour. British writers of every stamp found a brisk market for almost anything written about the States. In the years before mid-century an average of ten new books a year kept British readers abreast of the changing character of America. Obviously most authors were mere tourists or travelers; however, a few writers became immigrants, and several immigrants later became writers. Both groups had a high incidence of return.

William Cobbett was one of the first colorful and controversial writers to abandon the United States. Born of humble parents,

25 *The Edinburgh Review, or Critical Journal*, Vol. X (April–July, 1807), 103ff; John Foster, *Critical Essays Contributed to the "Electric Review"* (London, Henry G. Bohn, 1857), 44ff.

Cobbett grew up as a plowboy in the hop gardens near Farnham, Surrey. The son of an aggressive partisan of the American Revolution, he absorbed his father's deep respect for the new nation. The belief in republican pureness quickly created dissatisfaction with rural England's aristocratic feudalism. When twenty, he traveled to London in search of fame and fortune. After several months as a copy clerk in Grey's Inn, he enlisted in the army in 1784. While on a six-year tour of duty in Nova Scotia and New Brunswick, Cobbett was attracted by the classless society and resolved to settle permanently in North America. Although he rose to the rank of sergeant major, he steadily grew more disturbed by the negligence, inhumanity, and outright dishonesty of his military superiors. Discharged in 1791, he requested the Secretary of War to investigate the injustices and initiate court-martial proceedings. As sergeant major, he had collected copies of documents which would prove his allegations. The naïve young man failed to perceive the danger when the date for the court-martial was repeatedly postponed and the location of the trial changed. He eventually learned of a counter plan whereby he was to be prosecuted for sedition. In bitterness, Cobbett turned to his earlier republican teachings and studied the works of Thomas Paine.

As an active republican, he decided to visit France and observe at first hand the progress of a truly independent people. Both he and his wife found French culture and society fascinating, but with the mounting tempo of the revolution they deemed it wise to leave the country. Apprehensive of the consequences if they returned to England, Cobbett resolved to fulfill a lifelong ambition, and in August, 1792, he and his wife sailed for the United States. They arrived at Wilmington, Delaware, with eighteen guineas and a burning desire "to become the citizens of a free state." Unfortunately the new country proved "exactly the contrary" of what he had expected.[26] Employment could be found as a common laborer and it was a "good country for getting

[26] William Reitzel, *The Autobiography of William Cobbett: The Progress of a Plough-Boy to a Seat in Parliament* (London, Faber and Faber, Ltd., 1933), 57.

money," but the land seemed unproductive, the roads impassable, the houses wretched, the fruits and vegetables inferior, and the climate debilitating. Disease and seasonal maladies, along with extreme heat, bitter cold, thunder, wind, and snow, rendered life wearisome.

Quickly moving on to Philadelphia, Cobbett found employment as an English teacher in the French quarter of the city. He was surprised by the indolent and unambitious attitude which pervaded the surrounding rural communities and the prudery and false sex standards within the city disgusted him. In line with his work, he composed a textbook, *Le Tuteur Anglais,* and began to translate works for a local bookstore. At first, the liberal and pro-French bias of his students, plus his fees of 330 pounds a year, delighted the Englishman, but in time he became critical and argumentative and began to champion the English cause. The British seizure of American ships, the unpopularity of the Jay Treaty, and the political propaganda of the Jeffersonians made the capital city of Philadelphia ring with anti-British slogans. The malicious attacks on monarchy stimulated by Joseph Priestley's arrival in the United States, coupled with the extreme republicanism of the French, tended to drive Cobbett farther into the pro-English camp. In August, 1794, he published his first political pamphlet. It was a reply to Priestley's newspaper comments on England. Almost overnight Cobbett's rather aimless life took shape. He became a "pronounced John Bull, noisy, egotistical and dogmatic." *Observation on the Emigration of Dr. Joseph Priestley* became a best seller, running through numerous editions in both England and America. *A Bone to Gnaw for the Democrats* also sold widely, while in *A Kick for a Bite* he used the pseudonym "Peter Porcupine" for the first time. Over the following six years, Cobbett produced some twenty pamphlets, edited a daily newspaper, published *Porcupine's Gazette,* and sponsored several minor periodicals. Much of his writing was directed at nullifying anti-British sentiment and ridiculing American Anglophobes.

The blaze of patriotic fervor which stimulated Cobbett to attack the anti-English biases of Philadelphians at the same time awakened the new writer to an appreciation of his literary potential. In early 1796, he quarreled with his printer, and in July he opened his own shop and for the first time revealed himself as Peter Porcupine. By now he had embarked upon a violent series of denunciations. In a libel action brought by the Spanish minister to the United States, the courts refused to indict Cobbett. However, in 1797, Dr. Benjamin Rush brought suit for slander, and after much delay, in December, 1799, the courts granted Rush damages of $5,000. The writer's Philadelphia property was sold at public auction. In the meantime, Cobbett had moved to New York, where in January, 1800, he published the last number of *Porcupine's Gazette*. Undecided about the future, he continued writing and even inaugurated a new fortnightly, *The Rushlight*, named for the plaintiff. On June 1, 1800, after ordering a farewell advertisement to be inserted in the public press, he sailed for England. When leaving Philadelphia, Cobbett bestowed "curses on the tyrannical and corrupt government of Pennsylvania." At New York he wrote: "When people care not two straws for each other, ceremony at parting is mere grimace; and as I have long felt the most perfect indifference with regard to a vast majority of those whom I now address, I shall spare myself the trouble of a ceremonious farewell."[27]

In England, Cobbett declared the American government to be the most profligate and dishonest system in the world, whereas the British represented the finest achievements of man. "I hate the United States and all their mean and hypocritical system of rule. . . . In the days of youth and ignorance, I had been led to believe that comfort, freedom, and virtue, were exclusively the lot of Republicans. A very short trial has convinced me of my error."[28]

Although he had once been a violent opponent of British officialdom, the years in America had erased all animosity and

[27] William Cobbett, *Porcupine's Works*, XII, 108.

[28] *Cobbett's Weekly Register*, Vol. XIII (March 26, 1808), col. 486; Reitzel, *The Autobiography of William Cobbett*, 86–87.

rendered Cobbett a defender of the establishment. Indeed, he so lavishly extolled life in the Old World and so completely associated himself with the conservative cause that even moderate criticism of English institutions became personal insults. His sharpest barbs were directed toward his countrymen who suggested that Americans were virtuous and prosperous. Teachers, clergymen, and aristocrats were attacked for glorifying American leaders and principles. Before sailing for England, he had collected most of his earlier writings. These were published in a twelve-volume set as *Porcupine's Works; Containing Various Writings and Selections, Exhibiting a Faithful Picture of the United States of America* .... In the preface, dated May 29, 1801, Cobbett explained that from 1688 on there had been a leaven of republicanism which had swollen discontent in England. The "misrepresentations and falsehoods" concerning American progress and prosperity had augmented the discontent and were at the root of current dissatisfaction in England. Cruel persecution of the few men who raised their voice in loyalty and truth had led to a stifling of accurate reporting from the United States. Honest Americans recognized that real happiness had been lost with their separation from England. "I solemnly declare that I never met with a man in whatever rank or situation of life, who did not regret the separation of the United States from the mother-country."[29]

Although thirty-seven years old when he returned to England and a famous political journalist, Cobbett was yet a novice at politics. His works had made him a hero among the same Whitehall officials who eight years earlier had hoped to convict him of sedition. Upon arrival in London, he was graciously received by government agents and immediately became intimate with aristocrats and cabinet ministers. He dined with the Prime Minister and was offered control of one of the official newspapers, but declined the sinecure to embark upon his own publication ventures. Cobbett supported the Tories unreservedly, from their prosecution of the French Wars to a denunciation of the freedom of the

[29] *Porcupine's Works*, I, 16.

press. Yet, as the months passed, the rustic paradise of England faded and the crude democracy of America regained some of its luster. He found the regime not a tolerant, self-respecting aristocracy that allowed the poor man to enjoy his traditional inheritance. The masters of Britain suppressed basic eighteenth-century human rights. As an old-fashioned Tory who opposed enclosures and the extinction of small farms, he discounted the country's need for increased commerce or manufacturing and campaigned for army reform.

Criticism of the war ministry led to a charge of sedition, and in July, 1810, Cobbett was sentenced to prison and forced to pay a heavy fine. Two years in Newgate forged a benevolent Tory into a crusader for justice and a fervent defender of the rights of the common man. Political indecision and economic confusion following the Napoleonic Wars resulted in the suspension of the Habeas Corpus Act in 1817. Aware that he was marked as an agitator, Cobbett wrote *Mr. Cobbett's Taking Leave of His Countrymen* and, with two of his sons, secretly sailed for the United States on March 27. Although assuring his English acquaintances that he would remain a British subject, Cobbett's words and actions demonstrated that he had again reversed his position in relation to republican America. Throughout the British-American War of 1812, he had tended to favor the American position, and despite his earlier abuse of certain phases of republican society, he had always maintained close contact with many American friends.

Comfortably settled on Long Island, Cobbett continued to write, but in addition counseled scores of English immigrants and travelers who sought his opinions. A few of the migrants were, like Cobbett, political refugees, but most were fleeing before the economic recession that had engulfed Britain. Cobbett assured his British readers that they were living under intolerable conditions and in turn painted a reasonably flattering picture of older American states. Hard work and thrifty management would result in the good life for all Englishmen. The United States enjoyed low taxes, political freedom, a benevolent government, and a democratic society. Conversely, Britain's spirit was being broken by starvation, a tyrannical government, and social injustices. However, Cobbett did not encourage immigration. Basically his reasons were patriotic. The comparisons were made more to show the grievances borne by Englishmen than to glorify the progress of America. Of the many works undertaken during his two and one-half years on Long Island, only *A Year's Residence* and *Account of the Life, Labours, and Death of Thomas Paine* dealt with the American scene.[30] Cobbett so completely regained his youthful admiration for Paine that he disinterred the bones of the great radical and, with plans for a shrine, carried them back to Britain in 1819.

For the remaining sixteen years of his life, Cobbett championed many of the ideals that he once scorned as being Jeffersonian. But a deep-seated love of English tradition bound him to the institution of the monarchy. He symbolized the fight against the dissolution of the old order, yet through personal migration he inadvertently pointed to the United States as an avenue of escape. He admitted that flight seemed mandatory, but cautioned his countrymen against the cold pragmatism of America. Singularity and rural stubbornness had long been permissible for conservative Britons; it gave excitement without real danger, spice without real heat. Cobbett's cultivation of eccentricity won him wide personal acceptance, but he remained deeply attached to the formal principles of country and class. Despite governmental harassment, he sought only the impertinences of radicalism, not its consequences. William Cobbett, like Charles Janson and Elizabeth Blackwell, seemed peculiarly discordant in republican America, yet all three gained scope and purpose in aristocratic England.

Frances Trollope's *Domestic Manners of the Americans* published in 1832 focused more attention on the failure of British immigrants and the inadequacies of the American West than any other book of the century. No other report was so often quoted or so thoroughly reviled. The story of Mrs. Trollope's bazaar,

[30] William Cobbett, *A Year's Residence in the United States of America.*

the accuracy of her observations, and the quirks in her personality stimulated hot debate and, according to some writers, "almost caused an Anglo-American incident."[31] She remained the scandal or the heroine of two hemispheres for a generation, and her work has engaged literary critics and social historians for over a century.

In May, 1809, the twenty-nine-year-old daughter of the vicar of Heckfield married Thomas Anthony Trollope, a thirty-five-year-old Oxford graduate and barrister. Over the following years, the birth of seven children and Trollope's ungracious manner did not prevent Mrs. Trollope from making their Bloomsbury home into a haven for radical ideas, foreigners, and students of the arts. A failure at the law and a disagreement within the family led Trollope in 1816 to lease an estate near Harrow, build a country house, and attempt to become a farmer. In the meantime, the extravagant Mrs. Trollope continued to entertain and associate with such pro-American luminaries as Washington Irving, James Fenimore Cooper, William Bullock, the Marquis de Lafayette, and Camilla and Frances Wright. In 1827, when Frances Wright visited London after establishing her famed colony at Nashoba, Tennessee, young Henry Trollope, a lad of sixteen, and his restless mother, decided to accompany the feminist leader back to America.

For years the Trollopes had been drifting into bankruptcy, and when the fortune of an aging uncle was swept from their grasp by his untimely marriage, a major alteration of the family routine was required. Mr. Trollope's eccentricity and uncertain health precluded his taking the vigorous action necessary. Proud and luxury-loving, Mrs. Trollope refused to sink into dignified poverty among her friends and associates. Furthermore, the children were to be provided with an opportunity for gentlemanly business endeavor. Henry, who was to accompany his mother, had shown himself to be an indifferent student at Winchester and an impossible clerk in a Parisian financial house. He was to

31 Michael Sadleir, "A Briton on a Rampage," in *The Saturday Review Gallery* (New York, Simon and Schuster, 1959), 4.

be given another opportunity in an expanding and exciting arena where his superior European experiences were certain to render him successful. Immigration was a practical matter, but it also appealed to Mrs. Trollope's flirtatious interest in rationalism, reform, and adventure. Her association with American popularizers, French intellectuals, and English community-makers had contributed to her instinctive desire to experience, to perform, and to dominate. But the idealism of Fanny Wright, the utopianism of William Bullock, and the fiction of Washington Irving provided her with a most inexact picture of western American life.

Fanny Wright had failed in the campaign to secure colonists for Nashoba; therefore, she was delighted to have the company of Mrs. Trollope when she embarked for America in early November, 1827. The *Edward* arrived at New Orleans on December 25, and after a week of sight-seeing, the party moved up the Mississippi River to Memphis. Some fifteen miles inland on Wolf River the bluestocking parlor rationalist was for the first time confronted with American reality. No longer could the imagination delude when amid sickness and hunger, free love, and free Negroes, the virtuous utopia lay at her feet. The Cooper novels, the recollections of Lafayette, and the passionate communialism of her hostess were insufficient background for the experience at Nashoba. Destitute and marooned in a sickly backwoods swamp which she had helped to finance, Mrs. Trollope thought only of escape. The departure was arranged after the Wright sisters provided her with a loan. Then, along with her two daughters, son Henry, and the artistic Frenchman Auguste Hervieu, Mrs. Trollope traveled on upstream, disembarking at Cincinnati in February, 1828.

The arrival of a singularly intense, luxury-loving English lady of forty-eight, with odd dress, a strange entourage and no husband, did not go unnoticed in Cincinnati. Although alone and without introductions in an unattractive frontier society with her noblest aspirations dashed, Mrs. Trollope quickly became acquainted with the important and artistic people of the community. She and the Bullocks were newcomers to the Queen City, and their common tastes and London experiences drew them into a close association. The English lady found the master of Elmwood most congenial. She followed his horticultural experiments with interest; they laughed together when the untutored natives assumed that Bullock's beautiful collection of engravings had been personally carved and printed by him after his arrival in Cincinnati. Mrs. Trollope accompanied the Bullocks when they drove to the Indiana backwoods to observe a frontier camp meeting.[32] The Bullocks also were hosts at lavish entertainments. Fifty years later, a former governor of Ohio vividly recalled the exciting dinner parties at which Bullock, Mrs. Trollope, and Auguste Hervieu discussed making Dante's picture of Hell into a local exhibition.[33]

Mrs. Trollope found it necessary to take advantage of the community's prosperity to recoup the family's fortunes. Her inexperience in business doubtlessly led her to seek advice from Bullock in planning her activities at the Western Museum and later in building her merchandise and art building. Joseph Dorfeuille's Western Museum, much like Bullock's earlier London display, featured everything from Indian artifacts to two-headed animals and wax figures of monsters and cannibals. The curator was in constant need of new and novel ideas. Therefore, in the spring of 1828, under the experienced hand of Bullock and with the enthusiasm of Trollope and the artistry of Hervieu, a set of allegorical figures and allusions were offered to the Cincinnati public. In a mysterious performance, Dorfeuille featured the Invisible Girl. Any question asked in the veiled chamber was answered in many tongues by an unseen oracle. Henry Trollope, whose smattering of ancient languages at Winchester made him into the Invisible Girl, had indeed discovered new opportunities in America. The setting sprang from Bullock's thorough knowledge of Egyptian design, and the artistic transparencies were painted by Hervieu. An Old World artist, a confused gentle-

32 Trollope, *Domestic Manners of the Americans*, I, 86–87, 93, 233ff.
33 *The Miami Journal*, Vol. II, No. 1 (October, 1887), 13.

woman, and an imaginative utopian had found that the only profitable means of expression in America was to become an early day P. T. Barnum for the twenty thousand restless citizens of Cincinnati. The Western Museum later widened its scope and portrayed the Infernal Regions as envisioned by Bullock and Trollope. The show became so successful and widely advertised that it drew audiences from throughout the United States for the next twenty-five years.

In the meantime, Mrs. Trollope, again with the assistance of her English friend, decided to open a quaint specialty store and athenaeum which would elevate the artistic taste of Cincinnatians and bring praise and wealth to its owner. Mr. Trollope and another son traveled to America in late 1828, but within a few months returned to London to send out merchandise for the business. The building which rose in the spring of 1829 reflected the influence but not the design of William Bullock. The four-story mosque-like bazaar on Third Street, with Egyptian colonnade, Gothic battlements, Moorish pilasters, Arabesque windows, and Doric columns was neither functional nor artistic.[34] After Mrs. Trollope became ill in August, it became obvious that there was not enough capital to complete the edifice. With the workmen unpaid, the building and a $10,000 consignment of goods were sold by the sheriff at public auction. After the failure of the grand design, Mrs. Trollope turned to the staging of musicals and theater recitals, while Hervieu put on exhibitions at the bazaar. But the income proved meager and Mrs. Trollope's household effects were finally seized by the sheriff.

Sick, bankrupt, and bewildered, Frances Trollope sent Henry back to England and with her daughters left for the East Coast in March, 1830. She resided in Baltimore, Washington, Philadelphia, and New York, and found much to admire along the Atlantic seaboard. Natural wonders like Niagara Falls and even pleasant country towns and eastern cities elicited her praise. However, she had decided to depict America's crude and callow

34 *Domestic Manners of the Americans*, ed. by Donald Smalley, (New York, Alfred A. Knopf, 1949), xli.

society in witty and salable fashion. Cured of her drawing-room radicalism, she wrote in the full flush of anger, defeat, and humiliation. When in August, 1831, she returned to England to find the excitement over the Reform Bill at its height, she deliberately capitalized on prejudice and emotion by further emphasizing the vulgar aspects of a classless democratic society.

Frances Trollope wrote mainly about the West. It was a region which had rid itself of ties with Europe, snatched the mantle of democracy from the Atlantic Coast, and was proudly directing the course of empire. The very limitations and directness of *Domestic Manners* made it the more reprehensible to many readers. But in a more tragic sense, the book was the story of an English woman's disenchantment with the sylvian wonders of the West, with the moral and cultural attainments of the frontier, and with the community planning of Frances Wright, William Bullock, and her Cincinnati friend, Dr. William Price. The widely held vision of Franklin and Jefferson of a great western agrarian utopia in which America's "glorious public virtue" could be preserved, safe from the corrupting influences of the Old World, was effectively challenged. Rather than rebirth, isolation had corroded the consciousness, dulled the senses, and destroyed the charm and grace which lifted man above animals. Although Mrs. Trollope lived to write over one hundred volumes, *Domestic Manners* remained her most significant book. She had participated in the idealization of frontier America and, although middle-aged, had insisted on pursuing the quest for paradise to its fountainhead. Encountering failure, she wrote from necessity, but also out of a sense of indignation at having been misinformed and having misled herself. In America, she had for the first time been forced to deal with things, not designs, and to experience incidents, not movements. The details of the new experience were very real to her.

America provided neither the materialistic nor the idealistic solution for Frances Trollope, but after fifty-two years of intense and rather purposeless living, she had found direction. Despite flight to escape creditors and sickness and death within the family, she never stopped writing. For thirty years she poured forth a continuous stream of books. The failure of an American sojourn fused the strands of a tangled life and allowed a middle-aged Englishwoman to blossom into a great literary figure.

Few of the British immigrants who gained their literary or journalistic legs in the United States were as controversial as William Cobbett and Mrs. Trollope. William Young represented the more moderate and businesslike type of newspaperman. Young was the descendant of an old Scottish family and the son of a vice-admiral. As a young man, he traveled widely in North and South America. After marrying a Charleston belle, he moved to New York City and accepted the post of editor of *The Albion* in 1848. For over two decades, Young ably directed the paper. In addition, he became a translator of French publications and served as president of the St. George's Society. After selling *The Albion* to Kinahan Cornwallis, Young published an evening paper, but in 1873 disposed of his New York interests and returned to Europe.[35]

Perhaps no British returnee of the nineteenth century became more celebrated than John Rowlands, better known as Henry M. Stanley. Rowlands was born in Denbigh, Wales, in 1841. Despised by his family and mulcted by his society, he escaped from the St. Asaph Workhouse when only fifteen and sailed for New Orleans three years later. Rowlands was adopted by the kindly American merchant, Henry M. Stanley. In 1862, the young Stanley traveled to Wales to see his mother, but again tragically rejected, he returned to the United States. In 1866, he went to Asia as a reporter for several American newspapers, and in 1871, James Gordon Bennett of the *New York Herald* sponsored his search for David Livingstone. Many countries offered Stanley both honor and opportunity while Britain argued over his legitimacy. Nevertheless, in 1892, he asked to be renaturalized a British subject. America had provided the spirit and the tools for the fashioning of a famous man, but it failed to capture his fealty.

35 *A History of St. George's Society of New York*, 132ff.

Another type of British-American journalist was typified by J. D. Borthwick. Borthwick, a scion of the Baron Borthwick family which dated back to the fifteenth century, attempted journalism in New York with limited success. He traveled to the California gold fields in the early fifties and for over two years tried to furnish copy for both eastern and English newspapers. Borthwick failed in the West and returned to the East Coast where further dissatisfaction caused him to sail for England. In 1857 he published *Three Years in California.*

Although the Republic of Texas elicited much editorial comment and controversy among English journalists, it failed to capture the allegiance of many professional immigrants. The mysterious behavior of Nicholas Doran P. Maillard was illustrative of the uncertainty surrounding the migration and the return of a number of literary men. Maillard was a London lawyer of "delicate health," who, after reading "exaggerated accounts" of Texas, sailed for the Lone Star Republic in November, 1839. By March, he had located in Richmond, Texas, and secured a position as co-editor of the *Richmond Telescope.* On April 7, 1840, he was admitted to the Texas Bar. Maillard traveled widely throughout the Southwest in his capacity as a lawyer-newspaperman. However, he seemed more interested in the treatment of slaves, the opportunities afforded to Indians, and the value of the land than in legal or journalistic problems. Although a genial host and a mixer of excellent drinks, Maillard had only one close friend, an English gunsmith and cutler named James Riddell.[36] While at Richmond, Maillard devoted much time to writing, and when questioned by the townspeople, Riddell explained that the journalist was completing a novel.

In July, 1840, the new citizen informed his associates that the death of a relative required a hurried trip home. A few weeks later, Riddell also sailed for England. Neither returned, and some two years later *The History of the Republic of Texas* appeared in London. The preface boldly explained that the book was written to warn the British government against recognition

[36] *The Handbook of Texas* (1952), article on Maillard by Andrew F. Muir.

of Texas "and to prevent more of my own countrymen from sharing in the ruin and wretchedness of too many others who have already emigrated to Texas."[37] English immigrants in the Republic were either languishing in want and sickness or begging their way to New Orleans and escape. Maillard made a concentrated effort to discredit pro-Texas Englishmen like William Kennedy, Jonathan and Arthur Ikin, and Charles Elliot. His real or contrived grievances prohibited a dispassionate view of the region. Indeed, it would appear that Maillard hoped to use immigration and repatriation as a lever to launch himself into a career as a political journalist. However, the British had recognized Texas a few weeks before the book appeared and the exposé on immigration went unheeded.

In the same year that Maillard left Texas, a more eminent British writer sailed for the Republic. Charles Hooton was born at Nottingham about 1813. He first attracted literary notice with the publication in 1836 of a three-volume novel, *Adventures of Bilberry Thurland.* Encouraged by journalistic acquaintances in London, Hooton resigned his post as editor of a small Leeds newspaper and moved to the metropolis. Over the following months, his second major work was published in *Bentley's Miscellany,* and in 1841 the ponderous three volumes of *Colin Clink* made their unsuccessful appearance. Meanwhile, the young writer worked as a sub-editor for *The Sun,* a short-lived journal devoted to the intricacies of political economy. Later, in May, 1840, he inaugurated *The Woolsack,* a sheet designed to publicize the abuses allegedly perpetrated by the Court of Chancery. Although a rather penetrating journal, *The Woolsack* was discontinued after the fourth number.[38]

Embittered by failure both as a reformer and as a writer, Hooton, along with his wife and thirty English acquaintances, left for Texas on December 28, 1840. Hooton later explained that "the political relations of the young Republic so exactly coincided with all my preconceived notions of government purity

37 N. Doran Maillard, *The History of the Republic of Texas,* iv.
38 *The Gentleman's Magazine,* No. 27 (January–June, 1847), 442–43.

and integrity" that migration seemed the only reasonable course.[39] Upon arrival at Galveston in late March, 1841, the party's dreams of an El Dorado were quickly dispelled. Young, imprudent, and overzealous, Hooton admitted that he was searching for a "wild Garden of Eden, where flowers grow without cultivation—where beasts of chase are not monopolized by the arm of aristocratic power—where governments are as liberal as the air—where labour reaps its own results."[40]

Hooton sought the university which supposedly was being built in Texas, but saw nothing like Oxford or Cambridge. He had been assured of a vigorous trade, but discovered no ports or docks like those of London. He expected a great cultural outpouring, but found people exclusively devoted to eking out a physical existence. Indeed, their literary contributions compared to those of England as a "pea to a pumpkin."[41] Shops differed from those of Europe, the climate was not conducive to physical or mental activity, and the city appeared filled with rascals, pirates, murderers, thieves, and swindlers.

The Hootons resided in the home of an English lady for several weeks, but late in the spring they rented a two-room clapboard house about half a mile from town. They attempted to grow a garden, but the heat withered most English vegetables and a neighbor's hog destroyed the remainder. An altercation over the hog led Hooton to adopt the western practice of carrying pistols. For nine months, the misplaced Englishman fished, hunted, visited barbecues, and frequented the local saloon. Utterly unable to discipline himself, he attempted no writing; "the quill 'stumped up' altogether, and the ink-horn dry."[42] By late 1841, Hooton, along with the thirty other Englishmen in the party, had acknowledged failure:

Of the thirty individuals who went out in the same vessel with

39 Charles Hooton, *St. Louis' Isle or Texiana*, 2.
40 *Ibid.*, 1.
41 *Ibid.*, 10.
42 *The New Monthly Magazine and Humorist*, January–April, 1847, Part I, 397ff.

myself, not more than three entertained for a moment any other views than those of obtaining land, either by purchase, or through the medium of the Government grants,—of squatting upon it, and becoming for the remainder of their natural lives good citizens of the new Republic. Look at the results. Of all this number, *not one* succeeded in effecting the object for which he had left home and country, crossed thousands of miles of ocean, and gone to Texas.[43]

Migrants who possessed sufficient funds returned home or sailed for ports in the United States. The Hootons were among the last to accept defeat, but in December, 1841, they moved to New Orleans. Hooton quickly obtained employment with a daily newspaper, which by May, 1842, went bankrupt. In disgust the temperamental writer embarked for New York. From New York, he pushed on to Montreal, where he accepted a post on one of the city's leading publications. After a few weeks, a dispute over salary resulted in his dismissal. In early November, 1842, the couple sailed for home.

Subdued in spirit and broken in health, the penniless Hootons settled at the home of his parents in Nottingham. Unable to find employment, Hooton turned to free-lance writing. Over the following years, *The New Monthly Magazine* published many ballads, poems, and short stories illustrative of his American experiences.[44] *Woodhouslee; or the Astrologer*, later published as *Launcelot Wedge*, was a partial and somewhat crude autobiography. In 1846, *Simmond's Colonial Magazine and Foreign Miscellany* carried "Rides, Rambles, and Sketches in Texas." The articles were only slightly reworked and published the next year as *St. Louis' Isle, or Texiana*.

Hooton never completely recovered from the severe attacks of ague and fever he suffered while in Texas. The physical illness aggravated his neurotic tendencies, and on February 15, 1847

---

43 Hooton, *St. Louis' Isle*, 41.

44 "Pirates Wager"; "The Exploits of Moreno the Texan"; "Bat, the Portuguese"; "The Two Jews of Peru"; "Ballad of Captain Blackstone"; and "The Raven."

when only thirty-four, he died from an overdose of morphia. Texas was Hooton's *bête noir*. Although it provided the setting for most of his later work, he viewed it as the key to his misfortune. In emotional appeals, he pointed to himself as an example of the affliction certain to befall emigrants:

> The object has been, by the detail of abundant facts, gathered from a woeful experience in the presence of the dying, the dead, the shattered in constitution, the ruined, and the disappointed, to warn, or, if possible, to terrify my fellow countrymen from attempting the insane project of dropping themselves down, as it were from the clouds, into the heart of a burning wild, however luxuriant, amidst lurking savages, reckless and unprincipled outcasts of civilization, and fell disease, more frightful and deadly even than these.[45]

Hooton was unique in that his new-found hatred of Texas and the United States did not diminish his old hatred for English aristocratic institutions. Indeed, he clung to republican principles and suggested that within a few generations the most perfect of political ideas would bring order to the American continent. Unfortunately no government could change the sun, the brick-burned earth, the pestilence, the sweltering bayous, and the arctic cold. To Hooton, America was a dream with tremendous outlines but with sordid details.

Hooton thought life in America similar to an "adventure into darkest Africa." Maillard, Fidler, and Janson would have agreed, but each for different reasons. No immigrant from the professional class suggested that the New World was culturally superior to the old or climatically comparable to an Italian spa. Yet there were many areas in which the returnees were not critical. The educated immigrants reflected little of the hostility common in British-American foreign relations at the time. Although books by British travelers were often stuffed with Tory condescension, few professional repatriates disclosed such sentiments. And the number who returned because of a deep-seated resentment

---

[45] *St. Louis' Isle,* 155.

toward American society was quite small. Indeed, men like D. Griffiths and George Combe sailed for home to preach the American way in Britain.

The greatest shock for certain migrants was the discovery that England and America enjoyed a common culture, but a quite dissimilar outlook. In many ways the United States seemed a land of paradox. As a new country, the people were proud yet insecure, calloused yet sensitive, wildly idealistic yet coldly pragmatic. In an open society, the newness, crudeness, and lack of sophistication could not be concealed. Certainly life in America offered no easy options. Society tended to challenge the precise sentiments to which many Englishmen were most deeply wedded. Anglophobes of Philadelphia caused Cobbett to defend a king from whom he had fled, and atheists in New York moved Fidler to support a state church which had refused him a pulpit. Even when such American tendencies did not alienate, they did irritate the newcomer. Furthermore, the strength of national sentiment no doubt tends to increase with the historical depth and meaning of the migrants' traditions. Perhaps there were many men like John Griffiths and John Davis who found that the more they succeeded in America, the more they were drawn to Britain. Others returned because their expectations were too high. Their arms were outstretched toward vast new horizons, but their eyes could not focus on the immediate needs of life. Nevertheless, the educated returnees possessed one positive factor not demonstrated by any other group: they almost unanimously went home less insular than when they left.

6

A DIVERSITY OF CAUSES

A study of the return of emigrants allows for two points of departure. First, it is reasonable to question the broad and plastic adaptability of the men and women who recrossed the Atlantic. What physiological or psychological changes should they have undergone in order to become happy and successful in the new society? Wherein did they fail to alter their perspective and swing the delicate balance so as to think in terms of the new dimensions called for in America? The second approach directs attention to the receiving environment. It demands a consideration of America's human and physical resources and an evaluation of their use and misuse. It attempts to analyze the inadequacies, the prejudices, and the crudities of the United States. This conclusion will focus on the individual and deal only incidentally with American society. Although assimilation was a two-way street, it was not a fifty-fifty proposition. It was necessary for immigrants to conform to the fundamental tenets and the basic social structure of the receiving community. Indeed, Europeans migrated, not to remake America in the image of Europe, but because they believed American institutions and opportunities superior to those of their homeland.

The most obvious problem in attempting to evaluate the return movement grows out of the uncertain accuracy of most of the accounts and records. Many reports contain glaring distortions and at the same time present a very limited and highly selective sampling of the total movement. Most narratives are autobiographical, written by literarily-inclined chroniclers who wished to record their views. Some of the literature is scarcely original. It reflects the same image and restates the same prejudices found in British travel accounts. Nevertheless, most of the writers who returned were systematizers, sensitive barometers of ideas which were, so to speak, in the air. They formulated an explicit pattern of criticism out of scattered fragments, from the experiences of the many. Although not literary innovators, they were often social innovators who anticipated life and attempted to mold it to their purpose. Few were original thinkers, and none established a mode of expression as penetrating as a De Tocqueville. But men who typify a movement, who sum it up best, are not necessarily people of great intellectual or creative force. Indeed, second- and third-rate minds often serve the historical purpose better than the genius.

Clearly the unifying concepts within the immigration dynamic are extremely difficult to isolate. In movements like those of the Jacobins of 1793 and the Chetniks of World War II, certain general political or philosophical beliefs emerge. No simple unity of purpose or principle is found among returning migrants. Can the admittedly diverse literature, mainly from the pens of disaffected Britons, be made to add up to more than an anthology? Can a composite portrait be reduced to a sketch which will project the meaning and importance of the movement? Clearly facts are not enough in themselves; they must be explained, their implications explored. Certain socio-economic questions must be asked and certain generalizations posited. Evidence must be interpreted and intentions investigated. Of course, in the final analysis, it is the richness of the personalities of the repatriates, their insights, their assumptions, and their hostilities which provide the best basis for conclusions.

As industrialism broke the bond of sympathy among England's social classes, the affinity was replaced by a mere cash nexus between employer and employed. Those Britons set adrift by the harsh and impersonal materialism longed for an authority and a direction. For many, the most attractive road to a deeper and fuller reality appeared to be emigration. America with its abundance of land presented a real temptation for Englishmen who were reluctantly being forced from a rural into an urban environment. The New World could offer a new hope and a new stability. As the Americas had once yielded great wealth to the world, so might they reveal great social truths.

The myth of the United States was particularly associated with rural life. Leaders of eighteenth-century thought had glorified America as a kind of Arcadia, the ideal home for the natural man. The notion that rural folk somehow possessed greater virtues than city dwellers still persisted. Supposedly, urban, industrialized life cut man off from innocence, vitality, and a piety born of nature. Many British immigrants were civilized men sick of civilization and in search of new purpose and direction. They accepted De Tocqueville literally when he said, "The American is the Englishman left to himself."

To be completely satisfied, the immigrant demanded not only material success but emotional integration into the new society. The vast majority of British immigrants did not wish to wander; they sought a place to grow roots. They no more sought adventure than did the Puritans, but rather, like the Puritans, they moved to escape the necessity of change. Unfortunately most migrants found that America was no cool and pleasant Arcadia inhabited by perfect specimens of the natural man, nor was she a rural retreat from the urban cares of the new industrialism. Rather, her shifting and diverse population seemed to possess no roots, while an ill-defined democracy with dozens of seemingly autonomous local governments often did little to maintain dignity or direction. When political and social dissatisfaction was compounded by economic failure, return seemed the reasonable expedient. If Britons came to America in search of a stability which had eluded them at home, they commonly found the new country less poised and settled than the old.

The literature of return is replete with the shopworn reproach that in the South cruelty had replaced *noblesse oblige*, in New

England there was bigotry without curiosity, and in the West demagoguery rather than democracy prevailed. When such phrases were incorporated into an immigrant's report, they were generally borrowed from earlier Tory accounts. Nevertheless, to many thoughtful newcomers, America did appear a prodigious welter of life swept by the ground-swells of half conscious emotion. As sensitive persons, they could find neither creative spirit nor meaningful direction. An Italian once said, "Send a bookkeeper to Italy and he turns poet." Bookkeepers emerged as bankers and poets became newspapermen in America.

Obviously there were two Americas just as there were two Englands. One was inhabited by a generous, alert, forward-looking people who although proud were capable of self-chastisement, introspection, and negation. The other fostered Know-Nothings and slavery, closed its windows to the superior culture of Europe, and practiced intellectual bias in the backwoods and political chicanery in the cities. Many thoughtful returnees could only see the negative attributes. They did not understand that progress emerges from intangible and elusive fractions, from economic interaction, and from hundreds of small social achievements. Hemmed in by their experiences and lacking in faith, they could not penetrate beneath the surface and comprehend the true meaning and strength of the society. No doubt many who returned, although possessed of education and skills, were deficient emotionally and philosophically. Their culture and sensitivity led to softness and retreat rather than into the hardness of acclimation. Others simply found little *joie de vivre*. When they settled in native communities, life became dull, tasteless, and devoid of creativeness. Although there was no forced conformity or control of opinion, the new community failed to release the individual human spirit or to create a climate in which new tastes in the arts and joy of expression could flourish.

Immigrants did not envision themselves as heroes destined to slay the mysterious dragon of loneliness and frustration. They sought a better life in the immediate future. Despite the romanticizing of later historians, the average migrant was not an Edward Bellmay fictionalizing on the happiness of coming generations. He wanted success and accomplishment in the foreseeable future.

A further cause for return stemmed from an unfortunate indifference on the part of most Americans. One of the consequences of the nation's great achievements was a subconscious supposition that a certain sacrifice of genius was sometimes necessary as the country moved towards its inevitable destiny. Since an overwhelming preponderance of the immigrants succeeded, the failure of a minority was overlooked. British migrants were not persecuted, but they were sometimes tolerated and often neglected. Experimenters and naturalists like Richard Parkinson and Thomas Nuttall, artistic showmen like William Bullock and John Bernard, and political writers like Samuel Roberts and William Cobbett were among the minority who returned. These men of talent and sometimes of genius might have made an invaluable contribution to their adopted land.

The assumption has persisted that immigrants of homogeneous races, particularly Anglo-Saxons, assimilated more readily and therefore were less likely to leave America than other newcomers. A 1960 report on immigration and re-immigration practices by Ilja M. Dijour concludes "that the return of British from Australia, South Africa and Canada or of Portuguese from Brazil, or Spaniards and Italians from the rest of Latin America, is incomparably higher than the re-emigration of say Japanese from Brazil, Slavic people from Australia and Canada, or others." Dijour continues by explaining that one of the main reasons for this rather surprising trend "was an exaggerated expectation of finding no difference at all between the 'old' and the 'new' home in the case of the first group and a kind of psychological preparedness of the other group to finding everything different in the new country."[1]

Perhaps too much emphasis has been placed on differences in culture and the barrier of language. Many authorities agree that

1 *A Seminar on the Integration of Immigrants*, 6.

after World War II the English migrants were among the slowest to integrate in Canada, while the re-immigration from Australia has been predominantly English.[2] World-wide or national catastrophies often virtually catapult people into immigration. Under such emergency or revolutionary conditions, re-immigration is generally precluded. The Irish economic refugees of 1846, German political refugees of 1848, or even the French Utopian socialists of 1849 had little alternative but to accept the new way of life. There was nothing to return to. When war, peace treaties, religious upheavals, or acute depression culminated in immigration, the disaffected seldom possessed the alternative of return. Mere distance precluded even the thought of return for most Continental peasants; whereas ocean transport allowed for a relatively quick and inexpensive recrossing of the Atlantic for Britons. Other than for about three decades at mid-seventeenth century, British immigrants did not leave because of positive necessity. Not having been driven from their native land, they possessed and often embraced the alternative of return without suffering social stigma or political reprisal. Education, skill, and other factors contributing to status and income gave the British further independence of movement.

Since the British were in no sense refugees, they underwent the mental conflict of making difficult decisions before migrating. Naturally they made probing comparisons after arrival. They could return, and so accepted the new society only if it seemed to offer clear advantages over the old.[3] Furthermore, they often immigrated because of dissatisfaction with a single factor within the home environment. Consequently, America might offer greater economic or perhaps political opportunity, but if social demands or community life became irritating, certain types were ready to return. Acceptance of the new cultural patterns was

2 *Ibid.*, 14.

3 *Ibid.* Etta Deutsch has shown that Dutch-Indonesian immigrants who cannot return have integrated into American society more easily and rapidly than Dutch immigrants who often migrate on an experimental basis.

often slow and sometimes led to repatriation. Perhaps ethno-centric and national connections were more binding on Britons than on migrants from Continental countries. Great Britain was an international power which elicited respect or fear throughout the world. Her economic and political influence in North America was a matter of constant concern to the United States. A half-century later, many German-Americans were to show a similar cultural attachment and pride in nationality when their motherland had gained world-wide prestige.

Knowledge of the language allowed for the rapid assimilation of English immigrants, but at the same time it permitted them to compare critically American authors, newspapers, and theaters with those at home. Acquaintance with English governmental and legal traditions provided easy understanding of American law, but it sometimes provoked censure of political methods and frontier justice. Nearness to markets, cheap labor, and advanced technical methods in Britain often led immigrants of the entre-preneur class to despair of the New World's inefficient agricul-tural methods and unorthodox business practices. British workers once associated with the trade union or Chartist movements found American labor groups lacking in organization, leader-ship, and purpose. For the first century of American independ-ence, few immigrants other than the British were in a position to evaluate and criticize most broad and basic aspects of American society. Some concluded that Anglo-Saxon institutions were weakened and corrupted when transplanted and that the original rather than a blurred carbon copy could provide the most fruit-ful life.

Americans of the nineteenth century saw in the young Re-public's activities an unexcelled series of achievements. Disap-pointed returnees pointed to American failures and argued that they were the level of American performance. Clearly the story of immigration was not seamless, and most of the returnees accented the seams. They were not circlers who scouted the issues; rather, they tried to convince by an energetic frontal at-tack. Nevertheless, even the most embittered repatriates indulged in derision rather than breakage. They wished to expose, not to destroy.

In the study of immigration, first impressions have tended to be final judgments. The sum of the misunderstood, the subconscious, or the suspected have too often formed the basis for conclusions. Fortunately, biographical sketches and the literature of return can to some degree be supplemented and appraised by a simple method of statistical enumeration and classification. Certainly the limited number of case studies does not provide enough common variables to establish a completely satisfying pattern. However, the basis of history is never more than the pulling together of available data. The first and most obvious question is who returned and why? Were they young people with relatively great physical stamina or older people with experience? Were the men single or married? In searching for employment were they more or less mobile than native Americans? Did they return with significant amounts of capital? Or did repatriation grow from economic necessity? Although the limited evidence does not allow for rigorous empirical analysis, a statistical accounting can help to put the movement in clearer focus.

Of the seventy-five returnees[4] specifically catalogued in the preceding chapters, reasonably complete demographic data is available on fifty.[5] The fifty migrants varied from eighteen to

[4] The count includes only one member from each family. It does not include transient performers, touring preachers, immigrant agents, or British travelers.

[5] The only criterion used in the selection was the availability of biographical data. Each of the fifty is discussed in the body of the study. The fifty in alphabetical order are John Alexander, Andrew Bell, John Bernard, John R. Beste, Thomas Brothers, William Brown, William Bullock, James Burn, William Clark, William Cobbett, John Davis, Thomas Dixon, Maurice Farrar, Mrs. E. Felton, Isaac Fidler, Mr. Fidler, Edward Flower, Elias Fordham, Rev. D. Griffiths, John Griffiths, Edward Hall, William Hancock, Isaac Holmes, Charles Hooton, Charles Janson, Frances Kemble, Charles Lane, James Lawrence, James Leigh, Doran Maillard, David Mitchell, Edward Money, Peter Neilson, Thomas Nuttall, John Oldmixon, Richard Parkinson, John Pearson, Joseph Pickering, John Regan, Anne Ritson, Samuel Roberts, Edward Sanderson, Rich Short, Henry Stanley, John Taylor, Charles Trimmer, Frances Trollope, Richard Weston, Charles Wilson, and William Young.

sixty-one years of age. Upon first arrival in America, three persons were in their teens, fourteen in their twenties, fourteen in their thirties, five in their forties, six in their fifties, one in his sixties, and seven of unknown age. At least seven of the fifty immigrated to the United States a second time, two a third time, and one a fourth time before returning permanently to Britain.

The total time spent per migrant in the United States varied from two months to forty-six years. Five migrants remained in America for less than one year, four remained from one to two years, nine from two to three years, two from three to four years, six from four to five years, ten from five to ten years, six from ten to twenty years, six from twenty to forty years, and two for over forty years before returning home.

The primary occupation of the immigrant appears to have been an important factor in determining the probability of return. Only four migrants were experienced farmers, six were skilled artisans, nine had professional training and experience, ten enjoyed a good liberal education and demonstrated literary tendencies, five had an interest in a particular business venture, eleven indicated no specific skills or training, and the occupation of five is unknown. Although about half of the returnees possessed a secondary occupation, of the thirty-four with specific skills or professional training, only eight undertook careers in America outside their primary area of interest or competence. The immigrants' reluctance to attempt a new occupation was one of the most significant factors in prompting return.

Mobility was the most universal characteristic shown by the fifty repatriates. All but four visited more than one section of the United States, and twenty-six are known to have traveled one thousand miles or more through many American states. Mobility and the willingness to investigate many areas of the country were not a deterrent to re-immigration. On the contrary, it apparently increased the likelihood of return. Yet, at least 75 per cent of the migrants under study were not truly restless persons incapable of permanent settlement. Rather, they failed to find the economic and social improvement for which they searched.

Since the idea of emigration tended to attract men rather than women, the marital status of the migrant was often a key factor in the return. Some twenty-one persons remained single throughout their American sojourn. (Nineteen had never been married, one was separated from his wife, and one was a widower.) Seven married during their residence in America, but four returned to Britain to select their brides. Only two chose American spouses, and the nationality of one wife is unknown. Five migrants were married when they arrived in the United States but had no children, and thirteen couples sailed with families ranging from one to eleven children. One man immigrated with his family after his wife's death, and the marital status of three is unknown. Of the nineteen couples who traveled to America, with or without children, in at least six cases the wife or children or both were responsible for effecting the return to Britain. In only one instance did the woman wish to remain in America when the husband urged return.

The records suggest that immigration was not something entered into hastily or half-heartedly. It was in most cases an idea long before it became a reality. The cultivated gentleman Richard Beste did not arrive at the railroad terminus at Indianapolis prepared to buy wagons to convey his wife and eleven children on into the wilderness without considerable planning. James Burn dreamed of America for fifty years before he—at sixty-one years of age with a mentally ill wife and five of his sixteen children—embarked for New York. Only three of the fifty migrants were under twenty years of age. Thirty-eight per cent traveled with families, while 82 per cent remained in America more than two years. British returnees were mature, they took time to investigate American opportunities, and they looked beyond the environs of a single community.

Professor T. F. Tout once cautioned that it was easy to record the actions of men, but "vain conjecture when we begin to investigate the [ir] motives."[6] Perhaps we would do well to heed

6 T. F. Tout in the *English Historical Review*, Vol. XXXIV, No. 136 (October, 1919), 601.

Professor Tout's warning; however, attitudinal data and opinion research can surely assist in the formation of generalizations. Granted the rich particularity of every human experience, nevertheless, a kind of collective biography is possible through the study of group tensions, dissatisfactions, and failures.

The climate was one of the more controversial topics in immigrant reports. From the time of the earliest explorers through the nineteenth century, the American climate was the basis for constant disagreement and broad divergence of opinion. Accounts attesting to blue skies and crisp air were always matched by those telling of tropical summers, arctic winters, and incessant maladies. For nine migrants, health was a major factor in their decision to return. In ten instances, the climate was severely criticized and offered as a contributing cause for re-immigration. On the other hand, five of the fifty returnees declared America one of the most delightfully healthy and invigorating regions of the world. The remaining twenty-six persons made only passing reference to climate and health.

According to Anne Ritson, it was the Virginia climate which brought about her husband's death and prompted her return. Richard Beste blamed the Indiana swamps for the death of a daughter and for his own lengthy illness. John Regan left Illinois and James Leigh fled Georgia mainly for reasons of health. Charles Hooton argued that not one of the thirty Englishmen who accompanied him to Galveston, Texas, in 1841 remained healthy for more than a year. Conversely, William Bullock found Cincinnati so free from disease that he attempted to establish a "retirement home" near the city. Thomas Nuttall was among the first naturalists to explore from the Atlantic to the Pacific. He thought the climate of the entire continent exhilarating. After ten years of work and failure in East Tennessee, Samuel Roberts still declared the region the most healthful spot on earth.

British returnees showed no more unity in their assessment of the American political system than they did in their appraisal of the climate. Approximately half of the migrants had no major fault to find with republican institutions, and eight of the fifty were distinctly complimentary. On the other hand, ten bitterly denounced republicanism in principle and American governmental practices in particular. Five straddled the issue. They made no blanket condemnation of the United States, but found certain political functions sufficiently offensive to prompt their return. Joseph Pickering believed American officials to be essentially honest, although the suggestion that he become a citizen was so distasteful that he left rather than swear allegiance to a foreign power. Elias Fordham registered no major complaint against American republicanism. After a few months on the frontier, however, he came to believe that much time would elapse before the system was sufficiently mature to protect all men and provide the requisite governmental services. David Mitchell approved of the democratic ideal, but insisted that it would not work in a competitive economy. Men like Andrew Bell, Thomas Brothers, and John Alexander were much more emphatic. They believed the theory behind the American political system unworthy, the practices followed by officials corrupt, and the total result destructive of human dignity.

Most British immigrants did not possess a strong sense of political cohesion or national solidarity. Indeed half of the returnees studied seem to have been little interested in any political philosophy at the time of migration. The American experience often awakened a dormant sense of tradition and loyalty. In extreme cases even the term "American" came to be viewed not so much a nationality as a philosophy incompatible with all things British. Perhaps the majority of repatriates found the little things and the commonplace features of American life the most annoying. They were more often perplexed by the handling of local problems than by national policy; more often shocked by the partisan political debates than by the issues of a campaign; more often critical of public conduct than of the country's moral fiber. They would have tended to agree with Lord Acton that big truths need supplementing by smaller ones.

For two generations the issue of slavery loomed as America's most controversial domestic topic. British returnees almost universally noted the South's peculiar institutions and rarely attempted to defend them. However, slavery was not a significant factor in the return movement. Fourteen of the fifty migrants settled in slave states, and although all but three expressed some distaste for the institution, none suggested that it was a major factor in their decision to leave. Of the thirty-six returning immigrants from nonslave states, only eighteen seem to have taken notice of the sectional conflict. Typical was the attitude of Elias Fordham. Fordham arrived in southern Illinois during the summer of 1817. His letters to relatives in England revealed a distaste for slavery, yet he admitted that its introduction into Illinois would double land values. He candidly explained that he would oppose the expansion of the system, but should it become legal in Illinois, he would be among the first to make use of it.

As a Welsh nonconformist minister, Samuel Roberts was active in the abolition of slavery in the West Indies. He wrote extensively on the subject and deeply touched his countrymen through the poem "The Complaint of Yamba the Black Slave-Girl." Yet during the late fifties, Roberts purchased thousands of acres of land in Tennessee, migrated to Scott County in 1857 and was not unsympathetic to the Southern cause during the Civil War. For many years Peter Neilson made annual visits to Charleston to buy cotton for his factory at Bristol, Pennsylvania. In 1828, he removed from America to Scotland and nineteen years later wrote *The Adventures of Zamba,* a moralistic tale about an African Negro king and his enslavement in South Carolina. Neilson's rather belated concern with the slave issue after his retirement from the lucrative cotton trade clearly did not influence his decision to return to Scotland. Only in one direct way does the slavery issue seem to have been responsible for the return of Britons. In 1862 the wealthy New York banker, Thomas Dixon, sailed for Eastbourne to escape the problems and controversy growing out of the Civil War. Other affluent English-Americans no doubt took similar action to avoid the confusion of the conflict.

The immigrant reaction to American morals, manners, dress, religion, and family life was a diverse mixture of premature generalization and penetrating analysis. When Britons went to the United States to improve their economic status, they had a natural predisposition to accept change in working conditions and to adjust to new employment requirements. Such a predisposition did not always carry over into the more personal social spheres. Indeed, the greatest resistance to assimilation was registered on moral and cultural grounds. The immigrant family remained the most solidly foreign institution in America. It should be emphasized, furthermore, that when unable to give a tangible reason for failure, the migrant commonly denounced New World social institutions. Few returnees wrote self-effacing or personally embarrassing reports; rather, when dissatisfied, they attempted to throw an unfavorable light on American society. Many migrants wrote to justify their return and through exaggeration and sarcasm tried to preserve their self-esteem. Such goals could best be served by stressing the polemical issues of American emotionalism, cultural barrenness, male inquisitiveness, and female independence. Such reports were not consistent; their criticism was not of a piece. Rather, the mass of conflicting testimony makes difficult the accurate assessment of the returnee's honest attitude toward American culture and society.

Despite the difficulty in evaluating many complaints, nineteen of the fifty migrants offered no serious objections to the American social system. Indeed, nine expressed great admiration for the country's fine and delicate idealism and buoyant humanitarianism. Of the thirty-one critics of American life, six limited their objections to a charge of immaturity. They explained that the New World was moving toward greater sophistication, but that considerable time must elapse before it could claim the social graces and intellectual richness of Europe. Some twenty-five of the returnees expressed deep dissatisfaction with the patterns of American life. Although meeting the harsh demands and paying the penalties exacted by the new society, they had not achieved a satisfactory recompense. Several of the critics like Doran

Maillard, Isaac Fidler, and Charles Janson were glib and all-encompassing in their fault-finding, but not very convincing. They were so universal and uncompromising in their disparagement of everything American that they destroyed their own arguments. Furthermore, in the case of Fidler and Janson, as well as of Frances Trollope and William Brown, it became evident that financial failure was to a large degree responsible for the deep resentment toward the United States. Occasionally utopians like John Alexander and Charles Lane failed in their search for a Garden of Eden and therefore decried all things American. Perhaps ten returnees, typified by William Clark, Thomas Brothers, and Charles Hooton, were uncertain what they were seeking. America quickly eroded their veneer of cosmopolitanism and at the same time exposed a confused conservatism. Their disillusionment with the New World was a mere continuation of their dissatisfaction with the Old and with life in general.

Sociological studies of the American draft have shown that those who "gave up the most" by going into the army were less indignant about the military way of life than those who "gave up the least." As a broad generalization, complaints by returning migrants followed the same inverse order. Those with apparently little cause for resentment were often the most caustic in their denunciation of the American social system.

Economic success has often been considered the most significant factor in determining the enthusiasm with which migrants accepted America. If the newcomer failed to find steady and satisfying employment, he remained on the margin of society. Of course, economic integration became complete only after energies were fully absorbed and skills or capacities thoroughly exploited. Nevertheless, those who returned were surprisingly well equipped to face the demands of the new society. Approximately 85 per cent of those studied arrived in the United States at the peak of their physical productivity. Seventy-five per cent were educated for a profession or skilled in a trade. Virtually all demonstrated mobility. It seems likely, therefore, that the financial reasons for return were not as significant as has often been

assumed. In fact, twenty-eight of the fifty repatriates offered little
or no criticism of America's money-making propensities. Apparently none of the twenty-eight left because of adverse financial
conditions. Indeed, thirteen returned with their economic status
substantially improved. A few like Edward Sanderson, Thomas
Dixon, and William Young re-immigrated after they had become
sufficiently wealthy to retire in England. Some twenty-five Britons
returned home with approximately the same amount of capital
as when they left. Not more than twelve of the fifty actually lost
money as a result of their migration.

That is not to suggest, however, that others did not leave for
financial reasons. At least twenty indicated dissatisfaction with
economic prospects in the United States. Even the well-educated
often viewed America as a golden land which could provide
unique opportunities for the attainment of immediate wealth.
Consequently, a modest income was often considered inadequate
and sometimes transformed a relatively successful immigrant
into a testy critic of the economy.

Returnees not uncommonly declared themselves financially
ruined upon arrival in England, when in actuality they had been
reasonably successful. William Cobbett wrote over a dozen tracts
and articles in which he told of his American losses. By his own
admission, however, he arrived in the United States in 1792 with
eighteen guineas[7] and left in 1801 with several thousand dollars.[8]
Richard Parkinson argued that his two years on a Maryland farm
had been an economic catastrophe. But he overlooked the substantial income he enjoyed from becoming part-owner of a

7 Reitzel, *The Autobiography of William Cobbett*, 57.

8 *Ibid.*, 75. Cobbett's statement that he returned with only $2,500 is totally misleading. The Englishman John Morgan became associated with Cobbett in Philadelphia during the 1790's. In the spring of 1800 the two worked together in New York and Morgan followed Cobbett to England later the same year. Morgan left the United States with several thousand dollars which belonged to Cobbett. The two repatriates became partners and used the money in several London publication ventures. Their most famous undertaking was the publication of the twelve-volume set entitled *Porcupine's Works; Containing Various Writings and Selections, Exhibiting a Faithful Picture of the United States of America* (London, Cobbett and Morgan, 1801).

Baltimore brewery and from the American printing of his popular book, *The Experienced Farmer*.[9] In 1836, William Bullock silently retreated from his planned Kentucky paradise of Elmwood, but not until after he had sold the property for the handsome price of $51,000.[10] Even returnees who lost money in America often more than recouped their deficits as the result of their American experiences. Of the fifteen books written by Richard Beste only *The Wabash*, which grew out of his residence in Indiana, received wide acclaim. Mrs. Trollope's *Domestic Manners of the Americans* catapulted her to literary fame. Charles Hooton, John Davis, Charles Janson, and James Burn all received substantial remuneration from their American-inspired works.

Britons did not have to bridge a broad gulf to become Americanized. Their speech and culture allowed them unusual social and occupational fluidity. They neither grouped together in communities nor formed societies to help preserve their emotional and esthetic values. Without a buffer to slow the process of acculturation they were constrained to accept the new institutions and given every opportunity to draw invidious comparisons. If dissatisfied, they were more likely than any other nationality of the period to become Atlantic back-trailers.

Baffled by their own agricultural and industrial metamorphosis, many British traditionalists had come to idealize the proud generosity and practical instincts of the unsophisticated Americans. But such Britons remained conservative and conventional; they thought of principles as being fixed and conceived of the American design as a purified British system which required only extension and expansion. They demanded order and sought stability; they desired growth but through organized direction. Unfortunately many of the migrants possessed a sense of election which prohibited accommodation to America. They could not forget who they were or where they were from.

9 Parkinson, *A Tour in America in 1798, 1799, and 1800*, I, 78, 178, 238.

10 John M. Hunnicutt, *History of the City of Ludlow* (Publication by the Volunteer Fire Department, 1935), 6; *The Cincinnati Enquirer*, April 12, 1903, sec. 3, p. 7.

Whether literary figures or farmers, professionals or ne'er-do-wells, they fell into the historic pattern of exiles who "lament by the waters of Babylon." Faced with momentous problems in unfamiliar surroundings, they became the homesick who sought the warmth of memory. They recalled the peace of mind of their childhood and evoked the myth of "merrie England." America seldom met the needs of the traditionalist or reactionary Briton.

At the other end of the spectrum was the visionary in search of concrete and tangible goals. He thought of America as being idealistic, yet practical, a land which stressed the transcendent value of man, yet upheld individual and personal interests. Such migrants were usually disappointed. Persons who were pioneering in socialistic or Marxist theories found that neither utopian communism nor scientific socialism had effectively penetrated the American mentality. Other Britons anticipated a rediscovery in America of the close-knit community which was disappearing at home. Instead, they found institutional federalism, a restless frontier, and a mobile society. Such total pluralism seemed to negate the norms and virtues which they sought. Migrants carrying the torch for social rights and human dignity often could not separate America's generosity from her greed, her love for personal independence from her tendency toward anarchy. In short, America commonly failed to satisfy the visionaries and the perfectionist. It was a land where methods and not views prevailed.

The majority of British returnees were neither reactionary nor revolutionary, but rather human nondescripts in search of new beginnings. They were willing and indeed eager to exchange old ways for new ones when the new ones proved to be more meaningful. Actually they sought conversion, but found no all-pervasive dynamics. They were in a sense surprised and disappointed when their identity was not swept from them. Many harbored a nebulous resentment at not finding America an end in itself, but more concluded that it could not provide a means for achieving their ends. The immigrants had been drawn through dreams of the New World to reject the reality of the Old. But through experience they found that human satisfaction and a sense of well-being was a very personal matter often bound to family, friends, and fellow countrymen.

The settlement of the United States has been interpreted by most historians as the central thread in its development. Yet, for many the great American success story unfolded in reverse. The happy ending which for a century and a half was considered the predestined reward for trial and error, work and virtue, did not always emerge. The magic of the New World was not always sufficient to challenge the conventions and quicken the appreciation of the newcomer. Both worthy men and scoundrels failed to achieve a sense of belonging and to acquire a willingness to sacrifice. But with all the accounts of success and failure perhaps the most tragic stories were never told. Knights-errant are often reticent after the quest is over. An exhausted immigrant silently sails for home; he debarks, and we are left in doubt about the temper of his mind or the lure of the dream that provoked the tilt with America.

 BIBLIOGRAPHY

To catalog all references used in this volume would produce a bibliography of inordinate length. Indeed, even a simple listing of works written by or about the seventy-five immigrant returnees herein discussed would nearly double the size of the volume. For example, Horace A. Vachell was the author of over one hundred full-length books. At least a score of bibliographical and scientific articles were inspired by the long career and numerous volumes of Thomas Nuttall. The peculiar fortunes of Henry M. Stanley elicited an even more extensive literature. It would require months to survey the hundreds of pounds of printed material issued by William Cobbett and equally as long to study the comments and replies of his contemporaries. More significant, the sources of this book are so scattered that a comprehensive bibliography fails to relate to the central theme. Perhaps the chapter notes can provide the most useful guide to specific topics of interest.

The following selected bibliography is limited to works and documents which provide the most concrete data on, and best portray the attitudes of, returning immigrants.

GOVERNMENTAL SOURCES

Annual Report of the Chief of the United States Bureau of Statistics on Foreign Commerce and Navigation. Washington, D.C., Government Printing Office, 1892.

Annual Report of the Commissioner-General of Immigration. Washington D.C., Government Printing Office, 1932.

Annual Report of the Superintendent of Immigration for the Fiscal Year Ending June 30, 1892. Washington, D.C., Government Printing Office, 1892.

Parker, Warner A. (comp.). *Annual Report of the Commissioner-General of Immigration for the Fiscal Year Ending June 30, 1908.* Washington, D.C., Government Printing Office, 1908.

Parliamentary Papers, House of Commons, XCIV, 1894, Emigration and Immigration, "Report to the Board of Trade," Table XI.

Parliamentary Papers, House of Commons, XCIII, 1896, Emigration and Immigration, "Report to the Board of Trade," Tables X, XI, XIX, and XX.

Parliamentary Papers, House of Commons, Nineteenth General Report of the Emigration Commissioners, 1859, Sess. 2, XIV (2555).

Parliamentary Papers, House of Commons, Twenty-first General Report of the Emigration Commissioners, 1861, XXII (2842).

"A Report of the Commissioners of Immigration upon the Causes which Incite Immigration to the United States," 52 Cong., 1 sess. (1891–92), *House Executive Document 235,* Part I.

ARTICLES

"Alien Population is Smallest in Years," *The New York Times,* June 13, 1937.

"The British Section of Icarian Communists," *Bulletin of the International Institute of Social History,* No. 2 (1937).

Campbell, Mildred. "English Emigration on the Eve of the American Revolution," *American Historical Review,* Vol. LXI (October, 1955).

Chapman, W. G. "The Wakefield Colony," *Transactions of the Kansas State Historical Society,* Vol. X (1907–1908).

Dublin, Louis I. "A New Phase Opens in America's Evolution," *The New York Times,* April 17, 1932, sec. 9.

"Emigration of Girls as well as Boys to Canada," *The Ragged School Union Magazine*, Vol. IX (1857).

Foreman, Grant. "English Emigrants in Iowa," *The Iowa Journal of History and Politics*, Vol. XLIV (October, 1946).

Handlin, Oscar. "Historical Perspectives on the American Ethnic Group," *Daedalus*, Spring, 1961.

———. "Immigrants Who Go Back," *The Atlantic*, July, 1956.

Hickman, C. Addison. "Barlow Hall," *The Palimpsest*, October, 1941.

Lynch, Hollis R. "Sir Joseph William Trutch, a British-American Pioneer on the Pacific Coast," *Pacific Historical Review*, Vol. XXX, No. 3 (August, 1961).

Moro, Arthur Reginald. "The English Colony at Fairmont in the Seventies," *Minnesota History*, Vol. VIII, No. 2 (June, 1927).

"Present System of British Emigration," *The Colonial Magazine and East India Review*, Vol. XXI (1851).

Sachse, William L. "The Migration of New Englanders to England, 1640–1660," *American Historical Review*, Vol. LIII (January, 1948).

Schafer, Joseph. "Lands Across the Sea," *The Wisconsin Magazine of History*, Vol. XIII, No. 4 (June, 1930).

Talman, James J. "George Sheppard, Journalist, 1819–1912," *Transactions of the Royal Society of Canada*, Vol. XLIV (June, 1950).

BOOKS AND PAMPHLETS

Bell, Andrew. *Men and Things in America; Being the Experience of a Year's Residence in the United States, in a Series of Letters to a Friend.* London, William Smith, 1838.

Bernard, John. *Retrospections of America, 1797–1811.* New York, Harper and Brothers, 1887.

Beste, J. Richard. *The Wabash: or Adventures of an English Gentleman's Family in the Interior of America.* 2 vols. London, Hurst and Blackett, Publishers, 1855.

Borthwick, J. D. *Three Years in California.* Edinburgh, William Blackwood and Sons, 1857.

Bristow, John T. *Memory's Storehouse Unlocked.* N.p., n.d.

Brothers, Thomas. *The United States of North America as They Are; Not as They Are Generally Described: Being a Cure for Radicalism.* London, Longman, Orme, Brown, Green, and Longmans, 1840.

Brown, William. *America: Four Years' Residence in the United States and Canada.* Leeds, privately published, 1849.

Bullock, William. *Sketch of a Journey Through the Western States of North America* . . . . London, John Miller, 1827.

Burn, James. *The Beggar Boy: An Autobiography.* London, Hodder and Stoughton, 1882.

——. *Three Years Among the Working-Classes in the United States During the War.* London, Smith, Elder and Co., 1865.

Clark, William. *The Mania of Emigrating to the United States.* London, n.p., 1820.

A Clear and Concise Statement of New York and the Surrounding Country. Belper, Derbyshire, J. Ogle, Printer, 1819.

Cobbett, William. *Porcupine's Works; containing various Writings and Selections, Exhibiting a Faithful Picture of the United States of America.* 12 vols. London, Cobbett and Morgan, 1801.

——. *A Year's Residence in the United States of America* . . . . New York, privately published, 1818.

Davis, John. *Travels of Four Years and a Half in the United States of America* . . . . London, T. Ostell, 1803.

Ebbutt, Percy G. *Emigrant Life in Kansas.* London, Swan Sonnenschein and Co., 1886.

Emigration, Emigrants, and Know-Nothings. Philadelphia, privately published, 1854.

Farrar, Maurice. *Five Years in Minnesota: Sketches of Life in a Western State.* London, Sampson, Low, Marston, Searle and Rivington, 1880.

Faux, William. *Memorable Days in America: Being a Journal of a Tour to the United States Principally Undertaken to Ascertain, by Positive Evidence, the Condition and Probable Pros-*

pects of British Emigrants. London, Simpkin and Marshall, 1823.

Fearon, Henry Bradshaw. *Sketches of America: A Narrative of a Journey of Five Thousand Miles Through the Eastern and Western States of America.* London, Longman, Hurst, Rees, Orme and Brown, 1819.

Felton, Mrs. E. *American Life: A Narrative of Two Years' City and Country Residence in the United States.* Bolton Percy, Lancashire, privately published, 1843.

Fidler, Isaac. *Observations on Professions, Literature, Manners, and Emigration in the United States and Canada, Made During a Residence There in 1832.* London, Whittaker, Treacher and Co., 1833.

Flint, James. *Letters from America, Containing Observations on the Climate and Agriculture of the Western States, the Manners of the People, the Prospects of Emigrants, etc., etc.* Edinburgh, W. and C. Tait, 1822.

Flower, George. *History of the English Settlement in Edwards County, Illinois, Founded in 1817 and 1818, by Morris Birkbeck and George Flower.* Ed. by E. B. Washburne. Chicago, Fergus Printing Company, 1909.

Fordham, Elias Pym. *Personal Narrative of Travels in Virginia, Maryland, Pennsylvania, Ohio, Indiana, Kentucky; and of a Residence in the Illinois Territory, 1817–1818.* Ed. by Frederic A. Ogg. Cleveland, The Arthur H. Clark Co., 1906.

Griffiths, D., Jun. *Two Years' Residence in the New Settlements of Ohio, North America.* London, Westley and Davis, 1835.

Griffiths, John T. *Reminiscence: Forty-three Years in America, from April, 1865, to April, 1908.* Morriston, Glamorgan, Jones and Sons, 1913.

Hancock, William. *An Emigrant's Five Years in the Free States of America.* London, T. Cautley Newby, Publishers, 1860.

Harris, William Tell. *Remarks Made During a Tour Through the United States of America in the Years 1817, 1818, and 1819.* London, Sherwood, Neely and Jones, 1821.

A History of St. George's Society of New York. New York, St. George's Society of New York, 1913.

Homes, Isaac. *An Account of the United States of America, Derived from Actual Observation During a Residence of Four Years in That Republic.* London, Printed at the Caxton Press by Henry Fisher, 1823.

Hooton, Charles. *St. Louis' Isle or Texiana; with Additional Observations Made in the United States and in Canada.* London, Simmonds and Ward, 1847.

Horn, Harcourt H. *An English Colony in Iowa.* Boston, The Christopher Publishing House, 1931.

Janson, Charles W. *The Stranger in America: Containing Observations Made During a Long Residence in That Country . . . .* London, Albion Press, 1807.

Jones, Jack. *Off to Philadelphia in the Morning.* London, Hamish Hamilton, 1947.

Journal of an Excursion of the United States and Canada in the Year 1834 . . . . Edinburgh, John Anderson, Jun., 1835.

Kemble, Frances Anne (Fanny). *Journal of a Residence on a Georgian Plantation, 1838–1839.* London, Longman, Green, Longman, Roberts and Green, 1863.

Leigh, J. W. *Other Days.* London, T. Fisher Unwin, Ltd., 1921.

Letter from a Tradesman, Recently Arrived from America to His Brethren in Trade. London, Effingham Wilson, 1835.

Maillard, N. Doran. *The History of the Republic of Texas . . . .* London, Smith, Elder and Co., 1842.

Mitchell, D. W. *Ten Years in the United States: Being an Englishman's Views of Men and Things in North and South.* London, Smith, Elder and Co., 1862.

Money, Edward. *The Truth About America.* London, Sampson, Low, Marston, Searle and Rivington, 1886.

Murray, Charles Augustus. *Travels in North America During 1834, 1835, and 1836.* 2 vols. London, Richard Bentley, 1839.

Neilson, Peter. *Recollections of a Six Years' Residence in the United States of America.* Glasgow, David Robertson, 1830.

Oldmixon, J. W. *Transatlantic Wanderings*. London, George Routledge and Co., 1855.

Parkinson, Richard. *A Tour in America, in 1798, 1799, and 1800, Exhibiting Sketches of Society and Manners, and a Particular Account of the American System of Agriculture, with Its Recent Improvements*. 2 vols. London, J. Harding, 1805.

Pearson, John. *Notes Made During a Journey in 1821 in the United States of America in Search of a Settlement*. London, Sherwood, Neely and Jones, 1822.

Pickering, Joseph. *Emigration or No Emigration; Being the Narrative of the Author, an English Farmer, from the Year 1824 to 1830*. London, Longman, Rees, Orme, Brown and Green, 1830.

Raish, Marjorie Gamet. *Victoria: The Story of a Western Kansas Town*. Topeka, State Printer, 1947.

The Real Experience of an Emigrant. London, Ward, Lock and Tyler, n.d.

Regan, John. *The Emigrant's Guide to the Western States of America; or Backwoods and Prairies* . . . . Edinburgh, Oliver and Boyd, 1852. 2d ed.

Ritson, Anne. *A Poetical Picture of America, Being Observations Made During a Residence of Several Years at Alexandria, and Norfolk, Virginia*. London, privately published, 1809.

Roberts, Samuel. *Diosg Farm: A Sketch of Its History During the Tenancy of John Roberts and His Widow*. Newtown, Montgomeryshire, Henry Parry, 1854.

Sanborn, F. B. *Bronson Alcott: At Alcott House, England, and Fruitlands, New England, 1842–1844*. Cedar Rapids, The Torch Press, 1908.

Savage, William. *Observations on Emigration to the United States of America*. London, Sherwood, Neely and Jones, 1819.

A Seminar on the Integration of Immigrants. New York, American Immigration and Citizenship Conference, 1960.

Short, Rich. *Travels in the United States of America . . . with Advice to Emigrants*. London, Richard Lambert, n.d. 2d ed.

Taylor, John G. *The United States and Cuba: Eight Years of Change and Travel.* London, Richard Bentley, 1851.

Things as They Are; or, America in 1819. Manchester, J. Wroe, 1819.

Trollope, Frances. *Domestic Manners of the Americans.* 2 vols. London, Whittaker, Treacher and Co., 1832.

Van Der Zee, Jacob. *The British in Iowa.* Iowa City, State Historical Society of Iowa, 1922.

Welby, Adlard. *A Visit to North America and the English Settlements in Illinois, with a Winter Residence in Philadelphia.* London, J. Drury, 1821.

Weston, Richard. *A Visit to the United States and Canada in 1833; with the View of Settling in America.* Edinburgh, Richard Weston and Sons, 1836.

Wilson, Charles H. *The Wanderer in America, or, Truth at Home, Comprising a Statement of Observations and Facts Relative to the United States and Canada.* Northallerton, Yorkshire, n.p., 1820.

Woollam, J. G. *Useful Information for Emigrants to the Western States of America.* Manchester, B. Hampson, Printer, 1846.

Wyse, Francis. *America, Its Realities and Resources . . . .* 3 vols. London, T. C. Newby, 1846.

INDEX

Account of the Life . . . of Thomas Paine: 165
Account of the United States, An: 93
Acton, Lord: 189
Actors: *see* immigration
Adams, John (immig.): 54
Adams, Pres. John: 64
Adams, John Quincy: 28
Adventures of Bilberry Thurland: 173
Adventures of Zamba, The: 95, 190
Advice to Emigrants: 93
Africans: 40
Ainsworth's Magazine: 15
Alabama, state of: 93
Albert, Prince Consort: 19
Albion, The: 171
Albion, Ill.: 42, 44, 46
Alcott, Bronson: 117ff.
Alcott, Louisa M.: 118
Alexander, Caleb: 152
Alexander, John: 17, 71ff., 185n., 189, 192
America, Its Realities and Resources: 86
American Exile, The: see *Refugee in America*
American Monthly Review, The: 14
American Revolution: 32, 62, 146, 156
Anglicans: 57, 142, 146
Antelope Valley, Calif.: 56
Appleton & Co.: 89
Ashe, Thomas: 10
Ashley, Lord: 19
Astor House riots: 100
Athenaeum, The: 9, 12, 15, 86, 107

Ayrshire: 54, 55, 71

Baker, Capt. Charles G.: 113
Baker, Col. William T.: 113
Bakewell, Robert: 31, 35
Banks, Sir Joseph: 36
Baptists: 144
Barlow, Capt. Alexander: 56, 60
Barnabys in America, The: 14
Barnum, P. T.: 169
Barrington, Anne (Mrs. John W. Oldmixon): 134
Barton, Benjamin S.: 136
Bebb, William: 126ff.
Bedford, Duke of: 62
Beefsteak Club: 102, 103
Belgium: 68
Bell, Andrew: 65ff., 77, 78, 153, 185n., 189
Bennett, James Gordon: 171
Bentham, Jeremy: 11, 66
Bentley's Miscellany: 173
Berkshire Hills: 13
Bernard, Sir Francis: 102
Bernard, John: 102ff., 140, 182, 185n.
Beste, Henry: 57
Beste, John Richard: 9, 57ff., 185n., 194
Beveridge, Capt.: 23
Birkbeck, Morris: 42, 44, 46, 47, 48
Birkbeck-Flower colony: 42ff., 123
Blackwell, Dr. Elizabeth: 17, 153, 154, 155, 165
Blackwood's Magazine: 10
Board of Agriculture (British): 32, 37

Board of Trade (British): 5
Bone to Gnaw, A: 161
Booth, Junius: 100
Borthwick, J. D.: 172
Boyd, Thomas: 23
Bradbury, John: 135
Bray, John: 100
Bray, John Francis: 100
Breeding and Management of Live-stock: 37
Bristol, Penn.: 94, 95
British Temperance Emigration Society and Savings Fund: 26
Brothers, Thomas: 69ff., 77, 78, 185n., 189, 192
Brown, William: 87ff., 92, 185n., 192
Bryant, William Cullen: 109
Brynyffynon, Tenn. (colony): 125ff.
Buchanan, James: 23, 24
Buckingham, James Silk: 117n.
Buckinghamshire: 37, 40
Buck's Lodge: 102
Bullock, William: 9, 98, 119ff., 136, 138, 140, 166, 168, 169, 170, 171, 182, 185n., 188, 194
Burn, James: 80ff., 185n., 187, 194
Burr, Aaron: 152
Bussey, Peter: 71
Butler, Pierce: 107ff.
Butler Co., Pa.: 48, 49
Byron, Lord: 112

Cabet, Étienne: 71 ff., 77, 119
California, state of: 13, 56
Cambridge, England: 15, 102, 115, 149
Cambridgeshire: 44n.
Carey, Matthew: 70
Carlyle, Thomas: 71
Casey, Charles: 53
Catholics: 40, 57, 58, 59, 60, 70, 72, 142, 150
Channing, William Ellery: 109
Charleston, S. C.: 94, 95
Chartists: 70, 71, 76, 81, 184
Cheerful (ship): 23
Cheltenham Chronicle: 21
Chesapeake and Ohio Canal: 24
Chesterfield, Lord: 38
Chicago, Ill.: 79
Christian World: 116

Cincinnati, Ohio: 9, 58, 59, 122, 167, 168, 169, 188
City of Kent (Bosque Co.), Tex.: 22, 125
Civil War, U.S.: 24, 78, 89, 90, 98, 110, 190
Clark, William: 64, 185n., 192
Clergymen: *see* immigration
Cleveland, Ohio: 79, 88
Clinton Co., Iowa: 28
Close, James, William, & Frederick: 114
Cobbett, William: 8, 46, 71, 153, 159ff., 177, 182, 185n., 193
Coke of Holkham: 33
Coles, Edward: 42
Colin Clink: 173
Colonial Land and Emigration Commissioners: 25
Colonial Magazine and East India Review: 19
Colonizers: *see* immigration
Colorado, state of: 56
Combe, George: 149, 150, 153, 155, 177
Commissioners of Immigration: 5
Congregationalists: 126, 142, 143
Conyngham, Earl of: 36
Cook, Capt.: 121
Cooper, James Fenimore: 166, 167
Cooper, Thomas: 36, 100
Corneal, Thomas D.: 122
Cornwallis, Kinahan: 171
Crèvecoeur, Jean de: 36, 55
Crimean War: 9, 25
Cyfarthfa Iron Works: 101

Dana, Richard Henry: 137
Davis, John: 151 ff., 155, 177, 185n., 194
Decamp, Adelaid: 106
Decorah, Iowa: 113
Derbyshire: 49, 64
Devonshire: 53
Dickens, Charles: 12, 109
Dijour, Ilja: 182
Diosg Farm: 127
Distant Fields: 13
Dixon, Thomas: 90, 185n., 190, 193
Doctor Unmasked, The: 69
Dodge, Col. Henry: 132
Domestic Manners of the Americans: 9, 13, 14, 165, 170, 194
Doncaster Chronicle: 25
Dorfeuille, Joseph: 168

Index

Dorsetshire: 22
Dublin, Ireland: 36, 81
Dutch: *see* immigration

East Indies: 48
East Lothian: 53
Eclectic Review, The: 158
Edinburgh Review, The: 158
Edinburgh, Scot.: 81
Educational Places . . . in London, The: 83, 86
Edward (ship): 167
Edward Fitz-Yorke: 15, 157
Edward VII, as Prince of Wales: 110, 129
Edwards County, Ill.: 43
Egyptian Hall: 120ff.
Elliot, Charles: 173
Ellis, John: 74, 75
Elmwood Hall: 122ff., 168, 194
Emerson, Ralph Waldo: 109
Emigration: *see* immigration
Emigration Gazette and Colonial Advocate, The: 22
Enclosures: 31, 32
English colonies: 113ff., 125
English Practice of Agriculture, The: 37
English Prairie: 43, 44, 45, 46
Episcopalians: 142, 146, 147
Essex: 46
European Magazine, The: 158
Europeans: *see* immigration
Experienced Farmer, The: 33, 34, 36, 37, 194

Far Away and Long Ago: 13
Farmer Careful: 126
Farrar, Maurice: 115, 185n.
Faux, William: 10, 46
Fearon, Henry: 10, 46
Felton Travellers: 13
Felton, Mrs. E.: 87, 150ff., 153, 185n.
Fennell, James: 100
Fidler, Mr.: 43, 60, 185n.
Fidler, Rev. Isaac: 146ff., 153, 176, 177, 185n., 192
Fitzgerald, Edward: 112
Flint, James: 50, 51
Flower, Edward: 43, 43n., 47, 185n.
Flower, George: 42, 43, 44, 48
Flower, Richard: 43n.

Fordham, Elias: 44, 45, 47, 60, 154, 185n., 189, 190
France: 55, 57, 68
Franklin, Benjamin: 4, 64
Fraser's Magazine: 10, 11
Fruitlands (colony): 117, 119

Galveston, Tex.: 21, 22, 174, 188
Garneau, F. X.: 68
Genera of North America, The: 137
Gentleman's Magazine: 105
George, Mary (Mrs. John Oldmixon): 101, 133, 135
George III, of England: 62, 87
Georgia Emigration Company: 21
Georgia, state of: 20, 21, 108, 110ff.
Germans: *see* immigration
Girard, Steven: 69
Glasgow Herald: 95
Goethe, Johann: 22
Grant, George: 113
Grant, Mr.: 49
Great Eastern Railway: 83
Greeks: 7
Griffiths, Rev. D.: 145, 150, 177, 185n.
Griffiths, Rev. John: 9, 143ff., 177, 185n.

Hall, Edward: 89, 92, 185n.
Hallam, Arthur: 112
Hampshire: 49, 57
Hancock, William: 9, 79ff., 185n.
Hansen, Marcus: 63
Harney, George: 71, 77
Harper and Bros.: 79
Harris, Thomas Lake: 125
Harris, William: 46
Harrison, William Henry: 137
Hawthorne, Nathaniel: 109
Henry (ship): 75, 76
Herefordshire: 89
Hertfordshire: 44n.
Hervieu, Auguste: 167ff.
Historical Sketch of . . . Odd Fellows, A: 81
Historical Sketches of Feudalism: 68
History of Strikes, A: 83
History of the Republic of Texas, The: 172
Hobart, Lord: 114
Holmes, Isaac: 93, 185n.
Holmes, Oliver Wendell: 109

Hooton, Charles: 8, 13, 15, 16, 17, 173ff., 185n., 188, 192, 194
Horn, Harcourt: 113
Horsfall, Robert: 84, 88
Hottinguer (ship): 25
Howitt, Emmanuel: 10
Hughes, Thomas: 114
Huntingdonshire: 37
Hutchinson, Gov. Thomas: 3
Hygeia (colony): 123ff.

I'Anson, Charles William: *see* Janson
I'Anson, William: 156, 157
Icarians: 74, 119
Ikin, Arthur: 21, 173
Ikin, Jonathan: 173
Illinois, state of: 40, 42, 43, 44, 46, 47, 49, 53ff.
Illinois Central R. R.: 79
Immigration: of Welsh, 5, 7, 21, 53, 78, 143ff.; of Scots, 5, 18, 20, 51, 53, 78, 95; of Irish, 5, 34, 59, 91; of Europeans, 6, 29, 50, 178; of Germans, 58, 66, 75; of Dutch, 75; of actors, 99–112; of colonizers, 113–30; of clergymen, 142–48
India: 56, 92
Indiana, state of: 40
Indians, American: 40, 70, 132, 135, 136
Industrial Revolution: 23, 92
Iowa, state of: 24, 27, 56, 113, 114
Irish: *see* immigration
Irving, Peter: 111
Irving, Washington: 106, 107, 111, 166
Isle of Wight: 47, 49
Italy: 7, 55, 57, 60, 108, 181

Jackson, Andrew: 151
Janson, Charles William: 10, 13, 15, 16, 156ff.
Jefferson, Thomas: 33, 36, 137, 151, 152
Johnson, J.: 116
Johnson, Samuel: 86
Johnston, Prof. James: 30
Jones, E. B.: 127
Jones, John R. & William: 127
Jones, Michael D.: 126
Journal, The: 107, 110
Journal of a Residence on a Georgia Plantation: 110

Kansas, state of: 113

Kean, Edmund: 100
Keily, Richard: 21, 125
Kemble, Charles: 106ff.
Kemble, Frances: 8, 13, 17, 98, 106ff., 185n.
Kemble, Frances (younger): 110ff.
Kennedy, William: 22, 173
Kentucky, state of: 38, 47, 53
Kick for a Bite, A: 161

Lafayette, Marquis de: 166, 167
Lanarkshire: 92
Lancashire: 92
Lane, Charles: 117ff., 140, 185n., 192
Lane, William: 117ff.
Language of the Walls: 81
Last of the Mohicans: 90
Launcelot Wedge: 15, 172
Lawrence, James: 42, 43, 47, 185n.
Lawson, Melvina: 138
Leigh, Rev. James W.: 111, 185n., 188
Leisure Hour: 68
Lenox, Mass.: 109
Le Populaire: 74
Letter on Vested Rights, A: 69
Letters from an American Farmer: 36
Letters from Illinois: 42
Letters on Improvement: 127
Le Tuteur Anglais: 161
Lewis, William G.: 69, 70
L'Histoire du Canada: 68
Liberty (ship): 25
Lieber, Dr. Francis: 147
Life and Adventures of Jonathan Jefferson Whitlaw, The: 14
Lincolnshire: 27, 33, 36, 37, 46, 57
Literary Gazette, The: 51, 137
Livingstone, David: 171
Llanbrynmair, Wales: 126ff.
London Catalogue: 11
London Compositors Emigration Fund: 26
London Ragged School Union: 19
Long, John: 135
Longfellow, Henry W.: 109
Long Island, N. Y.: 79, 150, 164, 165
Louisiana, state of: 15
Lounge in the Tuileries, A: 9, 133

Macbeth: 100
McDouall, Peter: 71

Index

MacKay, Charles: 24
McKenzie, Lt. Charles: 125
Macready, Charles: 99, 100
Madison, James: 42
Maillard, Nicholas D. P.: 172ff., 176, 185n., 192
Manchester and Missouri: 89
Manchester Times: 99
Mann, Horace: 150
Marryat, Capt.: 70
Marshall, William: 33
Martineau, Harriet: 107
Marx, Karl: 100n.
Maryland, state of: 34, 37
Massachusetts, state of: 3
Mathews, Charles: 100
Maxwell, Walter: 114
Mediterranean: 60
Melville, Herman: 109
Memorable Days in America: 10
Men and Things in America: 68
Mercantile Enterprise: 81
Merthyr Tydfil, Wales: 101
Methodists: 116, 125, 142, 145
Methuselah's Diary: 13
Mexico: 72, 73, 119, 121, 122
Michigan, state of: 53
Milam, Benjamin: 72, 73
Mill, James: 11
Milnes, Richard Mockton: 112
Milton, John: 67
Mississippi, state of: 93
Mitchell, David: 9, 90ff., 185n., 189
Money, Col. Edward: 56, 57, 60, 155n.
More, Sir Thomas: 74
More from Methuselah: 13
Moreton, Capt. Reynolds: 114
Morgan, John: 193n.
Mormons: 80
Moro, Reginald: 115
Mount Vernon, Va.: 33, 34
Mr. Cobbett's Taking Leave: 164
Muir, Thomas: 66
Murray, Charles A.: 131, 132

Napoleon: 73, 120
Napoleonic Wars: 4, 23, 32, 38, 62, 101, 159, 163, 164
Nashoba, Tenn. (colony): 123, 166, 167
National Typographical Emigration Society: 26

Nebraska, state of: 115
Negroes: 34, 65, 70, 88, 123, 190
Neilson, George: 94
Neilson, Peter: 16, 94ff., 185n., 190
Nettle, George: 53, 54
New Harmony, Ind.: 72, 118, 119
New Monthly Magazine, The: 15, 175
New York (ship): 25
New York, state of: 38, 67
New York Herald: 171
New York Journal of Commerce, The: 21, 95
North American Review: 10, 148
North Carolina, state of: 16, 53
Northern Star: 71
North Texas Colonization Company: 75, 119
Notes on a Journey in America: 42
Now Came Still Evening On: 13
Nuttall, Jonas: 138
Nuttall, Thomas: 98, 99, 135ff., 182, 185n., 188

O'Brien, James: 71, 74, 77
O'Brien, William: 145
Observation on the Emigration of Dr. Joseph Priestley: 161
Observations on Professions: 148
Ohio, state of: 16, 53
O'Kelly, Patrick: 150, 153
Old Countryman and Emigrants' Friend, The: 21
Old World and the New, The: 14
Oldmixon, John W.: 9, 133ff., 140, 185n.
Oldmixon, Sir John: 101, 132, 133, 134
Owen, Robert: 21, 71ff., 100n., 118, 119
Oxford, Eng.: 115, 149, 166

Paine, Thomas: 36, 66, 68, 69, 77, 151, 160
Palmyra, Neb.: 115, 116
Parkinson, Richard: 10, 32ff., 41, 182, 185n., 193
Parliament: 60, 62, 96
Parry, Daniel: 101
Parry, Joseph: 101
Payne, John Howard: 106, 111
Pearson, John: 47ff., 60, 185n.
Pellew, Henry: 149
Pennsylvania, state of: 7, 20, 24, 37, 49
Peters, William S.: 74

Phillips, Mr.: 53
Piccadilly to Pera: 9
Pickering, Joseph: 40, 41, 185n., 189
Poe, Edgar Allan: 107
Pokoke Academy, Va.: 152
Poor Law Act: 18
Porcupine's Gazette: 161, 162
Porcupine's Works: 163
Potter's Joint Stock Emigration Society: 26
Powderly, Joseph: 5, 42
Power, Tyrone: 100
Practical Observations on Gypsum: 37
Preakness, N. J.: 64
Pregethau a Darlithiau: 128
Prentice, Archibald: 99, 142
Presbyterians: 142, 145, 146
Price, Peter: 47, 48, 49
Price, Stephen: 106, 111
Price, Dr. William: 170
Priest, William: 101
Priestley, Joseph: 36, 161

Quakers: 42, 142
Quarterly Bulletin of the Nuttall Ornithological Club: 139
Queensborough, Lord: 114

Rawlings, Thomas: 21
Recollections of a Six Years' Residence: 95
Red River: 72, 75
Reformer, The: 71, 75, 77
Refugee in America, The: 13, 14
Regan, John: 54ff., 59, 185n., 188
Reid, Thomas: 23
Remarks on Iron-Built Ships: 95
Retrospections of America: 104
Richmond Telescope: 172
Riddell, James: 172
Rights & Wrongs of the Poor, The: 70
Ritson, Annie: 87, 185n., 188
Roberts, John: 126
Roberts, Richard: 127ff.
Roberts, Samuel: 9, 16, 125ff., 138, 140, 182, 185n., 188, 190
Robins Agency: 21
Robinson Crusoe: 9
Roman Catholics: *see* Catholics
Rowed-Makery Agency: 22, 125
Rowlands, John: *see* Henry M. Stanley

Royal Academy of Music: 102
Royal Literary Fund: 83
Runnymede, Kan.: 114
Rush, Dr. Benjamin: 162
Rushlight: 162
Russia: 42
Rutland: 37

St. George's Society: 149, 171
St. Louis' Isle, or Texiana: 175
Sanderson, Edward: 90, 185n., 193
Saunders, Samuel: 21
Savage, William: 47
Saye and Sele, Lord: 111
Scots: *see* immigration
Scott, Sir Walter: 111
Sears, R.: 116
Sedgwick, Catherine: 109
Senator Unmasked, The: 69
Sentimental Journey: 9
Seppings, Herbert: 114
Seton, Capt. Charles: 114
Sheppard, George: 27, 28, 125
Sherman, H. F.: 115
Shirreff, Patrick: 53
Short, Rich: 51ff., 59, 185n.
Sidney's Emigrant Journal: 24
Simmond's Colonial Magazine: 175
Sinclair, Sir John: 32
Sketch of a Journey Through the Western States: 9, 123
Slavery: 93, 96, 110, 189, 190
Smith, Adam: 69
Smith, J. Gray: 125
Smithie, Mrs. Henry: 114
Socialism: 71
Stanley, Henry M.: 171, 185n.
Star of Empire: 116
Stephen, King: 44n.
Stephenson, George: 45, 154
Sterne, Laurence: 9, 12
Stirlingshire: 94
Stranger in America: 157, 158
Sturge, Joseph: 142
Sun, The: 173
Surrey: 42, 43, 47
Susquehanna River: 48
Susquehanna settlement: 42
Sussex: 90

Tattershall Bridge, Eng.: 27

Index

Taylor, John G.: 130, 185n.

Tennessee, state of: 38, 40, 127ff., 188

Terre Haute, Ind.: 58, 59

Texas, state of: 15, 16, 20, 21, 22, 71 ff., 172ff.

Texas Colonization Society: 75

Thirwell, John: 115

Thompson, George: 142

Three Years in California: 172

Three Years . . . in the United States: 83

Tietkens Agency: 21

Times, The (London): 20, 21, 23, 24, 60

Tocqueville, Alexis de: 59, 179, 180

Torrens, Col. Robert: 62

Tory party: 63, 71, 163

Tour in America, A: 37

Tout, Prof. T. F.: 187, 188

Townsend, Lord: 31

Trade Union Emigration: 25

Transalpine Memoirs: 57

Transcendental Wild Oats: 118

Traveller and Emigrant's Handbook: 89

Travels of Four Years . . . in the United States: 153

Trent (ship): 110

Trimmer, Charles: 42, 43, 47, 185n.

Trollope, Frances: 9, 10, 13, 14, 15, 16, 87, 123, 165ff., 185n., 192, 194

Trollope, Henry: 166, 168, 169

Trollope, Thomas A.: 166, 169

Trutch, Joseph: 154, 155

Tull, Jethro: 31

Turley, Edward: 114

Tussaud, Madam: 124

Twilight Grey: 13

Uncle Tom's Cabin: 14

Underground railroad: 88

United Empire Loyalists: 5

United States Land and Emigration Society: 21

United States of North America: 70

United States Senate: 19

Vachell, Horace: 13, 56, 57

Venus (ship): 23

Vermont, state of: 94

Victoria, Kan.: 113

Victoria, Pres. Guadalupe: 73

Victoria, Queen: 19, 129

View of the Present Conditions of the State of Barbary, A: 158

Virginia, state of: 21, 33, 53, 188

Wabash, The: 9, 59, 60, 194

Wadsworth, James & Elsie: 131, 132

Wake, Rev. Richard: 115, 116

Walker, Maria (Mrs. Charles Janson): 158

Wamsley, Mrs.: 54

Wanderer, The: 95

War of 1812: 32, 38, 101, 164

Warwickshire: 69

Washington, George: 32ff., 64

Wavell, Arthur: 21, 72

Webster, Daniel: 69

Webster, Noah: 85, 152

Webster-Ashburton Treaty: 25

Welby, Adlard: 46

Welsh: *see* immigration

Welsh colonies: 115, 125

Wesley, John: 141

Weston, Richard: 84ff., 87, 88, 92, 185n.

Whignell, Thomas: 102

Whitefield, George: 141

Whitlock, Elizabeth: 100

Widow Barnaby, The: 14

Wilhem Meisters Lehrjahre: 22

Wilkes, Capt.: 110

Williams, Guilliam: 127

Wilson, Charles H.: 39, 40, 41, 185n.

Winneshiek Co., Iowa: 113

Wisconsin, state of: 26

Woodhouselee; or the Astrologer: see Launcelot Wedge

Woollam, J. G.: 89, 92

Woolsack, The: 173

Wright, Camilla: 166

Wright, Frances: 10, 166, 167, 170

Wright, Henry: 117

Wyoming, state of: 56

Wyse, Francis: 86, 87, 92

Wyth, Nathaniel: 137

Y Chronicl: 126

Year of Consolation: 8, 108

Year's Residence, A: 165

Yorkshire: 21, 32, 39, 47, 49, 88, 100, 135, 156

Young, Arthur: 29, 33, 37, 62

Young, William: 171, 185n., 193

The text for *Emigration and Disenchantment* is set on the Linotype in 11-point Baskerville, a weight-for-weight, curve-for-curve copy of John Baskerville's celebrated printing type. The type is set with two points of space between lines. The paper on which this book is published bears the University of Oklahoma Press watermark and has an effective life of at least three hundred years.

UNIVERSITY OF OKLAHOMA PRESS : *Norman*